Jackson School Publications in International Studies

JACKSON SCHOOL PUBLICATIONS
IN INTERNATIONAL STUDIES

Senator Henry M. Jackson was convinced that the study of the history, cultures, political systems, and languages of the world's major regions was an essential prerequisite for wise decision-making in international relations. In recognition of his deep commitment to higher education and advanced scholarship, this series of publications has been established through the generous support of the Henry M. Jackson Foundation, in cooperation with the Henry M. Jackson School of International Studies and the University of Washington Press.

The Crisis of Leninism and the Decline of the Left: The Revolutions of 1989, edited by Daniel Chirot

Sino-Soviet Normalization and Its International Implications, 1945–1990, by Lowell Dittmer

Contradictions: Artistic Life, the Socialist State, and the Chinese Painter Li Huasheng, by Jerome Silbergeld with Gong Jisui

The Found Generation: Chinese Communists in Europe during the Twenties, by Marilyn Levine

Rules and Rights in the Middle East: Democracy, Law, and Society, edited by Ellis Goldberg, Reşat Kasaba, and Joel S. Migdal

RULES AND RIGHTS IN THE MIDDLE EAST

Democracy, Law, and Society

EDITED BY

Ellis Goldberg, Reşat Kasaba, and Joel Migdal

UNIVERSITY OF WASHINGTON PRESS

Seattle • London

Library of Congress Cataloging-in-Publication Data

Rules and rights in the Middle East : democracy, law, and society /
    edited by Ellis Goldberg, Reşat Kasaba, and Joel S. Migdal.
        p.   cm. — (Jackson School publications in international
    studies)
    Includes bibliographical references and index.
    ISBN 0-295-97286-6 (cloth). — ISBN 0-295-97287-4 (pbk.)
    1. Democracy–Middle East. 2. Civil rights—Middle East.
    3. Middle East—Politics and government—1945–. I. Goldberg, Ellis.
    II. Kasaba, Reşat, 1954–. III. Migdal, Joel S. IV. Series.
    JQ1758.A91R85
    321.8′0956–dc20   93-4679
                                                                    CIP

CONTENTS

PREFACE ◊ vii

Introduction
Ellis Goldberg, Reşat Kasaba, Joel Migdal ◊ 3

PART 1. OVERVIEW

The Practice of Electoral Democracy in
the Arab East and North Africa:
Some Lessons from Nearly a Century's Experience
Roger Owen ◊ 17

PART 2. POWER AGAINST POWER

Populism and Democracy in Turkey, 1946–1961
Reşat Kasaba ◊ 43

Taxation without Representation: Authoritarianism and
Economic Liberalization in Syria
Steven Heydemann ◊ 69

State, Legitimacy, and Democratization in the Maghreb
Abdelbaki Hermassi ◊ 102

Civil Society in Israel
Joel S. Migdal ◊ 118

v

PART 3.   PRACTICAL POLITICS

Prospects and Difficulties of
Democratization in the Middle East
Bülent Ecevit ◊ 141

American Policy toward
Democratic Political Movements in the Middle East
William B. Quandt ◊ 164

Voices of Opposition: The International Committee
for a Free Iraq
Chibli Mallat ◊ 174

PART 4.   THE SHADOW OF LAW

Public Confessions in the Islamic Republic of Iran
Ervand Abrahamian ◊ 191

Obstacles to Democratization in Iraq: A Reading of
Post-Revolutionary Iraqi History through the Gulf War
Chibli Mallat ◊ 224

Private Goods, Public Wrongs, and Civil Society in
Some Medieval Arab Theory and Practice
Ellis Goldberg ◊ 248

INDEX ◊ 272

CONTRIBUTORS ◊ 280

PREFACE

EARLIER versions of the papers that are collected in this volume were presented at a conference on "Democratic Movements and Representative Governments in the Middle East" that was held at the University of Washington. Both the conference and this book were made possible by a grant from the Henry M. Jackson Foundation and additional support by the Earhart Foundation and the Middle East Center of the Henry M. Jackson School of International Studies. We would like to thank Robin Pasquarella and other members and staff of the Jackson Foundation and the other institutions for their help and advice. We also thank Ehud Merhav, who made the index, and Theodora MacKay, who prepared the papers for publication. Last but not least we are pleased to acknowledge our colleague Jere Bacharach's contribution to this project. His boundless energy and enthusiasm made the conference a reality and helped us immensely in editing this volume.

ELLIS GOLDBERG, REŞAT KASABA, JOEL MIGDAL
University of Washington

Rules and Rights
in the Middle East

Introduction

ELLIS GOLDBERG, REŞAT KASABA, JOEL MIGDAL

W HEN mentioned in the same sentence, the words "democracy" and the "Middle East" usually elicit a sense of deep
suspicion, if not outright disbelief.[1] It is not hard to understand
how such impressions are formed and why the Middle East is so
easily dismissed when it comes to democracy and its constituent
elements such as popular sovereignty, human rights, and civil society. Anybody who has the slightest interest in this part of the
world will have heard of the Saudi women who are prevented from
driving their cars; the secret service organizations that have created a vicious environment of fear and intimidation in Syria, Iraq,
and Jordan; the elections that were postponed in Algeria because
their likely results threatened the military and politial elite; the
Turkish coups that seem to occur with remarkable regularity; the
cult of personality in Libya, Iraq, and Syria that harks back to the
Soviet Union under Stalin; the retrograde regime of the mullahs in
Iran; the uncertain status of the Palestinians in Israel's occupied
territories; and the discrimination against women and ethnic and
religious minorities that seems to continue unabated in the entire
region. Stacked against even such a partial and random list, a
discussion of democracy in the Middle East seems at best like an

---

[1] Michael Hudson rightly complains about a recent four-volume survey on
democracy in developing countries that ignores the Arab world entirely.
Michael Hudson, "After the Gulf War: Prospects for Democratization in Arab
World," *Middle East Journal* 45 (1991) 407. The book in question is Larry Di-
amond, Juan Linz, and Seymour Martin Lipset eds., *Democracy in Developing
Countries* (Boulder, Lynne Rienner Publishers, 1989).

academic exercise in the true sense of the word. But our interest in convening the conference from which this book grew was and is more than academic.

Like many other close observers of the Middle East, we are struck not so much by selective episodes that reinforce the commonly held stereotypes but by two other developments that are not as easily seen or adequately appreciated. In recent years there has been a phenomenal growth in the number and influence of a variety of social movements and organizations that are trying to expand the spheres of social, political, and civil rights, and to constrain the power of the states in many countries in the Middle East. At the same time, we are witnessing a renewed (albeit hesitant) interest on the part of many of the regimes in the area in introducing certain practices and institutions designed to make their rule more democratic and thereby enhance their domestic and international standing and legitimacy, as well as to spur badly needed economic growth.[2] As writers who are familiar with the region, we know that neither of these developments is without historical precedent. Accordingly, we agreed that in evaluating the significance of this new wave of liberalization, we need to place it in its historical context and study it from a long-term perspective. It is to this task that we set ourselves in convening the conference on Democratic Movements and Representative Governments at the University of Washington in the spring of 1992.

In conceiving this project, we felt that many of the arguments about the "presence" or "absence" of democracy and its constituent elements in the Middle East (and other parts of the world, for that matter) are based on a narrow and static understanding of this very important concept. Most typically, in assessing whether or not democracy is present or likely to "develop" in a given society, analysts look for a list of "preconditions" and/or "attributes." Since for the most part these characteristics are drawn from western Europe, it should not come as a surprise

---

[2] For a general review of these developments see Michael Hudson, "After the Gulf War" (supra n. 1), 407–426. See also also *Democracy in the Middle East*, special issue of *Middle East Report* 174 (January–February 1992); *Islam, State, and Democracy*, special issue of *Middle East Report* 179 (November–December 1992).

that conditions in the rest of the world usually appear unpropitious for the development of democracy.[3] In addition to the important role attributed to cultural predisposition, one of the earliest and most pervasive assumptions of this literature has been that there is a positive correlation between economic development and democracy.[4] Later on, the dependency literature questioned and weakened this link by emphasizing the intervening class structures and global processes and by approaching the issue from a more historical perspective. While representing a significant improvement over its predecessors, the dependency literature also suffered from a mechanical view of social change that explains both authoritarianism and transition to democracy primarily by the interactions among a limited number of military and civilian elites, who behave in highly predictable ways.[5]

[3] A good example of such analyses is provided by an article that appeared in *The Seattle Times*, 14 March 1992. After going over a list of "ingredients" that are essential for a "recipe for democracy" (which are attributed to Samuel Huntington), the author concludes that of these, the most important is "prior experience" with democracy and human rights. Another way of putting this would be to say that only those societies that are democratic are likely to be (or remain?) democratic! A good critique of this "futile search for democratic preconditions" is Terry Lynn Karl's "Dilemmas of Democratization in Latin America," *Comparative Politics*, October 1990, 1–21.

[4] See, e.g., Seymour Martin Lipset, *Political Man* (Garden City, Doubleday, 1960).

[5] The most useful examples of this literature can be found in David Collier ed., *The New Authoritarianism in Latin America* (Princeton University Press, 1978). A more comprehensive review and critique of the proposed relationship between economic development and democracy is in Steven Heydemann's contribution to this volume. In the more recent variants of the dependency approach, elites play an important role not only in the establishment of authoritarian rule but also in the transition to democracy. See, e.g., G. O'Donnell and P. Schmitter, *Transitions from Authoritarian Rule: Tentative Conclusions about Uncertain Democracies* (Baltimore, Johns Hopkins University Press, 1986); and John Higley and Richard Gunther eds., *Elites and Democratic Consolidation in Latin America and Southern Europe* (Cambridge University Press, 1992). The same emphasis on the role of elites in transitions to democracy pervaded the initial analyses of the recent changes in Eastern Europe. See, e.g., Timothy Garton Ash, *The Uses of Adversity* (New York, Vintage, 1990). For an excellent commentary on the relationships of the collapse of communism, the development of market economy, and the prospects of

Regardless of the perspective used, in most comparative studies the Middle East is seen to lack traits or prospects for democracy. It is routinely argued that either the lack of autonomous elites and civil associations, or a heritage of despotism that is traced to some historical and even genetic necessity, or the nature of Islam, or some combination of these render the states and people in this part of the world inhospitable to democratic ideals.[6]

There is no denying that the articles in this collection borrow from and build on previous studies on political change in the Third World and in the Middle East. But unlike most of the existing scholarship, we do not see democracy as the end point of a path on which some nations are not allowed to embark or as the result of negotiations and pacts from which the majority of the population is excluded. We take a more inclusive and dynamic view of this form of human coexistence and think of democracy as an ongoing project that unfolds on two related fronts. One of these is the continuous assertion and exercise of popular sovereignty, and the other is the equally persistent declaration and protection of fundamental human rights. In our view, the subjects of this project may include but are not limited to social classes. Other groups such as peasants, farmers, migrants, religious sects, ethnic communities, women's groups, writers, business people, and even bureaucrats can all be (and are) important actors in the struggle for democracy. They participate in the democratic project not as individuals

---

democracy in Eastern Europe, see Slavoj Zizek, "Eastern Europe's Republics of Gilead," in *Dimensions of Radical Democracy*, ed. Chantal Mouffe (London, Verso, 1992) 193–207.

[6] For a comprehensive review and critique of this literature, see Bryan Turner, *Marx and the End of Orientalism* (London, Allen & Unwin, 1978). As was the case in other regions, studies of the Middle Eastern societies that are inspired by dependency and its extension, the bureaucratic authoritarian models, represent a significant improvement over the earlier approaches. But here too such studies come with an elite-centered, mechanical understanding of social change that sometimes conceals more than it explains. For an alternative approach that highlights these weaknesses, see Robert Vitalis, "Business Conflict, Collaboration, and Privilege in Interwar Egypt," in *State Power and Social Forces: Domination and Transformation in the Third World*, ed. Joel Migdal, Atul Kohli, and Vivenne Shue (forthcoming).

but through the associations they form. These associations, along with the relational networks that develop among them, constitute the space that is commonly referred to as civil society.

It is our contention that for any democratic project to be viable, there has to be a consensus among the participants on the rules of the game, and there has to be a normative framework that provides a generally desired direction for the society. Without such an agreement, the pluralist ideal can deteriorate into some form of postmodern politics that emphasizes heterogeneity and incommensurability and as such is more conducive to division and atrophy than to unity and participation.[7] As Hermassi explains in his contribution to this volume, part of the confusion that followed the indefinite postponement of elections in Algeria in 1992 stemmed from the absence of such a normative framework, which left many of the democratically minded people without representation and without protection in the face of a pending victory by the FIS. We do not see the democratic project as something that is confined to the organization of the political community and to the procedures of elections that arbitrate among formal associations and political parties. It is equally essential that fundamental human rights and popular sovereignty are asserted and upheld within the groups, communities, and associations that participate in the democratic process. Otherwise, as Kasaba explains in his chapter, even a seemingly unhindered practice of democratic procedures may fail to improve conditions for a substantial majority of people where it most matters: that is, in their daily lives.

IN the first essay in this collection, Roger Owen gives a historical sketch reviewing the earlier periods when democracy was on the agenda in the Arab Middle East. Initially, liberal democracy appeared to have been borne on the wings of colonialism and was perceived primarily as a tool for continuing the domination of the old elites over subordinate classes. Certainly, in much of the Arab world the apparent success of radical nationalism in confronting the colonial powers after World War II and in seizing the property and wealth of foreign capitalists made democracy seem

---

[7] On this point, see Chantal Mouffe, "Democratic Politics Today," in *Dimensions of Radical Democracy* (supra n. 4) 13–14.

watery gruel for the heavy job of political, social, and economic development. According to Owen, the recent retreat from state-centered policies and the move toward more open economic and/or political systems in various countries in the Middle East are primarily owing to the economic difficulties of the late 1970s and the early 1980s. The apparent failure of the public sectors to deliver on their promises of economic development, the loss of Soviet support, and more recently the Gulf War and its aftermath are the additional factors that have been forcing various states in the area toward some compromise with their oppositions. In Owen's view, however, the levers of power reside almost wholly in the hands of state officials, and the sources of social support for free elections remain limited. Moreover, neither figures in the international environment nor many domestic actors may now be willing to risk the outcome of democratic elections for fear of Islamicist groups committed to using the fragile reemergence of democratic processes to destroy any decisive move in the direction of liberal democracy itself.

Of all the states in the Middle East, Turkey and Israel have had the longest experience with democratic procedures and institutions, and as such they would be expected to have an easier time dealing with the growing social pressures. For different reasons, however, both of these states have succeeded only partially in this task. In Turkey, for forty-two of the past forty-seven years, the population has been governed as the result of free elections. Kasaba traces this democratic "tradition" back to Ottoman times, where, he argues, a large area of social autonomy provided crucial social and institutional support for emerging ideas of constitutional limits on state power.

Kasaba details the rapidity with which the Turkish population welcomed the chance to express resentment against an intrusive state after 1945 and the skill with which the leaders of the Democratic party (especially Adnan Menderes) reinforced a popular sense of empowerment in the country. That democratic sentiments run deep in Turkey is evident from the rapidity with which the military regimes collapsed after the coups of 1960, 1971, and 1980. On the other hand, the political parties that benefited from these sentiments never questioned the power relations within the extended families, communities, and other networks that were crucial in mobilizing the population. This gap between formal politics and social associations constitutes one of the substantive weaknesses of democracy in Turkey. Today, despite the impressive record of almost half a century, the Turks still feel somewhat uncertain about the viability of democracy in their country. This pessimism is rooted in part in the realization that there is no longer a general consensus about the direction that the society should move. As we mentioned above, in the absence of such a framework, different groups attempt to fill in the void by imposing their own singular solutions. They attempt to pull the country in different directions by using radically different tactics, some of which have nothing to do with tolerance and compromise. Under such circumstances, political relations can quickly deteriorate into a chaos that makes a mockery of the pluralism so essential for the continuation of the democratic project.

Israel's inhabitants are, as Joel Migdal puts it, "inveterate political junkies," who live in a country with a relatively weak civil society. That Israel should have created a successful parliamentary system in which political power has been alternated and shared is remarkable, for, as Migdal reminds us, there was nothing in the formal order of the Mandate that made such an outcome likely. Although Migdal does not mention it, the political conditions in Eastern Europe, where Labor Zionism grew, were not conducive to making parliamentary democracy work either. Israel illustrates another key factor in the emergence of democracy: the importance of social and political forces checking each other so that none is able to dominate totally and all must find institutionalized means of accommodation in order to achieve their goals. Partisan competition and the desire to participate politically have ensured that Israel did not become a garrison state, but it remains problematic whether the growth of the components of civil society will bolster political democracy. Today, Israeli society is divided on the most fundamental issue of its existence: that is, on its borders, on the status of the occupied territories, and on the place in society of the large Arab minority. In the absence of consensus on this most basic question, the multiple voices of complaint may turn into a postmodern cacophony and render the state not more accessible but less prone to action, as explained by Migdal in his analysis of the Israeli case.

Hermassi retraces the story of the "social pact" that governed the postcolonial era, and provides a sharp picture of its breakdown in the Maghrebi context. He demonstrates that what is at issue in the Maghreb is not just a fiscal or budgetary shortfall but a thorough social and economic crisis arising from the collapse of the authority of the postcolonial states. Here, a civil society is born because of the need for individuals to exchange and negotiate and organize for themselves a living space that the state is no longer able to provide. Again, the absence of a single dominant force, as well as the checks among social groups and their need for accommodation, may prove to be one of the bases for the growth of civil society. In the Maghreb, the organization of society extends beyond the national and even regional borders, as migrants in Southern Europe participate in it and as the transnational appeal of Islamicism sweeps these countries. Taking these aspects into consideration, it is possible to talk about an international civil society in the Maghreb—and perhaps in the Middle East in general—making individuals even more powerful as they organize against the power of their respective states.

While the Maghrebi states tried to deal with social agitation by a carefully circumscribed extension of political rights, Egypt in the late 1970s and Syria and Iraq in the 1980s tried the different path of emphasizing economic liberalism with little or no broadening of political freedoms. Heydemann describes this process by focusing on Syrian history. For Heydemann, claims about an emerging democratic bargain neglect what he takes to be the more common experiences in the Middle East and elsewhere of corporatist, imposed, and selective liberalizations. One of the important conclusions of Heydemann's essay is that far from empowering people, the liberalization of the economy may end up providing states with larger and more stable revenues. The narrow circle of social groups that acquire some of the newly created resources, and that are now in a position to act apart from the state, may make the government occasionally responsive to their particular demands but only as a result of outright pressure and corruption. It would certainly be misleading to view this new arrangement as the harbinger of a civil society or democratic age in the Fertile Crescent.

To get the views of practical policy makers and participants on what the transition to democracy involves, we turn to William

Quandt, who was a National Security Aide to President Carter;
to Bülent Ecevit, who served as the Prime Minister of Turkey
in the late 1970s; and to Chibli Mallat, one of the organizers of
the International Committee for a Free Iraq, founded immediately
after the Second Gulf War. It is hard to overemphasize the importance of the role the United States has played in the regional and
domestic politics of the Middle Eastern states since at least the
end of World War II. Through Quandt's essay we are reminded
of the various and often conflicting considerations that go into the
making of the United States' policy in the Middle East. Quandt
forces us to reflect, once again, on why it has not always been
easy to combine the United States interests in different parts of
the world as dictated by the realpolitik with our broader moral
and intellectual commitment to democratic ideals.

Bulent Ecevit has been active in politics in Turkey since the late
1950s. His experience in these four decades has included not only
occupying the highest levels of decision making in the Turkish
government, but also being imprisoned for refusing the dictates
of some of the intervening military regimes. In his essay, Ecevit
focuses on Turkey's current position in the post–Cold War Middle
East and draws attention to her cultural and historical ties with
the nascent republics of Central Asia. Ecevit argues that, with its
democratic experience, Turkey is in a position to act as a model
both for the Middle East and Central Asia. This situation puts
new responsibilities on Turkish policymakers, and it may also act
as a brake against antidemocratic tendencies in the country.

Mallat recounts the efforts of Iraqis and others to help shape
the international resolutions spewing forth after the Gulf War. For
democracy to take shape in Iraq, there must exist a distinction
between the Iraqi regime and Iraqi civil society. This is a question
not only of reshaping domestic law but of demanding an opposition
influencing international law as well.

Although Islam is widely claimed to be a state and a religion,
the last three authors in this volume begin with the premise
that Islam is a legal system that has often been used against
the state. Ellis Goldberg's paper reviews many of the claims
about Islam as an all-embracing system of practice and belief,
which is an idea common both to the activists in Islamicist movements and to many of the great Orientalist scholars of the past

hundred years. Put most simply, Goldberg's argument is that Islamic laws arose in the context of royal decrees but not as a result of them. Consequently, those who created the intellectual structure of Islamic law between the eighth and eleventh centuries were aware of the need to guard against the arbitrary use of royal power to tax, monopolize, or simply seize the property of urban residents. In an era of constant civil and military conflict, they were also as cognizant as we are of the dangers of having no central authority at all. At all events, we should certainly be aware of the existence alongside a strain of thought oriented toward public order of another strain skeptical of the power of the state and anxious to limit it by imposing a set of constitutive rules of behavior on it. It can be argued that with these two strains of thought, classical Islamic law and classical Islamic political theory provide the majority of the people in the Middle East with the means to transcend the narrow divisions of ethnicity and local loyalties, giving them a reason to commit themselves to a broader entity. At the same time, this system of thought supplies a very effective intellectual resource for resisting the arbitrary and "unjust" use of state power.[8]

Along with Saudi Arabia and Syria, Iran and Iraq are the only places in the Middle East, where, to paraphrase Ecevit, it is hard to detect even a leaf moving despite the winds of democracy blowing around the region and across the world. What is interesting is that the rulers of these states have been relying on a combination of loosely interpreted Islamic and secular legal arguments and procedures and on international law in order to justify their disregard of fundamental political, social, and civil rights. As Abrahamian explains in his essay, this has been a particularly delicate task in

---

[8] On the relationship between Islam and Democracy in the contemporary Middle East, see John L. Esposito and James P. Piscatori, "Democratization and Islam," *Middle East Journal* 45 (1991) 428–440. See also Sami Zubaida, "Islam, the State, and Democracy: Contrasting Conceptions of Society in Egypt," *Middle East Report* 179 (November–December 1992) 2–10; Salim Tamari, "Left in Limbo: Leninist Heritage and Islamist Challenge," in ibid., 16–21; Lisa Anderson, "Obligation and Accountability: Islamic Politics in North Africa," *Daedalus* (Summer 1991) 93–112.

the Islamic Republic of Iran because neither Islamic history nor the Sunni or Shi'i doctrines provide a precedent or justification for the kind of centralization and concentration of religious and secular power that the mullahs have been instituting in that country.[9] In an effort to cover this deficit, the Iranian regime ignored the classical Islamic concepts of jurisprudence and replaced them with a panoply of totalitarian legal techniques designed to crush not only the bodies but the moral wills of those in opposition to it. Abrahamian's close reading of the show trials that occupied the first decade of the Islamic Republic's existence shows how closely, albeit unwittingly, they paralleled not only the practice but even the vocabulary of the Stalinist show trials of the 1930s. Perhaps this constitutes a tragic proof of how modern really are certain aspects of the Islamic Republic of Iran, which is frequently dismissed as a throwback to the Middle Ages.

Mallat, speaking now as an academic rather than a practitioner, expands on the intricate ways in which domestic and international systems of law have interacted to strengthen and protect a brutal dictatorship in Iraq. In this case, the international principle of sovereignty has become a powerful tool available to the Ba'thi dictatorship to maintain itself in power, as it utilizes a totalitarian systematization to define, exclude, and destroy enemies, real and imagined. The concern with legalism appears here to be far more the hallmark of a dictatorial regime than of high Islamic culture. The Iraqi and the Iranian regimes share this characteristic more with other tyrannies than with Arab or Islamic culture as such. By bringing in sharp resolution law as a substantive system and as a formal system at both domestic and international levels, Mallat poses again the question with which many of the other contributors deal, and around which much of the discussion around the conference centered: How to make states accountable before society, and the overriding importance of such accountability as a moral principle of political organization. In bringing this point to the fore, Mallat forces us to think again on the importance and implications of principles such as territorial sovereignty, in contradistinction to universal ideals of human rights and democracy.

---

[9] On this point see Bernard Lewis, "Muslims, Christians, and Jews: The Dream of Coexistence," *New York Review of Books*, 26 March 1992, 50.

When people talk of a democratic society, they usually have in mind a political arrangement that recognizes popular sovereignty and human rights, respects the distinction between the public and private spheres, maintains separation between civil law and religious law, and defends pluralism and individual freedoms. If we use these features as our only yardstick, then we cannot but reach yet another pessimistic conclusion about the prospects of democracy in the Middle East. But if we adopt a more dynamic and open-ended point of view, as the authors here have tried to do, and emphasize, above all, the purposeful activities of individuals within and through their groups and communities, we can begin to sense the deep stirrings and popular desire for democratic procedures and institutions that exist in all the Middle Eastern societies. Finally, we should not forget that in their pursuit of the democratic project, the people of the Middle East are not alone. Not only in other parts of the third world, but also in the advanced industrial societies of North America, Europe, and Asia, there are important movements to safeguard, uphold, and expand democratic procedures and institutions. We know that popular sovereignty and human rights are truly universal ideals but, as we are reminded daily, their existence cannot and should not be taken for granted in any part of the world.

PART 1
Overview

The Practice of Electoral Democracy in the Arab East and North Africa
Some Lessons from Nearly a Century's Experience

ROGER OWEN

I N this paper I propose to make some general comments about the practice of democracy in the Arab states during the twentieth century.[1] Looked at from a regional perspective, this has the advantage of treating a group of countries with a great deal in common in terms of recent history, social composition, economic structure, and so on. But it also has the disadvantage of forcing the exclusion of three other Middle Eastern states, Iran, Israel, and Turkey, whose democratic experience has been significantly different in many important respects.

Given the need for preliminary definition, I will simplify matters by following Karl Popper's usage, in that "democracy" is seen as, essentially, a system of competitive elections after which the winning group may be allowed to form a government.[2] This is obviously to neglect a number of features that are considered vital to democratic practice in the West. But it does have the advantage of comparing the Arab experience more directly with that of other non-European states.

---

[1] In writing this paper I have drawn on some of the ideas to be found in my book *State, Power and Politics in the Making of the Modern Middle East* (London, Routledge, 1992) as well as my article "The Transformation of the Systems of Economic and Political Management in the Middle East and North Africa: The Lessons So Far," which will appear in *The Review of Middle East Studies* 6 (Spring 1993).

[2] Karl Popper's definition is quoted in Chalmers Johnson, "South Korean Democratization: The Role of Economic Development," *The Pacific Review* 2 (1989) 3–4.

The Practice of Democracy
in the Immediate Post-Independence Period

It was usual for Arab states to embark on their independence with a constitution that called for the holding of regular elections. This seems to have been what Zubaida might call the "compulsory model," supported by the new nationalist politicians and the retiring colonial administrators alike.[3] It rested on a belief in the importance of constitutions as a protection against tyrannical government, as well as on the legitimation supplied by notions first elaborated during the French Revolution stressing equality, popular representation, and the sovereignty of the people. Such ideas had been used to form part of a powerful critique of colonialist practice. They were also reflected in the names of the first political parties, for instance, the 'Umma (Liberal Constitutionalists) in Egypt.

There was, however, considerable disagreement about how to conduct democratic elections, and there were frequent changes in the rules that governed them. In part, this represented the obvious problems of organizing such events in countries with a largely illiterate electorate, at least half of which lived in rural areas dominated by large landowning families. But it also represented a constant search for temporary political advantage either between competing parties (as in Egypt between 1923 and 1952) or between government and opposition groups (as in Iraq between 1931 and 1958). In addition, there was a constant use of a great variety of illegal interventions and electoral malpractices, which means that historians have been willing to describe only a handful of Arab elections as even reasonably fair.[4] Such a list would probably be

---

[3] Zubaida describes the "modern state system" as the "compulsory model" for new states but links this to the influence of powerful Jacobin notions such as popular sovereignty. See Sami Zubaida, *Islam: The People and The State* (London, Routledge, 1989) 121–22.

[4] Interesting accounts of electoral practices can be found, for example, in M. M. al-Adhami, "The Elections for the Constituent Assembly in Iraq, 1922–4" in *The Integration of Modern Iraq*, ed. Abbas Kelidar (London, Croom Helm, 1979) 13–31; George Grassmuck, "The Electoral process in Iraq, 1952–1955," *Middle East Journal* 12 (1960) 407–8; Philip S. Khoury, *Syria and the French Mandate: The Politics of Arab Nationalism, 1920–1945* (London, I. B.

confined to any Egyptian election won by the Wafd (1924, 1929, 1936, 1950); the Syrian elections of 1943, 1947, and 1954; the Lebanese election of 1943; the Jordanian one of 1956; and the first of the two Iraqi elections held in 1954.

Three other features of this first period of competitive elections are worth noting. The first is the almost universal assumption of the importance of universal, manhood suffrage. Only in the colonial period was it possible to attempt to impose the kinds of limitations that were common in, say, mid-Victorian Britain, when the definition of those deemed fit to take part in elections was restricted to males thought to have a particular stake in the community either because they owned property or because they were in sufficiently regular employment to earn more than a certain sum each year. After independence, such restrictions were only occasionally employed (for example, under the Sidqi constitution in force in Egypt between 1931 and 1935, when, according to Vatikiotis, some 80 percent of the adult male population was disenfranchised); the more usual method of maintaining central control was through a continuation of some version of the two-tier system first employed by the Ottomans and then the colonial powers in Syria and Iraq.[5] In such a system, male electors came together to vote for representatives who, in turn, met together to elect the actual members of Parliament. This made it very easy to exert official influence at the second stage.

A second and related feature was the forceful way in which notions of universalism and common citizenship expressed themselves in the countries that became independent just after the Second World War. One of the forms this took was the abolition of the special representation accorded to so-called "minorities" (mainly Christians and Jews) during the colonial-period elections in Iraq and Syria (but not in Lebanon and Jordan). Another was the termination of the two-tier electoral system in Iraq in 1952,

---

Tauris, 1987) 129–30, 360–74, 598–603, etc. It is important to be reminded that electoral malpractice was as central to the management of the colonial state as it was to its successors.

[5] P. J. Vatikiotis, *The Modern History of Egypt* (London, Weidenfeld & Nicolson, 1969) 283. For Ismail Sidqi's attempt to justify his restriction of the franchise see his *Mudhakkirati* (Cairo, Dar al-Hilal Press, 1950) 119–38.

and a third the extension of the franchise to women in Syria in 1947, Lebanon in 1952, and Iraq in 1953. There was also pressure from some of the more radical parties for fairer types of electoral practice—for example, the introduction of the secret ballot in Lebanon in 1952 and Syria in 1954—in an attempt, it has been suggested, to reduce the impact of landowner and government influence in the rural areas.[6]

Third, it is important to observe how few elections were contested between competing groups with sufficient cohesion and organization to be called a party. Such groups existed only in Egypt, Syria, Sudan, and to some extent Lebanon and Morocco. And even there the parties in question generally came to life only at election time, while hardly any of them possessed a regular system of membership or branches outside the major cities. This was generally a recognition of the fact that electoral victory was far more likely to come from the recruitment of large landowners as the parties' rural allies or from the exploitation of certain communalist or religious solidarities than from good organization per se. In other countries the majority of candidates stood as independents.

The Reaction against Pluralism and the Creation of Authoritarian, Single-Party Regimes

The speed and decisiveness with which the system of competitive elections was dismantled in Egypt, Syria, Iraq, and Sudan is sad but not surprising. On the one hand, the actual practice of electoral democracy was hardly one to inspire great enthusiasm even among its few defenders. On the other, pluralism and competition between parties was increasingly perceived as intrinsically divisive, and so a major obstacle to the unity thought necessary to throw out the last vestiges of colonialism and to place all the people behind a concerted drive towards national development.

One persuasive advocate of such ideas was the leader of the Egyptian revolution, Gamal Abdel Nasser. As he put it in an interview with an Indian newspaper editor in March 1957:

[6] Patrick Seale, *The Struggle for Syria: A Study of Post-War Arab Politics, 1945–1958* (Oxford University Press, 1965) 173.

Can I ask you a question: what is democracy? We were supposed to have a democratic system during the period 1923 to 1953. But what good was this democracy to our people? I will tell you. Landowners and Pashas ruled our people. They used this kind of a democracy as an easy tool for the benefits of the feudal system. You have seen the feudalists gathering the peasants together and driving them to the polling booths. There the peasants would cast their votes according to the instructions of their masters.... I want to liberate the peasants and the workers, both socially and economically, so that they can say 'yes'. I want the peasants and the workers to be able to say 'yes' and 'no' without this in any way affecting their livelihood and their daily bread. This in my view is the basis of freedom and democracy.[7]

Such views were, of course, very common among the political elites in many parts of African and Asia during the 1950s and 1960s. But what we cannot know without further detailed research is how widespread they were in specific Arab countries. What does seem clear, though, is that pluralism and democracy had few vocal defenders. The distinguished Egyptian writer Tawfik al-Hakim has attempted to explain this in terms of something he calls the "sleep of consciousness," which he says affected intellectuals like himself who were mesmerized by the revolutionary excitement, as well as the real victories, of the early Nasser period.[8] But this is also a piece of special pleading and does not do much to help us understand the general lack of opposition to such measures as the enforced dissolution of Egypt's political parties in 1953. Perhaps the only reasonable thing to say at this stage is that in Egypt, as elsewhere in the Third World, the liberal case for democracy as a necessary condition for the exercise of freedom, good government, and the rule of law had yet to be widely accepted.

The Persistence of Partial Democracy in Morocco and Lebanon

Given the fact that democratic practices disappeared so soon after independence in so many Arab countries, it is interesting to examine the special conditions that seem to have allowed it to

[7] British Broadcasting Corporation, Summary of World Broadcasts (Reading), 12 March 1957, 194.

[8] Tawfik Al-Hakim, 'Awdat al-wa'y (Beirut 1974).

continue in two others: Morocco and Lebanon. Conditions in a third country, Kuwait, which introduced an electoral system soon after independence in 1961, will be discussed below (pages 33–35).

There are various interpretations of the political history of Morocco before and after independence, but the general conclusion seems to be that the essential ingredients were the failure of the nationalist party, the Istiqlal, to establish a dominant position, combined with the emergence of King Mohammad V as an alternative national leader.[9] It was the Istiqlal that had led the struggle against the French and that, in spite of being forced to operate underground, had managed by the late 1940s to transform itself into a mass organization with a strong following in the larger towns. It then underwent a further period of expansion in the early 1950s, so that, by independence in 1956, it may have had as many as two million supporters out of a total Moroccan population of ten million.[10] In such circumstances, it looked for a while as though it was in a position to establish the same type of one-party hegemony as the Neo-Destour in Tunisia. But it was just at this moment that the king was able to create an independent power base of his own, sufficiently strong not only to avoid the fate of the bey of Tunis (who was ousted by Bourguiba and the Neo-Destour) but also to prevent the Istiqlal from obtaining sufficient momentum to mount a serious challenge to his authority. Hence the party was never allowed the monopoly of major cabinet posts that it demanded, while the general elections that might have given it a landslide victory just after independence were postponed to 1963, giving the king time to secure his own control over the administration and the army.

It was within this context that both King Mohammad V and then his son, Hassan II, were able to develop an alternative system of political management in which a variety of parties, some

---

[9] For example, Douglas E. Ashford, *Political Change in Morocco* (Princeton University Press, 1961); John Waterbury, *The Commander of the Faithful: The Moroccan Political Elite—a Study of Segmented Politics* (London, Weidenfeld & Nicolson, 1970); and I. William Zartman, "Political Pluralism in Morocco," in *Man, State and Society in The Contemporary Maghrib*, ed. I. William Zartman (London, Pall Mall Press, 1973).

[10] Ashford, *Political Change*, 246.

loyal to the throne, others in opposition to it, were allowed to compete with one another in a severely restricted political arena. In all this, the kings were helped greatly by the split inside the Istiqlal in 1959–60 that led to the creation of a more radical rival, the UNFP (Union Nationale des Forces Populaires). Even so, management of such a system has proved difficult, and there have been frequent periods during which constitutions have been dissolved and elections postponed. The king has also changed the rules governing electoral practice at frequent intervals, in particular by introducing different combinations of direct and indirect methods in 1969–70, 1977, and 1984. There have also been frequent accusations of gerrymandered constituencies and a whole variety of electoral malpractice.[11]

As far as the king himself is concerned, his aim has been to establish a system of organized pluralism, with himself playing the central role as the single arbiter between all the competing groups, a practice that Waterbury has characterized as one of "divide and survive."[12] But in spite of his own power and resources, this has proved no easy task. Such a system is inherently unstable and requires constant intervention to keep all parties in play in a situation in which only a few will be allowed any of the fruits of office, while leaving the rest in a position of permanent—but necessarily loyal—opposition. Nevertheless, the system has been sufficiently flexible to see Morocco through a decade of international indebtedness and economic reform without any of the major changes to be seen in its North African neighbors such as Egypt, Tunisia, and Algeria.

A final point concerning Morocco is that at no time has the monarch attempted to create a single King's party to look after his interests in the parliament, preferring to give his blessing to a number of different groups of loyalists. No doubt the refusal to exploit such an option must be seen as part and parcel of the business of maintaining the royal authority by keeping a regal distance between himself and the workaday politicians, just as it has been in Jordan and might also be in any Gulf state that

[11] For example, Mustapha Sehimi, "Les élections législatives au Maroc," *Maghreb/Machrek* 107 (1985) 23–39.
[12] Waterbury, *Commander of the Faithful*, 145–49.

permitted organized party life. But there is no doubt that it is also
a basic feature of that process of continuous arbitration between
rival groups that provides the key to the practice of Morocco's
particular form of controlled democracy.

Lebanon presents another picture entirely. There, the National
Assembly was given a central role in the system of organized con-
fessional representation and intraconfessional bargaining established by the constitutional mechanisms promulgated in 1926.[13]
As such, the same system was taken over more or less as it stood
by the leading politicians of the post-independence period, taking their cue from the National Pact of 1943. For a time, the
close fit that existed between the political and the socioeconomic
structures kept Lebanese democracy alive, with the leaders of the
well-balanced communities obtaining almost automatic access to
the rewards of high office, while free trade and low taxes under-
pinned over two decades of rapid economic growth. However, as is
well known, the system became subject to increasing internal and
external strain, which, in the end, proved too much. In hindsight
we can now see that what was needed to keep it going was a combination of the kind of internationally recognized neutrality that
would have protected it from outside pressures, and mechanisms
for ensuring that new political forces—exemplified, inter alia, by
the growth of the militias—were encouraged to work inside, not
outside, the parliamentary system. Whether such conditions can
ever be realized in the future seems unlikely.

The Revival of Democracy in the 1970s and 1980s

During the 1950s and 1960s the drive towards the establishment
of one-party, authoritarian regimes in the Arab world seemed un-
stoppable. Apart from the Gulf and Lebanon, it was only by
great determination and much good luck that the remaining royal
families—in Morocco and Jordan—were able to survive attempted

---

[13] Such arguments can be found in Kamal Salibi, *Lebanon and the Middle
Eastern Question*, Centre for Lebanese Studies, Oxford, Occasional Papers,
no. 8 (May 1988) 7, or Clyde G. Hess, Jr. and Herman L. Bodman, Jr.,
"Confessionalism and Feudality in Lebanese Politics," *Middle East Journal* 8
(Winter 1954) 26.

military coups. And even there, the practice of competitive elections was severely curtailed or even suspended for quite long periods of time.

But then, beginning with Egypt in the 1970s, and gathering momentum in Sudan, Tunisia, and Algeria, as well as in Jordan and the Yemens, highly controlled political systems began to open up in a way that appeared to promise a significant revival—or introduction de novo—of the democratic practices associated with competitive elections. Given the fact that this seemed to be part of a worldwide process, observers tried to link it to such general phenomena as economic liberalization and the enlivening of the private sector—and so perhaps the strengthening of a new and independent middle class.[14] But, on closer observation, matters seem much less simple.

In what follows I will make use of three lines of inquiry. The first is the obvious connection between political change and the huge economic problems associated with inefficient public sectors and wasteful planning, which so often resulted in a huge and unmanageable international debt. This is particularly apparent in the case of the Arab states of North Africa, which, with the exception of Libya and Algeria, possessed few or no oil revenues of their own. In the Arab East, on the other hand, most states were protected from the worst of such problems by their continued access to petro-dollars or by the fact that, when they did owe money, it was to their fellow Arabs and not powerful creditors in the West.

Second, I want to argue that, as a rule, economic difficulties only get labeled "crises" as a result of associated political events. These may take the form of serious demonstrations and disturbances that demand a major response. But just as often they are the result of the calculations of incoming rulers who, like President Gorbachev, are persuaded of the need to distance themselves from the policies of their predecessors. Better still if, like Mrs. Thatcher in 1979 or President Reagan in 1980, they can offer a whole new set of policies to replace those that they now seek to discredit. In the

[14] The best attempt to argue this case is by Çağlar Keyder, "The Rise and Decline of National Economies on the Periphery," *The Review of Middle East Studies* (Spring 1993) 6.

Arab context, Presidents Sadat, Chadli, and Ben Ali all played
some version of this game, as did the new regime that came to
power after the overthrow of President Nimeiri in Sudan in 1985.
It is obviously much more difficult for an incumbent leader to
attempt the same strategy when this must inevitably cast doubt
on his own stewardship.

Third, as far as single-party regimes are concerned, the political
response to a self-proclaimed economic crisis seems to depend very
much on the relations between the new leader and that same party.
Only in the case of Sudan did such a party (the Sudan Socialist
Union) crumble away so completely that it was deemed possible
to return directly to the multiparty system (and set of electoral
practices) that had existed before Nimeiri's own coup in 1969.
Elsewhere, leaders were faced with a variety of options but tended
to favor reform of the single party within the context of some form
of controlled multiparty elections.

I will begin with an examination of these processes in Egypt,
Tunisia, and Algeria before turning to two countries in which a
simple return to previous electoral practice has been attempted
(Jordan and Sudan) and then to two regimes where no serious
political reforms have as yet been contemplated (Syria and Iran).

President Sadat's policy of distancing himself from his predecessor, Nasser, began in 1971 as soon as he had defeated his principal
opponents inside the ASU (Arab Socialist Union). To do this he
placed great stress on the economic crisis produced by Nasserite
policies, highlighted by a dramatic and certainly untruthful account of his being told by the Minister of Finance and Economy
that the treasury was "empty" and Egypt "almost bankrupt."[15]
The alternative was a program he described as one of *infitah* (literally, "opening up" but now more usually translated as "liberalization"). Although he never spelled it out with clarity, this was
generally assumed to imply measures to encourage foreign investment, combined with an attempt to increase the salience of the
private sector.

Later, Sadat took advantage of the great boost to his authority
following Egypt's partial victory in the 1973 October War against

[15] Raymond William Baker, *Sadat and After: Struggles for Egypt's Political
Soul* (London, I. B. Tauris, 1990) 205.

Israel to provide *infitah* with a political as well as an economic component. It is important to note, however, that the connection he made between the two types of liberalism was simply asserted and never properly argued through.[16] In these circumstances there is much to learn from a close study of the prolonged and complex process that took place between 1974 and 1976 during which the ASU was transformed from a mass organization to a party of government supporters capable of dominating a highly controlled multiparty system.[17] This, in my opinion, provides the key to Sadat's often hesitant moves towards greater pluralism, in which his measures to reform the ASU (which he viewed as a base for his still dangerous Nasserite opponents) were first accelerated by pressure from individuals within the elite calling for greater democracy and then brought under control again by his decision to allow only two opposition groups (one on the right, one on the left) to contest the 1976 general election against his, now reorganized, center party (the NDP).

If Egypt was one of the first countries in the world to attempt what was later to be called "perestroika," it was also one of the first to experience the problems of trying to open up politically at a time when economic problems were being intensified by the introduction of IMF-sponsored policies combining deregulation with fiscal austerity. The resulting "bread" riots of January 1977 effectively put an end to any further moves towards greater pluralism until the momentum was restarted by Sadat's successor, President Mubarak, in 1983–84. Nevertheless, I do not think we should be too harsh on Anwar Sadat's obvious failures. Subsequent events in the Soviet Union and Eastern Europe have demonstrated just how difficult is the path he tried to take. And whatever may be said about the return to repressive policies at the end of his period in office, he still left a substantial legacy in the form of an embryonic party system, a relatively free press, and, again, a relatively independent judiciary upon which his successor could build.

[16] For Sadat's ideas, see Mark H. Cooper, *The Transformation of Egypt* (London, Croom Helm, 1982) 88–90.
[17] The best account of the transition to multipartyism is in ibid., chapters 8 and 11.

President Mubarak's decision to return to multiparty politics in the general election of 1984 is another move that still awaits satisfactory explanation. However, if we note how the initiative was justified by his own close advisers as his need to make his own personal contribution to Egyptian progress—Mubarak's "democracy" to follow Nasser's "revolution" and Sadat's "*infitah*"—we may find this to be an important clue. Prima facie evidence would suggest that these same advisers were able to persuade Mubarak himself of the political advantages to be obtained from such a move, provided it was kept strictly under control. Not only was it popular with Egyptians (as well as in Washington) but it also held out the possibility of reducing the cost of internal security by incorporating the great majority of moderate members of the Muslim Brotherhood within the official parliamentary system. Other advantages were discovered over time, not the least of them being the way in which an appeal to the democratic system could be used to assert civilian control over the military and so limit military access to the political arena.[18]

As practiced between the general elections of 1984 and 1990, Egypt's electoral democracy was based on rules contained in three sets of legal documents: the Constitution of 1971, the Parties Law of 1977, and the Electoral Law of 1983. It was the Parties Law that laid down that there could be no organizations based on religious, regional, or class allegiances, and the Electoral Law that created a system that gave the government party every possible advantage over its opponents. Nevertheless, opposition parties were sufficiently enthusiastic about the process to participate in the first two elections, allowing two of them (the Neo-Wafd in alliance with the Muslim Brothers in 1984, the Neo-Wafd and an alliance of the Brothers, the Socialist Labor, and Socialist Liberals in 1987) to hurdle all the various barriers and so obtain limited representation in the National Assembly. The opposition was also able to obtain the backing of the courts for its argument that parts of the Electoral Law were in violation of the constitution, and so to force a small change in the rules in 1987 and then a whole-scale reform of the system in

---

[18] For example, Robert Springborg, *Mubarak's Egypt: Fragmentation of a Political Order* (Boulder, Westview Press, 1989) 118–25.

1990. But this was still not enough to remove the government party's huge inbuilt advantage, and it led all the major parties but the Tagamu (Progressives) to boycott the 1990 elections on the grounds that the system was still seriously biased against them.

Imperfect as it is, the Egyptian system offers important lessons both to current democratic practice and the possibility of future progress. I will offer some reflections on this subject in my conclusion. Meanwhile, the Egyptian model also had a powerful influence on the leaders of Tunisia and Algeria when they too attempted to reform their systems of political management in the late 1980s. What seems to have attracted both presidents Ben Ali and Chadli Benjedid was the opportunity it provided to reform the single party in the context of multiparty elections, which it alone would be allowed to win. They may also have seen the possibilities it offered to incorporate moderate Islamic elements within the political system while isolating the more extremist forces. In the event, however, neither president managed to make the model work as it had in Egypt.

As far as Tunisia was concerned, the major opening took place after Ben Ali's ousting of President Habib Bourguiba in November 1987. Like Sadat, he immediately set about distancing himself from his predecessor's policies, promising to replace the "corrupt" one-party system with something more pluralist and tolerant.[19] But his lack of a personal political constituency severely hampered his freedom of maneuver, and in the end he had to content himself with reliance on a somewhat revitalized government party (hastily renamed the RCD—Rassemblement Constitutionel Démocratique) augmented by leading individuals coopted from other political organizations. This in turn encouraged the party to use its control of the National Assembly to draw up a new electoral law so partial to itself that none of the opposition groups could be persuaded to participate in the April 1989 elections. The result was what the *Le Monde* correspondent described as a "monochrome" parliament, in which all 143 seats were won by

[19] I. William Zartman, "The Conduct of Political Reform: The Path towards Democracy," in *Tunisia: The Political Economy of Reform*, ed. I. William Zartman (Boulder, Lynne Rienner Publishers, 1991) 15.

the RCD.[20] Ben Ali was also unsuccessful in his efforts to drive a wedge between Muslim moderates and radicals, branding all the members of the major Islamic organization, the MTI (Mouvement de Tendence Islamique), as enemies of democracy and so unfit to take part in the electoral process.

Events in Algeria took a completely opposite turn. There, President Chadli's move to break the monopoly over political life exercised by the FLN (Front de Libération Nationale) was triggered by the shock created by the nationwide riots of October 1988. The first result was the new constitution of February 1989, with its official abandonment of socialism and its call for a more plural system. After that, however, Chadli's strategy began to run into serious problems. On the one hand, his desire to distance himself from the FLN apparatus deprived him of much of the influence that he might otherwise have used to engineer its reform. On the other, his decision to allow the main Islamic group, the FIS (Front Islamique de Salut), to run candidates in the 1990 municipal elections led not only to a major victory for the FIS but also to its growing ability to put pressure on the government to ensure that the forthcoming general election would be conducted under rules it deemed fair to itself. One result was the further violent demonstrations against certain provisions in the draft electoral law organized by the Islamic Front in June 1991, after which Chadli resigned his position as Chairman of the FLN, then appointed a caretaker cabinet of technocrats led by Sid Ahmad Ghozali to manage the runup to the elections.

Viewed from this perspective, the FIS's overwhelming victory in the first round of the polls in December 1991 can be seen as the result of its own good organization and resources, the confusion that still reigned within the FLN, the fragmentation of the rest of the opposition, and, finally, Ghozali's fierce determination to conduct a fair election—symbolized (for him at least) by the use of transparent ballot boxes—that kept official government interference to a minimum while still allowing the FIS to use its own control over many of the municipalities to make things more difficult for its

---

[20] Interview with President Ben Ali, *Le Monde*, 12 July 1991.

opponents.[21] Several key features of this election still remain to be explained. For one thing, why were nearly a million ballot papers (or 12 percent of the total) deemed to be invalid? Was this because they they were too complicated, as some have suggested? Or was it one of the many kinds of alleged fraud? For another, how was it that an FLN-dominated National Assembly allowed the boundaries of the electoral constituencies to be drawn in such a way that the FIS, with 3.2 million votes, obtained 188 seats, while the FLN itself, with half that number (1.6 million), ended up with only 15?[22] Given the military's subsequent intervention, perhaps we will never know.

The two other openly contested general elections held in the Arab world in the 1980s were those in Sudan and Jordan. The one in Sudan took place in April 1986 under exactly the same system as that used in the country's last competitive election in 1968, and was contested by three of the same major political groups, the 'Umma party (led by Sadiq al-Mahdi), the Democratic Unionist party, and the NIF (National Islamic Front), dominated by the Sudanese branch of the Muslim Brothers. The experiment was short-lived, however, as the politicians floundered in front of the huge problems created by civil war, famine, the massive movement of refugees, and an international debt so large that even the IMF was no longer prepared to help. It then came to an abrupt end with General Omar al-Bashir's military coup of June 1989, his dissolution of parliament, and the establishment of what was in effect an Islamic one-party state controlled by the NIF.

Jordan's general election of 1989 was also the country's first since 1968. It represented King Hussein's response to the widespread riots and demonstrations that had taken place earlier the same year and resulted in the election of individuals and groups representing a wide spectrum of Jordanian—and Palestinian—opinion. As in Sudan, the new government was immediately called upon to face huge economic difficulties, as well as the particular political problems associated with the end of the Cold War, the

---

[21] For example, Francis Ghilès, "Establishment Takes Fright at Algeria Election Results," *Financial Times*, 2 January 1992.

[22] Figures from Francis Ghilès, "A Sense of Shock," *Financial Times*, 12 January 1992.

influx of 300,000 Palestinian refugees from Kuwait, and tensions over Jordan's role at the Middle East Peace Conference. But here, unlike Sudan, there existed an alternative center of power represented by the palace, with enough skill and determination to see the experiment through.

One noteworthy aspect of King Hussein's strategy was his attempt to create a national consensus embodied in a National Pact aimed at establishing the ground rules for acceptable political behavior and signed by representatives of all the major groups and trends. A similar strategy has been attempted in both Tunisia and Kuwait.[23] While the idea of such a pact has much to recommend it in principle—and I will return to this point in my conclusion—it remains to be seen whether interventions of this type can make a significant difference to the politics of these particular three states.

Lastly, to turn to Syria and Iraq. It has already been suggested that neither of these regimes has found itself confronted with a situation that either necessitates or encourages political reform. Both are governed by long-established leaderships with well-perfected systems of control. Both are free of those huge and unmanageable international debts that require outside assistance to reschedule. And while Syria continues to have access to large sums of money from the oil-rich states of the Gulf, Saddam Hussein soon abandoned all talk of new political initiatives shortly after the end of the war with Iran in 1988, and embarked instead on a much more drastic solution to his financial problems: the occupation of Kuwait. Hence, while both leaders have sometimes referred to the processes of perestroika and glasnost taking place in other one-party states, neither of them has felt himself under sufficient pressure to make any significant moves in that direction. Moreover, one of these leaders, President Asad, has resisted even labeling his various measures to attract private and foreign capital as "liberalization," being well aware that the word itself might be enough to arouse political expectations and enthusiasms that he would find very difficult to contain.

---

[23] For a useful examination of the Tunisian National Pact, see Lisa Anderson, "The Tunisian National Pact of 1988," *Government and Opposition*, Spring 1991, 244–60.

Is Constitutional Democracy Possible
in Saudi Arabia and the Gulf?

Mention has already been made of the often positive connection between monarchical rule and democracy in both Jordan and Morocco: might the same also be true in the case of the ruling families of the Gulf? Such a question is best approached from two directions. I will first examine the experience of Kuwait (and, to a lesser extent, Bahrain) as far as an elected assembly is concerned. I will then make a few more general comments about the situation in the rest of the Gulf, where the only concession to democracy so far has been the creation of a string of advisory or consultative councils.

Kuwait's initial experiment with an elected assembly lasted from its first general election in 1963 to the assembly's dissolution by the amir in 1976, and its second from the elections of 1981 to a second dissolution in 1986. Bahrain's was much shorter: from the general election of 1973 to final dissolution in 1975. Nevertheless, both experiments had much in common. For one thing, neither government permitted the existence of political parties, identifying them with fractiousness and division. For another, both restricted the franchise to a small number of males with full citizenship. In the case of Kuwait, this meant a total electorate of only 17,000 in 1963, growing to no more than 57,000 in 1985. Meanwhile, the Bahraini electorate numbered 27,000 in 1973.[24] The result was a situation in which candidates were likely to be personally acquainted with the bulk of the voters in their constituency and, in one instance at least, to be able to invite all eight or nine hundred of them to a single dinner in the street outside his Kuwaiti home.[25]

The central problem for both systems was the relationship between the assembly and the cabinet, most of whose important members belonged to the ruling family. In the case of Bahrain, both sides were locked in almost constant conflict over a series of major issues, leading to stalemate and then the eventual dissolution. In Kuwait, on the other hand, the situation was much

[24] Rosemary Said Zahlan, *The Making of the Modern Gulf States* (London, Unwin Hyman, 1989) 39.

[25] The party was given by a friend of mine, Hashim Behbehani.

more fluid. The fact that the handful of serious critics of government policy during the first thirteen years of the experiment came
from well-established families with a basic stake in the well-being
of the whole community certainly acted to prevent major crises,
thus giving time for certain rules of conduct and procedure to develop. There were even important occasions when the interests of
the family and the assembly overlapped, as with the decision to na-
tionalize the Kuwait Oil Company in 1975. Nevertheless, the fact
that any criticism of government policy could be interpreted as
an attack on the ruling family's authority made periodic tensions
inevitable. For a while, the al-Sabahs tried to deal with this by
seeking to pack the assembly with their supporters while keeping
opposition to a minimum. But criticism of any sort still continued
to rankle, and the amir was quite easily persuaded to dissolve
the assembly in 1976, during the first phase of the Lebanese civil
war, on the grounds that public debate might exacerbate tensions
between the various Arab communities inside Kuwait itself.

The family then made a second, and more serious, attempt
to engineer a tame assembly by introducing smaller, and heavily
gerrymandered, constituencies before the 1981 elections. But this
still did not produce the required effect, and a small number of
vocal critics, some from various Islamic groupings, was enough to
excite increasing resentment among ministers as they came under
unbridled attack, first for the way they handled the consequences
of the Suq al-Manakh financial collapse in 1982, then for their
failure in preventing a number of sabotage attacks, including one
on an oilfield in June 1986. The second dissolution of assembly
immediately followed.

After this, the Sabahs tried a new tack, seeking to head off
demands for a return to the old system with the creation of a
partially elected, partially appointed, National Council, the main
purpose of which was to devise methods by which criticisms of
ministers could be kept to an acceptable minimum. This council
had hardly begun its deliberations before the Iraqi invasion. Now,
a year and a half later, it is still trying to think through the subject
again in time for a general election scheduled for late 1992. In the
new circumstances produced by the Iraqi invasion, prospects for a
revived democracy of the old type do not look very promising, to
say the least.

Experiments with elected assemblies anywhere else in the Gulf must run into exactly the same difficulties. Rosemary Zahlan's list of members of the cabinets in Kuwait, Bahrain, Qatar, and the UAE at the end of the 1980s shows that, in every country, the post of Prime Minister, Minister of Interior, Minister of Defense, and, in all but one case, Minister of Foreign Affairs, was held by someone belonging to the ruling family.[26] So long as this remains true—and it is difficult to see how the families could be persuaded to relinquish such close control over areas so central to the safety and security of their states—it is doubtful if this can be combined with any serious criticism of their stewardship by an elected assembly, let alone any notion of proper parliamentary accountability for their actions. We can also be sure that any such move would be bitterly resisted by the leaders of the local religious establishment, which until now has been the sole institution able to offer the families basic advice. In these circumstances, probably the best that can be hoped for is a sustained experiment with the type of assembly now being tried in Oman, consisting of men who put themselves forward for selection by the various provincial governors.

Some General Conclusions

Several Arab countries have now had nearly a century's experience of some kind of electoral democracy—what are the lessons? One of the most significant is the importance of timing and context. As far as the first round of colonial, and then immediate post-independence, elections were concerned, the close association between constitutionalism, democracy, and the local nationalist movement could be sustained quite well in the 1920s and 1930s but then came under increasing strain in the new international situation following the Second World War, when ideas of unity, development, and national self-assertion began to assume an overriding importance. Only in certain rare situations—as in Lebanon (for a while) and Morocco—were there countervailing tendencies sufficiently strong to allow democracy to survive. Finally, the tentative

[26] Zahlan, *Making of the Modern Gulf States*, appendix.

return to democratic practice in the 1970s and 1980s was largely a
response to the existence of major economic and social problems
common to many Third World countries, which themselves made
its conduct difficult and its future uncertain.

A second point concerns the support for pluralism and competitive elections in the society at large. In the Arab world, only
Egypt (and perhaps Lebanon?) seems to have had a sufficiently
large and various class of landowners, entrepreneurs, and professionals to sustain this type of politics for a relatively long period
of time up to 1952. After that time, I would argue that the wave
of nationalizations and the huge increase in state control in most
Arab countries deprived such persons of the private, independent
economic power upon which multipartyism is most securely based.
Whether a return to a mixed economy with a significant private
sector will be enough to reverse this trend is still unclear. Some
writers, like Clement Henry Moore, profess to see the emergence
of an independent banking system that could play a role in fi-
nancing a variety of political activities.[27] For myself, I see private
sectors as remaining weak and still highly dependent on government patronage and support. Such a view is reinforced by my
observations of the major problems faced by local manufacturers, who will continue to require administrative protection for a
long time to come. It is no accident that, in these circumstances,
well-organized religious parties are usually best placed to mobilize
the financial resources necessary to run long lists of candidates in
contested elections.

The lessons regarding the practical difficulties of running elections in the Middle East (or anywhere else in the Third World)
are almost too obvious to require further elaboration. Nevertheless, it would be useful to have more firsthand accounts of the
actual conduct of the recent polls in the Arab countries just to
learn where the most intractable problems lie. A study of Egypt's
1990 election reveals, for instance, that only 16 million out of of a
potential 37 million electors were on the appropriate registers. It
also suggests that the cost of running for an Egyptian election is
high, standing at somewhere between £E30,000 and £E70,000 a

---

[27] Clement Henry Moore, "Money and Power: The Dilemma of the Egyptian
Infitah," *Middle East Journal* (1986) 634–50.

candidate.[28] The situation in the first round of the recent Algerian election seems to have been little better, with over 900,000 registered voters disenfranchised because they did not receive their poll cards.[29] The fact that even in Egypt almost every election before 1952, and then after 1976, was fought under different rules only makes matters worse.

It is in this context that some of the continuing criticisms of the appropriateness of unbridled party activity and contested elections in Third World countries should be placed. President Nasser may have been guilty of special pleading in his interview with the Indian editor quoted above, but his remarks about the manipulation of illiterate and politically defenseless peasants remain relevant to this day. The same is true of some of President Sadat's worries about allowing the creation of parties based on a regional, communal, or religious basis in a situation where this may exacerbate already existing divisions and open up fault lines within a far from cohesive society.

Algeria's recent experience makes an equally basic, and difficult, point about whether you should allow antidemocratic forces to contest (and win) democratic elections. While we may regret that President Chadli's experiment at a "cohabitation" with the FIS was never attempted, we should also be on our guard against dismissing such concerns as simply reactionary and authoritarian. They need to be addressed very seriously—perhaps in the context of the treatment of similar problems in non-Arab democracies like India or Turkey—with a view to seeing how they might best be challenged and, possibly, surmounted. One possible way forward is a modification of the National Pact formula, in which all parties to an election pledge themselves publicly in advance to respect the others' rights. In the case of Algeria this would have involved the prior agreement of the FIS neither to interfere with the command structure of the army nor to pursue policies that were inimical to Berber interests, something that might have had the double advantage of preventing military intervention, as well as reducing the

---

[28] Iman Farag, "La politique à l'égyptienne: lecture des élections législatives," *Maghreb/Machrek* 133 (July/Sept. 1991) 30, 33.
[29] Ghilès, "A Sense of Shock."

possibility that the Berbers would feel forced to vote communally rather than on an individual basis.[30]

A last point concerns the particular lessons to be learned from Egypt's long, and unrivaled, experience with electoral democracy and whether it can continue to provide a model (as well as, perhaps, a warning) for the other major Arab states. At the time of writing, the balance of scholarly opinion seems to be rather negative, suggesting—with Bianchi and Springborg—that, however gratifying the progress made, the country has reached the limits of what the present regime might reasonably allow.[31] Looked at from this perspective, President Mubarak is seen to have derived tangible benefits from the type of controlled pluralism presently practiced—less costly policing, easier control over the military, international admiration, a subservient government party, etc.— but cannot proceed further without running the risk of losing his own basis of support and ability to control society. This is, of course, an example of the usual state-centered view of Egyptian politics, but it does have the experience of the three last general elections to call upon, in which, contrary to some earlier expectations, there has been no apparent progress towards a situation where the opposition might gain enough seats to mount a serious challenge to the government party. Given the huge biases within the system, Egypt's polls continue to be, as the title of one useful comparative study puts it, *Elections without Choices*, or, perhaps more accurately, elections in which voters choose an opposition.[32] The inevitable result is increasing voter apathy and general cynicism.

Two implications follow. First, even in a country like Egypt, certain restrictions on democratic practice may have to be tolerated for some time to come. One is a military president, who may

[30] This idea has been argued powerfully by Dr. Ghassan Salamé, based on papers written for the Fondazione Eni Enrico Mattei's research project on "Socio-Economic Change and Political Mobilization in the Arab Countries."

[31] Robert Bianchi, *Unruly Corporatism: Associational Life in Twentieth Century Egypt* (Oxford University Press, 1989) chapter 1; Springborg, *Mubarak's Egypt*, chapter 5.

[32] This is the title of a useful work by Guy Hermet, Richard Rose, and Alain Rouquié (London, Macmillan, 1978).

well be society's best defense against more direct military interven-tion. Another is the use of Egypt's continued state of emergency as a barrier to the advance of religious extremism. The second implication concerns the opposition. Given all the obvious con-straints, what can opposition parties do to make elections more competitive so as to allow them to improve their position? Here there are also two important points to be made. The first, and most positive, is to note that elements within the opposition have already been quite effective in pushing the regime into making changes in the electoral system, notably through the use of the courts. They have also made strenuous efforts to persuade the government to place the conduct of the elections under the con-trol of the judiciary rather than the Ministry of the Interior and the president to step down as the chairman of the government party.

Nevertheless, it also has to be pointed out—and this is the negative side—that the opposition itself has done its own cause no good by failing to ensure that it has conducted itself any more democratically than the regime it has been so quick to criticize. This will remain true so long as the major opposition leaders continue to be self-appointed and refuse to allow themselves to be held accountable by their supporters.

Looking further ahead, the Egyptian opposition parties may find that the only way to obtain the strength and the resources to mount a real challenge to the government is by making alliances with important economic interest groups within the society: for example, industrialists or workers. At present, only the Muslim Brothers have the ability and the organization to conduct such a strategy. The Egyptian opposition may also be able to take advantage of the new international politics of human rights in which the United States government, the members of the Euro-pean community, and Egypt's major creditors might all be willing to bring financial and other pressure to bear if a case can be prop-erly made. Finally, as before 1952, the argument for democracy as producing better, fairer, freer government still has far too few exponents.

In other Arab countries progress towards electoral democracy has been even slower. I have discussed the different cases of Tunisia and Algeria, Jordan and Morocco, and the Gulf states, as well as the special problems that each must face. In some, the legacy of one-party, statist policies remains a heavy one; in others, progress continues to depend on the interests of a still powerful royal family. Clearly there is need for great patience.

PART 2

Power against Power

Populism and Democracy in Turkey, 1946–1961

REŞAT KASABA

WHEN discussing the recent history of Turkish democracy, the image that most readily comes to mind is a glass that is one-half full, which, of course, is also one-half empty. On the full side, we have the incontrovertible record of the past forty-seven years. In all but six of these years Turkey has been governed by governments that were elected freely. Twelve general and numerous local elections were held in this time period, and in most of these elections a multitude of parties that represented a wide spectrum of views competed. In other words, in most elections people had a clear choice. On the empty side, we have the six years when three different military regimes ruled the country; in 1960–61, 1971–72, and 1980 to 1983. These were the years when civil and political rights were suspended, democratic institutions were abolished, the press was silenced, and political parties were closed down. These were the years of mass trials, summary sentences, and even executions that were carried out with no regard to due process and without any chance of appeal. When studying social change, we have a tendency to focus on periods of crisis, hoping that these will give us a clue as to what was wrong with the period that led up to them. Braudel warned us a long time ago against paying too much attention to such "flash points of history" lest we become

The research for this paper was made possible by a Social Sciences Faculty Award that was granted by the Graduate School of the University of Washington. I am happy to acknowledge their support and also thank the staff at the Library of the Grand National Assembly in Ankara, Turkey, for their cooperation.

chroniclers of big events and important men (yes, men) and form a wrong impression of the years when there are no "extraordinary" events. For example, if we build the story of the Turkish democracy around the three coups, we find that we do not have much to say about the remaining forty-one years unless, of course, we see them as involving the ever-slow unfolding of conflicting forces and contradictions that would eventually culminate in the crises in question. But if we do this, we miss the more interesting part of the story.

In comparison with other Middle Eastern states and even with states elsewhere in the periphery, Turkey stands out not so much for the predictability of its coups but for the inability of the military regimes to achieve staying power and the failure of these governments to remake the Turkish state and society. Each one of the coups Turkey has experienced in the last thirty years ended in varying degrees of humiliation for its plotters. In the 1961 elections the Justice party (JP), which had clearly identified itself as the continuation of the just-overthrown Democrat party, became the largest party. In 1973, after a two-year campaign that aimed to destroy and discredit all the institutions, associations, and individuals who were affiliated with the left wing of the political spectrum, a plurality of the Turkish electorate voted for the only openly leftist party, which subsequently became the main partner of a coalition government. The 1983 elections turned out to be a humiliating defeat for the party that was set up and openly favored by the military junta. Here, the biggest winner was the Motherland party, which had been explicitly singled out for attack and criticism by the junta leader General Evren up to the evening before the elections.

In this paper I focus more on the fuller part of the glass. My interest lies not so much with the breakdown but with the pressures that ensure the repeated restoration of multiparty democracy in Turkey. The paper pays special attention to the 1946–1961 period because the context and the dynamics of democratic restoration were defined in these years.

From a social and economic viewpoint, the decades between the 1940s and the 1980s were among the most tumultuous in Turkish history. It was during those years that Turkey moved from being a predominantly rural to a predominantly urban society;

per capita income increased from about TL 98.00 to about TL 10 million today (in current TL); a vast network of roads reached the most distant parts of the country; and significant gains were registered in literacy, life expectancy, and other vital statistics. Compared with the scope and extent of these changes, the political scene in Turkey has remained remarkably predictable. In all but approximately two of the forty-one normal years of Turkish democracy, Turkey has been governed by parties and coalitions that have used an overlapping conservative, traditionalist, and democratic discourse to advance their causes.

Therefore, the key to understanding the resilience of Turkish democracy lies, in part, in explaining the enduring strength of this conservative appeal even as the country and people were affected by wide-ranging economic and political changes. In light of the changes that Turkey has been going through, it is impossible to attribute the appeal of conservatism to the manipulation and resources of a single group, party, or class. Over the years, the parties that have blended the democratic, traditionalist, and conservative themes have managed to craft a message that has found a receptive audience among people from a wide array of social and economic backgrounds. On the basis of the supra-class nature of their appeal, at crucial points in recent history these parties have become the main representatives of a genuinely populist movement in Turkey. What has made the democracy glass at least half full in Turkey has been this junction between the sentiments of a large section of Turkish society who resented the rise of the late Ottoman and early Turkish states to a position of supremacy on the one side, and the political parties who have made anti-statism the central feature of their programs on the other. The recentralization of the Ottoman state that led to this common and generalized resentment can be traced back to the late eighteenth century.

From Empire to Republic

In terms of state-society relations, the eighteenth and nineteenth centuries represent a watershed in the history of the Ottoman Empire. Following the incorporation of large parts of the empire into the world economy, groups of bankers, merchants, and manufacturers acquired new levels of prominence in the Ottoman

Empire independently of the central government. These groups were sustained primarily by their economic activities, but unlike their counterparts in earlier eras they were able to affect and even challenge the policies and the organization of the Ottoman state. Over time, various groups of people in this nonstate arena acquired the means of exercising a more direct influence on the Ottoman state. Urban professionals and merchants could form associations, non-Muslim groups were allowed to organize their own communities and draft their separate constitutions, and the empire's subjects as a whole gained the protection of codified laws, a constitution, and, ultimately, elections in the course of the nineteenth century. Societal inroads into the Ottoman state became most visible in the convening of the parliaments, one in 1876 for a short period and a second in 1908.

In the Ottoman Empire, the extent and the strength of the nonstate arena was not confined to people who became wealthy by engaging in commercial activities. Equally important was the presence of a large number of circulating laborers, who made it difficult for the Ottoman state to have a reliable tax base and, even more important, to define and protect its territories, especially along its border areas. Also in the nineteenth century, the ideas of political freedom, constitutional monarchy, and social justice spread among a relatively small but influential group of intellectuals and bureaucrats. Such cultural links with Europe contributed to the formulation of a discourse of opposition that was very effective through the end of the empire and into the republican period. And finally, there was the growing prominence of local religious orders. In most of the Ottoman centuries, these fell outside the official, imperially sanctioned practice of Islam, even though they were widespread and very influential. In large parts of Anatolia, when people "practiced" Islam they did so within the framework of one of these sects. It is there that people found a meaning to their lives and, occasionally, also the means of resisting the pressures of the central government, even when it was supported by the officially sanctioned version of the religion. Their organizational contribution to urban manufacturing associations and guilds made these sects particularly important and powerful in various parts of the empire. As long as the main arteries of imperial organization were strong and the imperial center could deliver on its promises of protection and redistribution, these local orders did not threaten the overall system; on the contrary they provided an additional element of stability by supplying a means of bonding people together and keeping them in obedience to a higher authority.

In the changing context of the eighteenth and nineteenth centuries we can imagine many different ways in which these social groups, communities, and associations could have continued to develop and exert an even more direct influence on the reshaping of the Ottoman state and society, whether alone, in competition, or in combination with each other. But after a series of junctions where alternative paths that involved different combinations had a good chance of materializing, the balance shifted decisively in favor of the political center in the twentieth century. Starting from 1908, in a twenty-year period that included a series of wars, the formal end of the empire, and the formation of the Turkish Republic, power and economic initiative once again centralized and concentrated in the hands of the central government—more specifically, in the hands of an urban-based, military-bureaucratic elite. Within the context of this recentralization, those entities that had the potential of increasing their autonomous presence were either curtailed or incorporated into the state apparatus. As for those whose goals were more in the direction of decentralization, federalism, or liberalism, they were completely excluded from the nationalist project. With this latter category went the professional, social, and political associations of non-Muslims; with them also went the mainstay of the fledgling Ottoman bourgeoisie. In these same years, the world economy went through two world wars and a major depression. These global conditions were quite conducive to the kind of changes that the political elite was spearheading in Turkey. Other states, whose size and status were similar to Turkey, also took advantage of these conditions and implemented similar policies of nationalist enclosure and development during the first half of the twentieth century. The same is true also for the more than twenty states that emerged from within the former territories of the Ottoman Empire.

Thus, between the early nineteenth century and the beginnings of the twentieth, the space that might have been conducive to the development of a civil society in the Ottoman Empire was systematically contained by the various Ottoman (and later Turkish, Arab, and Balkan) governments. During these crucial years, as people were prevented from associating freely and influencing their respective states-in-formation, they gradually retreated to the three modes of obtaining help and solidarity that were still open to them. These were extended families, religious orders, and tribal and other looser native-place networks. What motivated the individuals to seek refuge in each or all of these configurations was, above all, a sense of powerlessness in a world that was in a sea of change. Thus, strengthening of these three domains should be seen primarily as a defensive process set up by people confronted by a state that was capturing all the visible and tangible means of power and authority. It has to be borne in mind, however, that, while these domains were becoming extremely important, they did not necessarily empower the youth, the women, and the disciples who were in them. They were all organized along strictly hierarchical lines that put men above women, elders above youth, and often recognized religious leaders as the supreme arbiters both in spiritual and in worldly matters.

The single-party regime in Turkey, which continued until 1946, can be seen as the culmination of this process of political entrenchment. In these years, the Turkish state appeared to be all-pervasive and all-powerful, extending into every corner of public and private life in the new country. But this does not mean that the nonstate arena that I identified above had completely disappeared or was completely passive, even in this period. Kurdish insurgency, which takes most of its power from its tribal basis and extended family networks, became, and continues to be, the major source of contention for the new regime in Turkey. Under the Republic, religious affairs were taken over by the state but then, unlike the Ottoman period, they were made not the legitimizing ideology but a subordinate branch of the state bureaucracy. Local religious orders and sects were formally banned, but given the nature of these entities such a measure was difficult to impose. In fact, because of the overwhelming emphasis by the new state on secularism, these local orders became even more popular because they provided the only opportunity for continuing to live one's life according to the precepts of Islam without obviously being seen to do so.[1] Providing the means of worship was only one of the functions of these orders. More importantly, they supplied a ready network of help and solidarity for a people who wished to resist, avoid, or even just cope with the increasingly oppressive policies of the state.

Indirect as it might have been, the nonstate arena played an important role in shaping the content and implementation of many of the policies of the state in the single-party period. Repeated armed clashes with the Kurdish tribes and their forced resettlement is one example of such policies. Also, the emphasis that was placed on corporatist institutions such as the Village Institutes (Köy Enstitüleri), and People's Houses (Halkevleri) were attempts at breaking up the local networks of solidarity. But the most important impact of the nonstate arena can be seen in the way in which the republican regime made opposition to religion the hallmark of its modernization project. More than anything else, it was the widespread nature of religious organizations and the depth of people's ties to them that forced the new regime to focus so singlemindedly on the "regressive" role of Islam.[2]

Neither the Turkish state nor the nonstate arena in Turkey remained the same during the first two decades of the Republic. While the social groups that constituted the latter had to devise new methods of coping with the changing social, political, economic, and legal conditions, the former's policies became ever more uncompromising in its "nationalism," "secularism," and "Westernism" as unifying and universalizing directives. Because of the way in which these two spheres continued to shape each other, we cannot think of the nonstate arena by itself as containing the elements of "traditionalist" resistance to forces of "modernity." Both the nationalist project and the spread of religious orders, extended families, and the tribalist and native place affiliations were products of the one and the same modern era. It is for this reason that, in a strictly technical definition, these orders and other local groupings can be considered as fulfilling a role that

[1] Şerif Mardin, "The Just and the Unjust," *Daedalus* 120.3 (Summer 1991) 113–129.
[2] See Nilüfer Göle, *Modern Mahrem* (Istanbul, Metis, 1991).

was similar to that played by the constituent elements of civil society in Europe.

The economic and military mobilization the Turkish state organized during the Great Depression and the Second World War required large-scale appropriation and transfer of resources from the agricultural sector. The exigencies of this period made the unidirectional nature of Turkish reform policies increasingly more apparent. In addition to being regarded as the main obstacle to progress, the people in the rural sector, and in particular the peasants, now became the major bearers of a wide array of economic policies over which they had no influence. The policies that were carried out during these campaigns widened the chasm between the state and the majority of the people. It is easy to see how the religious orders, extended families, and other networks were recreated, restrengthened, and made more significant under these circumstances. The feelings of vulnerability that had originally pushed people toward these communities were galvanized with a growing sense of resentment and even an antagonism toward the state. As early as 1930, when an opposition party was allowed to form, it gained such popularity so quickly that it was closed down the same year it was formed. Even though the leaders of this party were handpicked by Mustafa Kemal Atatürk and they had no intention of actually taking over the government, they were readily perceived as "saviors" by large numbers of people, especially in the economically more advanced western regions of the country.[3]

The Multiparty System and the Democrat Party

A major break in Turkish political history came with the adoption of the multiparty democratic system in 1945. The reasons that pushed the ruling Republican People's party (RPP) to allow the formation of opposition parties had to do with the changing international conditions and growing domestic pressures. Externally, the relations between the Soviet Union and Turkey deteriorated significantly in the aftermath of the Second World War. For Turkey, this increased the urgency of improving its relations with

[3] Walter Weiker, *Political Tutelage and Democracy in Turkey: The Free Party and its Aftermath* (Leiden, E. J. Brill, 1973); Fethi Okyar, *Üç Devirde Bir Adam: Hatıralar* (Istanbul, Tercuman, 1980).

the United States. But in order to become a part of the new North Atlantic alliance and benefit from American aid, the Turks had to "prove" their Western and democratic credentials, especially in the face of the suspicions aroused by their reluctance in joining the anti-German alliance until the very last days of the war.[4] Domestically, there was pressure coming from some circles in the political elite to open the system to opposition and to debate, as it was becoming increasingly difficult to govern a country such as Turkey by fiat.

The new system of politics quickly found a receptive audience among the people. The Democrat party (DP), which was the first major opposition party, gained a very large portion of votes (according to some, the majority) in the first elections in which it participated in 1946, less than one year after it was founded. Democrats came to power in 1950 and received solid, albeit diminishing, majorities in the 1954 and 1957 elections. The DP was overthrown by a military coup in 1960, and its charismatic leader, along with two of the cabinet ministers, was hanged. But the Justice party, whose founders identified themselves as the heirs to the Democrats, became the largest party in the 1961 elections and came to power in the 1965 elections. The Justice party itself was overthrown two times by military interventions in 1971 and in 1980, each time to be returned to power eventually by elections.

In terms of their economic policies, the Democrats did not depart significantly from the last years of the RPP regime. So similar were the two parties' programs, that both Nihat Erim, who was the secretary general of the RPP, and Celal Bayar, who would become the president under DP rule, summarized their respective goals in identical terms as "turning Turkey into a small America."[5] Actually, it would be unrealistic to think the leaders of the DP

---

[4] Cemil Koçak, *Türkiye'de Milli Şef Dönemi* (Ankara, Yurt, 1985) 385–387.

[5] In 1949, Nihat Erim, the Secretary General of the RPP said, "Barring some unforeseen catastrophe ... in the near future Turkey will become a small America." Eight years later in 1957, President Bayar said, "it is our hope that in thirty years, with a population of fifty million, Turkey will become a small America." Feroz and Bedia Turgay Ahmad, *Türkiye'de Çok Partili Politikanın Açıklamalı Kronolojisi* (Ankara, Bilgi, 1976) 57, 170.

would have brought about a complete overhaul of the social and
economic system. All four of the founders of the new party came
from the ranks of the RPP; two were large landowners, one was
a close friend of Atatürk, and the last was a high-caliber intellectual who was a leading literary historian in Istanbul University.

During the 1940s the rural population was so impoverished and
conditions in the countryside were so bad that many economic
issues were discussed in terms of the most basic human needs,
such as the need to end hunger, prohibit forced labor, and end
emergency rule.[6] Beyond such generalities, and beyond removing
the intrusive presence of the military in the villages, the DP did
not promise a major restructuring of the Turkish economy or
a large-scale redistribution of wealth. This does not mean that
no improvement took place in the lives of people who supported
this party over the ten years during which the DP was in power.
But the DP's ability to bring about material improvements in the
lives of villagers (for example, by investing in basic infrastructure
or paying high prices for agricultural products) depended on the
suitability of external conditions and especially on the availability
of foreign exchange. So, most of the major steps in these areas were
taken in the first half of the 1950s, when American aid became
readily available and the Korean War improved the world prices
of wheat, which was a major export item of Turkey.

What made the Democrat party appealing to many voters was
its success in tapping popular resentment against the single-party
government. The new leaders were extremely skillful in translating
this sentiment into outright antagonism against the Republican
People's party: that is, the party that was founded by Atatürk and
that had been in power since the establishment of the Republic.

---

[6] For example, in 1948, Bayar told a group of villagers in east-central Anatolia that if they were hungry they should not pay any taxes. "If there is going
to be hunger in this country," he argued, "all of us should go hungry." Ibid.,
42. On the wartime conditions and government policies, see Şevket Pamuk,
"War, State Economic Policies, and Resistance by Agricultural Producers in
Turkey, 1939–1945," in *Peasants and Politics in the Modern Middle East*, ed.
F. Kazemi and J. Waterbury (Miami, Florida International University Press,
1991) 125–142.

Especially between 1945 and 1950, the DP's primary concern was to prove that it was genuinely different from the RPP and not a "party of the tutelage" like the opposition party that was set up in 1930. One of the earliest posters of the Democrats showed a raised hand with the palm showing, and a statement over it reading "Enough is Enough! It is the Nation's Turn to Speak!" The founders of the new party accused the RPP of representing the "Dictatorship of the Intelligentsia."[7] Adnan Menderes, who would later become the Prime Minister, likened the People's Houses to "fascistic organizations."[8] In some of his speeches, he claimed that there was little difference between Stalin's regime and that of the RPP in Turkey.[9] Following the elections of 14 May 1950, in his speech opening the National Assembly, in what has to have been a deliberate move, Menderes did not mention Atatürk's name. He said,

> I have no doubt that May 14 will always be remembered as a day of special importance that ended one period in our history and opened up another one.... With the May 14 elections an important step has been taken in a revolution that is far more important than anything that had been accomplished previously in our country.... We are not one of the many governments of the same party that followed one another. We are a party that came to power with the will of the nation.... All these years, continuing a system of government that did not include any mechanism for national or political controls has led to the multiplication of errors, wastes, and excesses.[10]

Barely one month after the elections, Menderes accused the RPP of plotting with the army to overthrow the newly formed DP government. He said,

[7] F. and B. Ahmad, *Türkiye'de Çok Partili Politikanın Açıklamalı Kronolojisi*, 14.

[8] Şevket Süreyya Aydemir, *Menderes'in Dramı?* (Istanbul, Remzi, 1969) 318.

[9] F. and B. Ahmad, *Türkiye'de Çok Partili Politikanın Açıklamalı Kronolojisi*, 56.

[10] Aydemir, *Menderes'in Dramı?* 206.

our only goal is to strengthen democracy in our country. if the
RPP wants to be helpful, they have to get rid of their leadership,
which has a sick obsession with power.[11]

Starting from their very first convention, and through their
years in opposition and in government, the Democrats saw themselves as representing a vision and a program that were different from their rivals in four major areas. Since then, these four
areas have become the main identifiers of a party's or a movement's place in the Turkish political spectrum. The Democrats
were openly critical of the alliance that had been behind the Ottoman and Turkish reform movement, in particular of the state
bureaucracy and certain segments of the intelligentsia. About the
military, which was the other member of this alliance, they were
careful not to express outright hostility lest this might antagonize
the officers and lead them to change their feelings about multiparty democracy.

The second way in which the Democrats were different was how
they distanced themselves from the militant secularism of the early
republican governments. The DP and the parties that followed in
its path have been less strident about keeping religion outside
the public domain. In 1949 Bayar said, "the Turkish nation is
Muslim. It will stay Muslim. It will reach its God as Muslim."[12]
In the late 1940s symbols of defiance, such as the Arabic rendering
of the call to prayer (which had been outlawed by the republican
regime), were used more and more frequently and openly by people
sympathetic to the DP. Indeed, the law that required the call to
prayer to be in Turkish would be one of the first laws rescinded by
the Democrat party after it came to power in 1950.[13] Nevertheless,
it has to be remembered that all the major figures of the DP came
of age as the empire ended and the new Republic was formed. They
had actively taken part in these changes. Some, like Bayar, were
Atatürk's personal friends and associates. As such they were not

---

[11] Aydemir, *Menderes'in Dramı?* 212.

[12] Kemal Karpat, *Turkey's Politics* (Princeton University Press, 1959) 233,
271ff.

[13] This law was passed on 16 June 1950, less than one month after the
elections: F. and B. Ahmad, *Türkiye'de Çok Partili Politikanın Açıklamalı
Kronolojisi*, 71.

interested in undoing the accomplishments of the Atatürk era. Therefore, once in power, rather than working to undermine or undo the reforms, they acted in a lenient and lax way in enforcing them. In 1951, Menderes "dismissed the Republicans' claim that they were the 'guardians of the Kemalist reforms' and told his interviewer that 'the real guardian of the reforms was the Turkish nation.'"[14] Later, he argued that the RPP had exaggerated the danger of Islamic reaction in order to maintain the single-party regime for a lot longer than was necessary. "In this way," he said, "secularism became a tool for creating animosities and oppressing people."[15]

The third main component of the Democratic program was an unqualified support for private initiative and unhindered private enterprise. Democrats described the RPP's etatism as "interventionist" and thoroughly incompatible with their brand of liberalism. In fact, Adnan Menderes had his first falling-out with the RPP by opposing the land-reform legislation that was drafted in 1945 to placate the rural population, which had suffered immensely during the war years. Over the years, the Democrats and the political movements and regimes that followed them were so strict in defending private initiative that they resisted even the most elementary laws and regulations concerning minimum wage, child labor, workers' safety and right to strike, let alone the consideration of larger issues such as land reform and directive economic planning. By being unequivocal in this respect, the Democrats managed to attract the support of not only large landlords but also medium peasants, merchants, and manufacturers in towns and cities.

Finally, and most potently, through their discourse the Democrats and their successors elevated the formal procedures of democracy, in particular the act of voting, to a very high level of esteem. From the very first days, "the sanctity of the ballot" was placed at the center of all the major policy statements, declarations, and speeches issued by the Democrat party. The first time the four founders of the DP cooperated was in 1945, when they drafted

---

[14] Feroz Ahmad, *The Turkish Experiment in Democracy, 1950–1975* (Boulder, Westview, 1977) 367.
[15] *Cumhuriyet*, 12 January 1960.

a proposal demanding the full implementation of the principle of national sovereignty that was in the constitution.[16] In the party convention that was held in 1949, the Democrats passed a resolution stating that violation of the election law was synonymous with violation of people's natural rights, and that such a situation would justify self-defense on the part of the citizens.[17] The Democrats, especially Menderes, worked the theme of electoral power very effectively. In Menderes' speeches, the individual, who up to then had been taken for granted as a producer of economic goods in peacetime and as human fodder in wartime, acquired a new sacred power that could allow him not only to live freely but also to change governments. Menderes' ability to communicate this message directly to the people was the Democrats' most effective weapon, as was demonstrated in the elections of 1950, 1954, and 1957. Whenever the economic problems appeared insurmountable or Ankara's political scene became too contentious, Menderes would take off to Anatolia and speak before hundreds of thousands of people and remind them of their power, while reassuring himself of his continuing popularity. Here he is in Kırşehir on 1 February 1960:

> Yes, a great and radical transformation took place. It used to be that only one person ruled and only a few hundred participated in politics. With our democratic revolution, with one leap, millions and millions of citizens acquired the vote and became influential in the administration of our country. They became real citizens.... Despite all of the difficulties, we are confident that with courage and determination we will be able to continue with the full implementation of this most beautiful and humanistic regime because it fits best with the characteristics of the noble Turkish nation.[18]

Two weeks later, he spoke as follows in Antakya:

> To those who forget their own mischief and accuse us of theft, I would like to respond by saying that it is not the DP that steals

---

[16] F. Ahmad, *The Turkish Experiment in Democracy*, 12; Karpat, *Turkey's Politics*, 145.
[17] F. and B. Ahmad, *Türkiye'de Çok Partili Politikanın Açıklamalı Kronolojisi*, 55; Karpat, *Turkey's Politics*, 233ff.
[18] *Cumhuriyet*, 2 February 1960.

votes. There is a reason why we are patient and tolerant towards these people. We trust in the Turkish nation, in its patriotism, political genius, and perception. When it becomes necessary, the Turkish nation knows how to take matters in its own hands and cry, "Enough! It is the nation's turn to speak!"[19]

Less than ten days before the coup that overthrew and ultimately killed him, he was in Turgutlu, not far from his birth place in western Turkey:

> In the old days, three people would plot together and take away the chair from under the fourth while the whole nation watched from a distance. This was politics then. The fate of the whole country would be decided by this or that individual. Now it is the whole nation across the entire land that determines the fate of the country.... This country does not have the slightest interest in becoming the stage for bloody adventures.... For this reason, as the great mass of people constituting the Turkish nation, we are determined to prevail over these adventures and adventurers."[20]

Finally, two days before the coup, on 25 May 1960 he spoke in Eskişehir:

> These events are caused by the efforts of those who want to see if it is possible to come to power through means other than elections. If we believe in the maturity of the Turkish nation and in the virtues of democracy, we have to agree that the only way of coming to power and leaving power is through elections.[21]

At this point, the question might be asked why a message that had originally been designed to rally the electorate against the single-party regime continued to be effective after fifteen years. There were two related reasons for this. Starting from the late 1940s, the Democrat party was organized as a truly national party, with a high number of regional branches and a variety of local-level

---

[19] *Cumhuriyet*, 14 February 1960

[20] *Havadis*, 18 May 1960.

[21] *Havadis*, 26 May 1960. The events referred to are student demonstrations that took place in Ankara and Istanbul during the closing days of April 1960.

offices.[22] Party branches in small towns and even villages were
given a great deal of autonomy in organizing and linking their regions with the party hierarchy, which for ten years between 1950
and 1960 fed right into the government. By contrast, the RPP
maintained close control over the activities of its local branches,
monopolizing a large part of the decision-making power in central
hands. Consequently, most people perceived the RPP branches not
as their own representatives but as the organ of central administration and, before 1950, that of the state. With the Democrats,
the power vector was in the other direction. This put them in
charge of a vast organizational network that they used to induce
people to come out, listen, demonstrate, and vote throughout the
1950s.

The Democrats also relied on the less formal network of people who, through their patterns of migration, had started to link
rural and urban zones to each other in Turkey. The movement
of large numbers of people from villages into towns and cities accelerated significantly in the 1950s. During these years, increasing
mechanization of agriculture released large numbers of people from
villages. At the same time, the highways that were being built all
across the country made it possible for these people to move with
relative ease over long distances. It would be misleading, however,
to view rural-urban migration as a single, self-contained movement
with a beginning (rural) and an end (urban). More typically, the
two-way flow of consumer goods, people, information, and ideas
served to create a continuum between the "rural" and the "urban,"
battering the imaginary city walls that had been jealously guarded
by the bureaucratic elite in previous decades and centuries.

One result of this new configuration was that the religious orders, extended families, and the native-place networks in which
people had sought refuge in the early years of the Republic became
larger and gained a new dynamism in the 1950s. By extending and
expanding, these units accommodated the needs of the large numbers of people who were going through significant changes in their
lives and expectations. Most importantly, it was through these

---

[22] According to one count in 1960, the Democrat party had over sixty thousand local units in small towns and villages across the country: *Cumhuriyet*,
24 June 1960.

networks that people found an entry into jobs and political processes. Their openness to these networks gave the Democrats an important advantage, but this situation also constituted one of the substantive weaknesses of democracy in Turkey. Throughout the multiparty period in Turkey, the political leaders who identified themselves with the Democrats' ideology never questioned or attempted to alter the power relations that tied the peasant to the landlord, the disciple to the religious sheikh, the children and women to the elders of extended families, or the new immigrants to the influential figures in native-place networks. In this sense, the relations that were taking shape resembled patron-client relations, where votes were traded for various favors, corruption was widespread, and some people became politically influential for reasons that did not have anything to do with the will of the nation. With their anti-statist credentials, the Democrats were able to work through these networks more effectively than any other political party in Turkey.

The ongoing ties to rural structures and the continuing impact of traditional relations on politics can also be detected in the special relationship that developed between the people and the Democrat party's prime minister, Adnan Menderes. Whenever Menderes addressed a rally, it was as if both he and the crowds drew strength from each other's presence. Furthermore, there had developed a widespread belief that Menderes possessed some mythical, supernatural powers. In an interesting twist, in 1959 Menderes walked away from a plane crash that killed fourteen people. This added fuel to the rumors that he was in fact immortal.

Nevertheless, the existence of such beliefs and corrupting influences should not undermine the reality that people in Turkey knew that they had access to free and open elections with a secret ballot, and that the political parties had pledged to abide by the results of these elections. Thus, when Menderes reminded people how elections had empowered them and allowed them the opportunity to be ruled by the government of their choice, this was not empty rhetoric. People knew what he was talking about, since many of them had lived through the transition from a single- to a multiparty system.

In the late 1950s, as the DP and Menderes continued to emphasize the virtues of democracy and popular will, Turkey faced a

series of problems that the government was unwilling or unable
to address. The economic situation was deteriorating, with high
inflation and growing deficits. Short-term, stopgap measures that
the state took were making the situation worse, especially for those
on fixed income. At the same time, it was becoming increasingly
difficult to administer Turkey with the existing body of laws, most
of which had been drawn up under very different circumstances
and to serve the needs of another era. However, in order to carry
out any large-scale legal and political reform, the parties in the
National Assembly needed to reach a broad-based agreement. But
neither the governing Democrats nor the opposition parties were
interested in compromise. Consequently, the economic difficulties
that awaited solutions were compounded by political inaction.

If things had been left to their course, it would have been difficult for the government to ignore the daily multiplying bottlenecks
for long. For one thing, the RPP was trying to shed its dictatorial image and become more attentive to the demands of various
groups in the society. As a result of the deteriorating relations
between the DP government and the press, many of the leading
journalists were now siding with the RPP, which significantly improved its discourse of opposition. Despite the seriousness of the
growing economic and political crisis, however, the DP still enjoyed enough support in the country that if elections had been
held in 1961 as scheduled they would probably have produced
another DP victory, albeit with a smaller majority. But looking
further into a future that did not materialize, it would certainly
have been difficult to hold together for much longer the populist
coalition that had been the mainstay of the DP power throughout
the 1950s.

27 May 1960: The State Redux

What actually happened was unprecedented, if not totally unex-
pected. On 27 May 1960, thirty-eight junior officers staged a coup
and overthrew the DP government. The military stayed in power
for eighteen months and handed over power to an elected government in the fall of 1961. During this time, most of the decisions
of the DP era were annulled, a new constitution was prepared
by a special commission of university professors, and the election system was changed from simple majority to proportional

representation. At the same time, the military junta set up a special tribunal where the deputies, the entire cabinet, and the state president of the DP era were tried. After a trial that lasted from October 1960 to August 1961, the court passed several death and prison sentences in September. Three of the death sentences were carried out immediately, whereby Prime Minister Adnan Menderes and two of the ministers in the last DP cabinet were hanged within two days of their sentencing. The coup formally ended with the elections that were held in the fall of 1961. In a pattern that would be repeated in each of the subsequent military interventions, the Justice party, which was created as a continuation of the overthrown DP, emerged from the elections as the largest party and became the main coalition partner in the government that was formed. The circumstances that led to the May 27 coup, the motivations of the officers who took part in it, the short- and the long-term impact of this event on Turkish society cannot be discussed adequately within the confines of this paper.[23] For our purposes, however, it is important to note and examine the most important result of the coup, which was not exactly intended. As a result of the military intervention of May 27, the populist coalition, which had started to dissolve in the late 1950s, gained a new momentum and continued to dominate Turkish politics for another twenty years.

The short time during which the military was in power cast a very long and dark shadow on Turkish politics. It looked as if, by overthrowing a democratically elected government, by adopting an elitist approach to legislation and administration, and by maintaining a close cooperation with the RPP leadership, the officers were trying to re-create pre-1950 conditions. The tripartite coalition among the military, bureaucrats, and the intelligentsia was resuscitated when a group of professors were given broad powers as advisers and as the writers of the new constitution. It was later revealed that the entire body of DP deputies were arrested and prosecuted on the advice of these professors, who had argued

---

[23] See Walter Weiker, *The Turkish Revolution, 1960–1961* (Washington, D.C., Brookings Institution, 1963); C. H. Dodd, *Politics and Government in Turkey* (Berkeley, University of California Press, 1969); F. Ahmad, *The Turkish Experiment in Democracy*.

that otherwise the military could not justifiably maintain that the DP government was guilty of major crimes and had lost its legitimacy.[24]

The influential figures in the military government seemed to be motivated by a deep suspicion of the "people" and their elected representatives. The regime went out of its way to discredit and humiliate the DP and its leaders, in particular the popular prime minister. Menderes was barred from speaking to anyone during the first several months of his imprisonment; some lawyers who were inclined to take his defense were intimidated into turning him down; those who defended him were not given free access to their client or to the files. When they tried to publicize these restrictions, the lawyers themselves were arrested. The trials were broadcast live on the radio and they revolved for the most part around issues such as the prime minister's extramarital affairs, or whether he or his colleagues had embezzled paltry sums of money, or whether President Bayar had sold a dog that was given to him as a gift and, if so, had he used the money (about TL 100.00— ca. $10.00) for political purposes. Degrading pictures of Menderes were auctioned to the press. These showed him at different points in his ordeal: during his interrogation by civil and military officials, at the trial, as he lay in a coma following a suicide attempt, moments before his execution, and even as he was being hanged. The junta was particularly intent on destroying the widespread belief that Menderes was superhuman and as such beyond the reach of temporal authority. In fact, one of the few explanations for the death sentences, which are otherwise hard to understand, is that they were passed and carried out in order to prove that Menderes was nothing more than a mortal human being.

The irony is that the junta's actions made Menderes even more powerful in the eyes of his supporters. The humiliation that he was submitted to was seen not as taking away from but as contributing to his divine powers. He was rumored to have left his prison cell (which was on an island) and to be riding his white horse in the Anatolian countryside both before and after his execution. In addition to his superhuman qualities, he was now perceived as

[24] Excerpts from the memoirs of the junta leader, Cemal Madanoğlu. Published in *Zafer*, 1 December 1961.

a Messiah-like figure who was suffering for the ordinary people at the hands of a cruel authority. Indeed, it can be argued that Menderes' ordeal brought him even closer to the people. Especially in the countryside, it was hard to find anybody who did not know how it felt to be carried away by the police or the military, to be accused of crimes that were difficult to comprehend, to be questioned in an uncomfortable setting by rude people who claimed to be acting on behalf of the state—to be, in short, at the mercy of an impersonal force that had the power to make life-and-death decisions. And this was precisely what was happening to Menderes. Consequently, far from becoming the symbol of a corrupt and illegitimate administration that the military tried to portray him as, Menderes turned into the victimized hero of a people whom he had represented and empowered. These two roles, the savior and the victim, blended easily into the Messiah-like image people already had of Menderes.[25]

Beyond the trials, various other measures taken by the military government were ominously reminiscent of the single-party period that had ended only ten years before. For example, once again there were forced resettlements of people in eastern provinces, secularist policies were reinforced with a renewed zeal, the body of a charismatic religious leader was even exhumed and reburied in an unmarked grave in order to prevent his tomb from becoming a shrine.[26] Village-level party offices were closed down and their operation was outlawed, restricting, once again, people's access to politics.[27] Just as the peasants in their everyday clothes had been barred from the streets of Ankara under the single-party regime, this time, wearing dirty clothes and speaking with a loud voice in city centers were outlawed lest these "could create the wrong impression, especially among the tourists."[28] In a broad attack on "religious obscurantism," the police in big cities were ordered to

[25] By coincidence, the leader of the coup, C. Gürsel died on 15 September 1966, to the day on the fifth anniversary of Adnan Menderes' death sentence. This too was widely interpreted as some kind of a divine justice.

[26] *Cumhuriyet*, 14 July 1960.

[27] Ibid., 24 June 1960.

[28] From the directive issued by the Military Governor of Istanbul, Refik Tulga, ibid., 25 July 1961.

arrest all bearded men and veiled women. In Istanbul, men were shaved by force in police stations.[29] As for women, there were plans to force them to sew European-style coats for themselves by using sewing machines donated by the military.[30] Supporters of the old regime were pejoratively referred to as the "tail-ends." Any mention of the "fallen" regime, its leaders, and the ongoing trials was prohibited. Several months after the coup, faced with the general lack of enthusiasm for the military regime and the new constitution, the military officers decided to travel the country and "explain to the people" why the new regime was good for the nation.[31]

When one goes over these examples, it is not difficult to understand how the coup and the mode of operation of the junta acted as a catalyst in reinvigorating and in fact re-creating the broad-based populist coalition that had been behind the DP. The Justice party (whose name was chosen deliberately to remind people of the injustices of the DP trials) was the major party to claim the DP heritage. The first showdown came in the summer of 1961, when the new constitution was submitted to a referendum. Even though the campaign was held under strict restrictions by which it was practically impossible to oppose the constitution, close to 40 percent of the people ended up voting against it. Such a large fraction of the people voted "no" not because they did not approve of the constitution but because the word had spread that a "yes" vote would mean a vote against Menderes, who was then still alive.

In the election campaign that followed, the political parties were barred from making direct references to the DP regime and its leaders, but the JP propaganda was full of thinly veiled references to what had happened. One candidate said, "I have so many things to say to you but, alas, I am not able to speak. Look into my eyes and you will understand what I mean."[32] Another opened his speech by "saluting the spiritual presence of those who served

[29] Ibid., 25 July 1961.
[30] Ibid., 21 August 1960.
[31] Ibid., 20 September 1960.
[32] Ibid., 30 September 1961.

you."[33] The JP's motto was that they would continue what had been started. The RPP was an easy and a favorite target of this propaganda. There was a widespread belief that the RPP had become the main beneficiary of the coup and that its leader, Ismet Inönü, had cooperated with the plotters. The JP's candidates brandished ration cards from the war years to remind people of the difficulties they had suffered under the single-party RPP regime. In one of the JP declarations, it was said that "RPP sees itself as the natural candidate to govern the country. This party sees 1950 as a mistake. Whereas the JP is the party of this nation's children, who do not hesitate to sacrifice their lives for national unity."[34] The following is from an editorial in a paper that was the official organ of the new party:

> Those who make fun of the people ... they write ... they write every day ... and people keep quiet, patiently.... Then people speak, once every four years, at the ballot box. Then everybody hears loud and clear how well the people understand what is going on around them.[35]

During the election campaign, an elaborate discourse grew around the theme of executions. Tables that looked like scaffolds were set up at public meetings ostensibly to carry loudspeakers. Week anniversaries and month anniversaries of the executions were marked with public prayers. Through such occasions, but also as part of JP's broader strategy, "religious freedom" once again became a central theme. It was intimated that the initials of the JP (in Turkish, AP) and its symbol (an open book) stood for, respectively, Allah, Prophet (in Turkish, *Peygamber*), and the Koran.[36] One of the reasons that the pro-Justice-party writers gave for not supporting the new constitution was that "it did not adequately safeguard the freedom of worship." Here is another speech by a JP candidate enunciating all the themes that had originally been articulated by the DP:

---

[33] Ibid.
[34] Ibid., 22 May 1961.
[35] *Son Havadis*, 26 September 1961.
[36] F. Ahmad, *The Turkish Experiment in Democracy*, 377.

They say that among the RPP candidates there are important men.
They say, not in the other parties but only in the RPP, there are
Professors, Doctors, Economists, Doctors of Economics. They say
that these people are educated in Germany, France, England and
the United States.... Well, my fellow citizens, we read books too,
but the books we like to read are different. First, we read the Holy
Koran, then we read your book, that is, the book of peasants![37]

Obviously, the coup and the legal and administrative reorgani-
zations that followed it did not have a major effect on the changes
that Turkish society had been undergoing since the early 1950s. In
the continuous migrations between the countryside and the cities
and among the people who were in between and who sought security in extended families, native place networks, and religious
sects, the JP found the kind of audience that had made the DP so
successful. The injustices of the military regime, and in particular
the cruelty of the military tribunal, made a large section of Turkish
society ever more responsive to the populist complaints of the JP.
It is for this reason that the 1961 constitution could muster but
the slightest margin of approval, the elections that were held in
the same year forced a coalition between the RPP and the JP, and
in 1965 and in 1969 the JP would win outright majorities in the
Turkish parliament. The end of the 1961 campaign, however, is
a good place to stop and reflect on the implications of the success
of populism for democracy.

Democracy and Freedom: Some Concluding Thoughts

In Turkey, the popularity of the ideology that combines the democratic discourse with a heavy dose of conservative and traditionalist elements does not owe either to the manipulation of skillful
politicians or to the malleability of a simple people holding simple
beliefs. While both of these may have played some part in making
the Democratic party and its successors successful, the real power
of this ideology lies in the way in which it both reflects and rein-
terprets reality so that the individual, typically a peasant and/or
a migrant, can see himself at the center, capable of affecting that
reality according to his will. To be sure, there is a certain degree

[37] From a speech by Cemal Babac, *Cumhuriyet*, 29 September 1961.

of illusion in this message of empowerment. Social, economic, and historical constraints do limit people's actions, and over the history of multiparty democracy in Turkey it is hard to point out more than one or two instances when people had the opportunity to vote for a program that had the potential of removing some of these constraints. Nevertheless, it is important not to minimize the idea and the reality of elections, as they have taken root as the only acceptable way of ordering state-society relations in Turkey. More than anything else, this should be attributed to the persistent democratic discourse of the so-called conservative parties. After several false starts, trials, and errors that go back over one hundred years, popular participation is now firmly ingrained in the Turkish political system as the only acceptable way of gaining legitimacy.

On the basis of over one hundred elections that have been held since Ottoman times, is it possible to conclude that "democracy" is alive and well in Turkey? In other words, how full really is the glass? The populist discourse, with the theme of empowerment that has been integral to it, rarely questions the nature of the social, economic, and cultural networks within which people exist and through which they have exercised their right to vote. Because of the way in which the Ottoman/Turkish state eliminated alternative ways of associating, extended families, native-place networks, and religious sects have been stretched to match the needs of the changing Turkish society. For the most part, the mass parties in Turkey have empowered people as members of families, as Muslims and Turks, and as parts of patron-client relations that are based on native-place networks. What is common to all these entities is that the hierarchies that are central to them constrain individuals, restrict their potential, and, most of the time, prevent them from expanding their positive energies. It is for this reason that we need to be cautious in seeing these communities as the building blocks of a substantively democratic society.

Progress along Western lines has been the common goal of both the early republican and the populist regimes in Turkey. The real steps that Turkish society has taken along this route do have a liberating effect, in that eventually people will acquire the necessary material and moral wherewithal to question, renegotiate, and finally supersede the power relations of which they are a part.

At that juncture, it is important that people have meaningful alternatives that are open to them, and that the search and exercise of these alternatives are legally and socially accepted, guaranteed, and protected. At several points in its history, the Ottoman/Turkish state has stepped in with the purpose of blocking some of these alternatives and imposing its own vision of the future on Turkish society. But as the spatial barriers between the "town" and "country" disappear, as Istanbul and other big cities become big "villages" full of peasants, it has become painfully obvious that it is impossible to legislate modernization or Westernization or civic virtue. So far, people going through these massive changes have found some protection in extended families and other less formal local networks. But such units have a limit beyond which they cannot continue to function without losing their characteristics. The crucial question is, what will people do when that point is reached? Will they have something to turn to when myths lose their hold, when people realize that they can no longer vote for a Messiah?

Since the early 1980s, Turkey has been moving toward a new breaking point, where market mentality and crass materialism are becoming the main axes over which people relate to each other and assess each other's success. They seek individual, market-generated means of safeguarding their interests.[38] Given the fact that these markets are now truly global, this can be an extremely frustrating situation for those who fail as individuals, groups, or nations. World history is full of examples where, failing to improve their own standing, groups of people, states, and nations have sought big and universal solutions that have turned out to be destructive not only to themselves but also to large sections of humanity as a whole. To avoid the repetition of such catastrophes people need to have the space where they can associate freely and expand their energies in a positive way and effect changes starting from the most immediate, local level, and in this way imbue concepts of democracy and freedom with a substantive meaning where it most matters—in their own lives. To do that, however, they have to be free, and this is where the dilemma lies.

[38] For an interesting discussion of 1980s culture in Turkey, see Aydın Uğur, *Keşfedilmemiş Kıta* (Istanbul, İletişim, 1991).

Taxation without Representation
Authoritarianism and Economic Liberalization in Syria

STEVEN HEYDEMANN

INCREASINGLY, the collapse of authoritarianism and the origins of political liberalization have been linked to the onset of economic crises.[1] In virtually every region of the world, failures of economic development associated with socialist regimes and with certain kinds of authoritarian regimes have been identified as a leading source of political liberalization and of market-oriented economic reforms.[2] For many scholars, policymakers, and officials of international lending agencies these global processes of democratization

I wish to thank the editors of this volume for their comments, particularly Joel Migdal, along with the participants at the conference where this paper was originally presented. The discussant, John Keeler, was especially helpful.

[1] See Lucian W. Pye, "Political Science and the Crisis of Authoritarianism," *American Political Science Review* 84 (March 1990) 3–19.

[2] These linkages are frequently found in the popular press, but have also been the subject of important attention from scholars. On the Middle East see Henri Barkey, ed., *Economic Crisis and Policy Response: The Politics of Economic Reform in the Middle East* (New York, St. Martin's Press, 1992). For an insightful critique of recent literature on Latin America, see Karen L. Remmer, "New Wine or Old Bottlenecks: The Study of Latin American Democracy," *Comparative Politics* 23 (1991) 479–95. See also Alfred Stepan, ed., *Democratizing Brazil: Problems of Transition and Consolidation* (New York, Oxford University Press, 1989); Adam Przeworski, *Democracy and the Market: Political and Economic Reforms in Eastern Europe and Latin America* (Cambridge University Press, 1991); Laurence Whitehead, "Democratization and Disinflation: A Comparative Approach," in *Fragile Coalitions: The Politics of Economic Adjustment*, ed. Joan M. Nelson, et al. (Washington, D.C., Overseas Development Council, 1989) 79–93; Larry Diamond, Juan J. Linz, and Seymour Martin Lipset, eds., *Democracy in Developing Countries:*

and economic liberalization are closely interconnected, if not interdependent or mutually reinforcing.[3] Recalling earlier (and ongoing) debates on the economic determinants of democracy and of authoritarianism, recent attempts by state elites in the Middle East, as well as in Africa, Asia, Latin America, and the former socialist states to liberalize politically while simultaneously pursuing market-oriented economic reforms have prompted new efforts to understand how these interconnections operate in a wide variety of settings.[4]

Persistence, Failure, and Renewal (Boulder, Lynne Rienner Publishers, 1989); and Merilee S. Grindle and John W. Thomas, *Public Choices and Policy Change: The Political Economy of Reform in Developing Countries* (Baltimore, The Johns Hopkins University Press).

[3] According to one recent study, "In the realm of both politics and economics we observe attempts to make a radical break with the past; in fact, in both realms, the word 'transitions' best describes the processes launched in a number of countries. These are transitions from authoritarianism of several varieties to democracy and from state-administered, monopolistic, and protected economic systems, again of several varieties, to a reliance on markets. Both transitions are radical, and they are interdependent." Przeworski, *Democracy and the Market*, ix. These connections have been noted beyond the Latin American and Eastern European transitions of the late 1980s and early 1990s: "Two paradoxical developments led the dictatorships of Southern Europe toward a more pluralistic social order ... : first, the exhaustion of traditionalist legitimation via the Fascist ideology and second, the transformation of the structure of the economy produced, to a considerable extent, by the policies of the dictatorships themselves." Salvador Giner, "Political Economy, Legitimation, and the State in Southern Europe," in *Transitions from Authoritarian Rule: Southern Europe*, ed. Guillermo O'Donnell, Philippe C. Schmitter, and Laurence Whitehead (Baltimore, The Johns Hopkins University Press, 1986) 35.

[4] Literature on the relationship between capitalism and democracy is too vast and too varied to be cited here in detail. For just one of many recent examples of the postcommunist debate about democracy and capitalism, see a collection of twelve articles published on the fiftieth anniversary of the publication of Joseph Schumpeter's *Capitalism, Socialism, and Democracy*, including pieces by Adam Przeworski, Robert Dahl, Ralph Miliband, and others: "Capitalism, Socialism, and Democracy," *Journal of Democracy* 13.3 (July 1992) 3–137. Literature on the economic origins of authoritarianism is almost equally extensive. See Albert O. Hirschman, "The Turn to Authoritarianism in Latin America and the Search for its Economic Determinants," in *The New Authoritarianism in Latin America*, ed. David Collier (Princeton

In the Middle East, as in other regions, the importance of political liberalization as a vehicle for managing the economic reforms that follow economic crises is a common theme of much recent writing—whether explaining political liberalization in Jordan following the outbreak of riots in April 1989 over the introduction of austerity measures, Algeria's short-lived experiment with democratization following large-scale unrest in October 1988, the deepening of political pluralism in Egypt since the mid-1980s, or the more general exhaustion of Middle Eastern populism as a political and economic strategy for regime legitimation.[5] Unable to sustain acceptable levels of economic growth, and incapable of altering development strategies within existing political frameworks, Middle Eastern regimes give way, whether by reform from above or below, to more pluralist and representative arrangements through which

---

University Press, 1979) 61–98. More recent studies on the relationship between political and economic liberalization serve as a useful corrective for the views of Hirschman and many others. See Karen L. Remmer, "The Political Impact of Economic Crises in Latin America in the 1980s," *American Political Science Review* 85 (September 1991); idem, "The Politics of Economic Stabilization: IMF Standby Programs in Latin America, 1954–1984," *Comparative Politics* 19 (1986) 1–24; The World Bank, *World Development Report 1991: The Challenge of Development* (New York, Oxford University Press, 1991); Stephan Haggard, "The Politics of Adjustment: Lessons from the IMF's Extended Fund Facility," in *The Politics of International Debt*, ed. Miles Kahler (Ithaca, N.Y., Cornell University Press, 1986) 157–86; Stephan Haggard, *Pathways from the Periphery: The Politics of Growth in the Newly Industrializing Countries* (Ithaca, N.Y., Cornell University Press, 1990); and Joan M. Nelson, ed., *Economic Crisis and Policy Choice: The Politics of Adjustment in the Third World* (Princeton University Press, 1990); Laurence Whitehead (supra. n. 2), 79–93; and Terry Lynn Karl, "Dilemmas of Democratization in Latin America," *Comparative Politics* 23 (1990) 1–21.

[5] See Gudrun Kramer, "Liberalization and Democracy in the Arab World," *Middle East Report* 174 (January–February 1992) 22–25, 35. The Jordanian and Algerian cases are also discussed in this special issue of *MER* on democracy in the Arab world. One additional observation: the view shared by these articles—that more pluralism eases the task of managing economic liberalization—reflects a strong convergence with the directions of research on other regions, notably Latin America, and represents a significant departure from the notion that authoritarian regimes are better equipped to manage the difficult process of economic restructuring.

new economic institutions (markets) and new economic policies are negotiated.

Political and economic openings in the Middle East are thus thought to strengthen and consolidate one another, though profound skepticism remains about the extent to which they will produce substantive gains in political freedom, meaningful shifts in the distribution of political authority, or sustained improvements in economic well-being.[6] Nonetheless, the success of economic liberalization is increasingly regarded as dependent on the success of political reform.[7] As expressed recently by an Egyptian economist, "the peoples of the world have learned the bitter truth that there can be no economic reform without political reform."[8]

This observation has recently been given a sharper analytical focus through one particular explanation that illustrates the interdependent dynamic connecting economic and political liberalization in the Middle East. This explanation suggests that these processes are linked and sustained through the creation of a "democratic bargain" that creates stable conditions for achieving economic liberalization through democratic political reform.[9] Yet the logic inherent in this argument and the widely shared assumptions on which it rests raise important questions about the extent to which economic and political liberalization must inevitably proceed in tandem, and whether the future of Middle

---

[6] One prominent exception, in addition to the Syrian case discussed in detail below, is Iraq. See Kiren Aziz Chaudhry, "On the Way to the Market: Economic Liberalization and Iraq's Invasion of Kuwait," *Middle East Report* 170 (May–June 1991) 14–23.

[7] Obviously, this view is prevalent well beyond the Middle East, and reflects a widespread understanding of the reform processes under way in the former Soviet Union and Eastern Europe, as well as in states such as Indonesia, Mexico, and Kenya.

[8] Sadiq Afifi, "Economic Reform Via the Polls," *Al-Ahram al-Duwali*, 26 October 1991, cited by Daniel Brumberg, "Survival Strategies vs. Democratic Bargains: The Politics of Economic Reform in Contemporary Egypt," in *The Political Economy of Stabilization Measures in the Middle East*, ed. Henri Barkey (New York, St. Martin's Press, 1992).

[9] Daniel Brumberg, "Islam, Elections, and Reform in Algeria," *Journal of Democracy* 2.1 (Winter 1991) 58–71.

Eastern economic liberalization efforts hinges on the implementation of political liberalization.[10]

Drawing on the experiences of Syria during the decade from 1982 to 1992, and implicitly on the experiences of other cases from Indonesia, to China, to Zimbabwe, I suggest instead that economic liberalization can be, and frequently is, pursued without recourse to political liberalization. Syria's experience can thus be taken as an example of more pervasive approaches to economic liberalization in the developing world. It calls into question the underlying assumption that economic and political reform are necessarily linked, or that the success of one hinges on the success of the other. It argues that authoritarian regimes are more flexible and adaptive in response to economic crises than is often recognized. It suggests, therefore, that a much more nuanced understanding is needed of the various conditions under which economic and political liberalization reinforce or undermine one another, as well as the factors that shape the relationship between the two. Economic crises are an important source of strain for authoritarian systems of rule, yet they do not inevitably lead to unmanageable political crises, to democratic movements, or, ultimately, to representative governments.

In pursuit of these claims, this chapter is divided into four general sections. The first reviews the arguments of the "democratic bargain" explanation, and tests them against the experience of economic liberalization in the Middle East. The second summarizes several approaches to economic liberalization that are consistent with the continuation of authoritarian systems of rule. The third reviews the emergence of selective and corporatist liberalization in Syria as a reaction to its protracted economic crisis of the 1980s, highlighting the conscious efforts of the regime to prevent the economic crisis from becoming a source of political change. This section focuses on the Damascus Chambers of Commerce and Chamber of Industry as examples of institutions whose relationships to the regime have been altered significantly by its distinctive approach to liberalization. Finally, I explore the prospects

---

[10] For similar reservations with regard to Indonesia, see R. William Liddle, "Indonesia's Democratic Past and Future," *Comparative Politics* 24 (1992) 443–62.

for more substantive political reform in the future, taking account in particular of the Syrian regime's reactions to the wave of democratization in Eastern Europe since 1989.

Testing the "Democratic Bargain"

Though the argument about democratic bargains has been applied principally to certain Middle Eastern states such as Algeria, Egypt, and Jordan, it captures a logic about the processes through which ruling coalitions are shaped and reshaped that has much wider currency.[11] The emergence of democratic bargains is said to rest on the recognition by authoritarian elites that an existing "ruling bargain," in which citizens accept limits on their political participation in exchange for certain economic guarantees, breaks down under conditions of economic crisis.[12] In particular, it breaks down as the capacity of state elites to satisfy the fiscal requirements of the state from external sources of capital diminishes. The onset of economic crisis, therefore, may be provoked by an *absolute* decline in resources available to the state, but also results from *relative* shifts in the balance of resources available to state elites, requiring that a greater share of needed revenues be generated internally rather than externally from foreign aid, oil rents, or remittances.

As resources decline, or the balance of available resources places greater demands on local economies, the ability of authoritarian regimes to satisfy their side of the ruling bargain erodes. In Jordan, this was reflected in the post-1988 decline in the ability of the regime to guarantee a stable economic environment (and a

---

[11] It has elements in common with several literatures, including those on the political economy of transitions from authoritarian rule, on constitutionalism, and on the political economy of economic policymaking. See, in particular, Jon Elster and Rune Slagstad, eds. *Constitutionalism and Democracy* (Cambridge University Press, 1988).

[12] Ruling bargains are identified with a range of conditions, and may take the form of the guaranteed employment, subsidized prices, and wideranging welfare provisions found in Egypt, Syria, or Algeria during much of the last three decades, or a commitment to sustain relatively high levels of economic autonomy for the private sector, as in Jordan. See Daniel Brumberg, "The Collapse of the 'Ruling Bargain' and its Consequences for the Arab World" (unpublished paper, 1992).

stable currency) in which the private sector could operate with a relatively high degree of autonomy. In Algeria and Egypt, it has meant that ruling regimes since the onset of the international debt crisis of the late 1970s and 1980s have been unable to maintain a broad range of welfare programs and subsidies on basic commodities, and otherwise sustain the post-independence populist commitments of their predecessors.

In place of a ruling bargain that offers economic benefits in exchange for political quiescence, these regimes preside over a process of economic and political liberalization from above that expands opportunities for political participation. They provide citizens a voice in defining economic priorities in exchange for short-term economic sacrifices that reduce the overall fiscal demands on the state, generate higher levels of economic participation, foster a willingness to invest, and offer the expectation of longer-term economic growth. Writing on Egypt, for example, one author defines this form of liberalization as a process through which "the state ... will exchange some of its autonomy in decision making for access to some of the abundant resources held by its citizens."[13]

This goes beyond the notion that transitions to a market economy require the dismantling of state regulatory institutions (itself an arguable proposition), to suggest that such transitions require levels of popular participation in the economy that can only be secured by broadening substantially the scope of political participation. As state control over the economy diminishes, some form of representative politics is needed to determine, aggregate, accord weight to, and legitimate the economic preferences of various social groups. The argument, in effect, is that some measure of representative government is necessary for the success of economic restructuring.

According to the argument, authoritarian elites accept political liberalization as a strategy in part because they recognize that new economic policies cannot be implemented successfully by reliance on repression, particularly with regard to generating

---

[13] Robert Springborg, *Mubarak's Egypt: Fragmentation of the Political Order* (Boulder, Westview Press, 1989) 296–97, cited in Michael C. Hudson, "After the Gulf War: Prospects for Democratization in the Arab World," *Middle East Journal* 45 (1991) 412.

higher levels of private sector investment.[14] The confidence of business, both local and foreign, cannot be coerced. In addition, the high social costs of economic liberalization, which often take the form of an IMF-sponsored stabilization and adjustment program, and the accompanying risks of political instability, can be more effectively managed in political systems that offer their citizens a role in allocating the costs and benefits of economic reform. This factor carries particular weight. From Morocco to Jordan, the introduction of multiparty politics and increasing tolerance of political oppositions during the mid- to late 1980s was directly linked to regime efforts to build support for economic liberalization programs involving significant austerity measures.

In other words, the demands of economic liberalization compel authoritarian elites to sacrifice a measure of political power. This is a simplified summary, but it can be further distilled as an expression of the view firmly etched into the minds of American school children: there can be no taxation without representation.

This explanation captures one possible form of the relationship between economic and political restructuring. It acknowledges that authoritarian regimes are sustained not by coercion alone, but by more complex dynamics that involve elements of negotiation and accommodation, as well as repression. It focuses attention on the material bases of authoritarianism in the Middle East and thus integrates an important political-economy dimension into discussions that often focus narrowly on the ethnic, sectarian, or cultural determinants of various Middle Eastern regimes. It suggests how the imperative to develop alternative strategies of capital accumulation in Middle Eastern states following the global economic crises of the 1980s has altered the local political relationships between state and society, redefining the boundaries of each and their relationships with one another. And it reverses the prominent post–World War II assertions that capitalism in the developing world is a necessary precondition for democracy by suggesting that in

---

[14] New economic policies typically reflect the priorities associated with IMF stabilization and structural adjustment programs: reducing imports, devaluing local currencies, implementing austerity programs that cut consumer subsidies, promoting exports, creating incentives for private sectors, and strengthening markets in place of state-managed supply and price regimes.

the post–Cold War era, democracy is a necessary precondition for capitalism.[15]

For the most part, however, the notion of a democratic bargain misrepresents the processes of economic and political liberalization in the Middle East. First, it establishes democratization as a *necessary* condition for successful economic reform. Not only are the two processes interdependent, they are linked in a mutually reinforcing relationship, and are expected to develop simultaneously. It creates a formula where each measure of economic liberalization requires an equivalent measure of political liberalization. Yet this relationship by and large does not hold. Economic restructuring in the Middle East (and perhaps Africa as well) has outpaced political restructuring, and both processes remain far less institutionalized than in other parts of the developing world. Moreover, as suggested above, the political changes that have come to the region continue to frustrate those who hope for more far-reaching democratic reform. These changes are frequently described in terms of democratization, but with a few possible exceptions Middle Eastern regimes have not democratized. They have undergone a relatively limited process of political liberalization that has preserved much of the power of ruling regimes.[16] This form of political liberalization, in which regimes create and then manage a set of pluralist political arrangements that include a limited political role for opposition parties, must be distinguished from democratization and is not necessarily a prelude to it.[17] Its trajectory may or may not be linked to the pace

[15] For an early variant of the literature on the economic determinants of democracy as applied to the Middle East, see Charles Issawi, "Economic and Social Foundations of Democracy in the Middle East," *International Affairs*, January 1956, 29–42.

[16] See *Middle East Report* 174 (supra n. 5), special issue on democracy in the Arab world. See also John L. Esposito and James P. Piscatori, "Democratization and Islam," *Middle East Journal* 45 (1991) 427–40, and Hudson, "After the Gulf War" (supra n. 13), 407–26.

[17] The editors of *Middle East Report* also adopt this distinction: " 'Democratization' and 'Liberalization' tend to be used interchangeably, but they refer to two distinct, if related, processes. Democracy denotes a mode of governance in which decision-making power is shared by 'the people'.... 'Liberal,' in the classical sense, refers to limitations on the power of a state—democratic or

or scope of economic reform. Political liberalization in the Middle East resembles more closely the "enforced limited pluralism" of Latin America's authoritarian regimes of the 1970s than it does the emerging Latin American democracies of the late 1980s.[18] Indeed, enforced limited pluralism may well represent a relatively stable equilibrium over the near- to midterm, even as economic liberalization continues to deepen. Moreover, the success of economic reforms may well hinge on the capacity of regimes to govern the transition to less centralized economies, to enforce new regulatory mechanisms and new forms of property rights.[19] Economic liberalization may thus create incentives for politicians to insulate the process from debates over political liberalization, rather than to acknowledge their interconnections or to permit the transition from liberalization to democratization.

A second, and perhaps more important, issue concerns defining political and economic reform as a process of negotiation between regimes and societies that leads to a mutually acceptable "bargain." This formulation establishes an equivalence of power between authoritarian regimes and their subjects that seems far removed from the everyday experience of Egyptians, Jordanians, Syrians, Algerians, and other Middle Easterners. It also misconstrues as consent the general compliance with which citizens in authoritarian regimes often greet changes in economic policy. There is an important element of bargaining that takes place in the process of economic liberalization, but it tends to happen within a narrowly delimited arena that typically includes only a small set of privileged institutional or individual participants. Even here, and even when prompted by pressures from below, the process of economic liberalization is shaped principally from the top down,

otherwise—to intervene in the individual and collective lives of people." *Middle East Report* 174, 3.
[18] James M. Malloy, ed., *Authoritarianism and Corporatism in Latin America* (Pittsburgh University Press, 1977) 4.
[19] According to the World Bank, "An efficient domestic economy ... requires public goods of ... high quality. These include, most fundamentally, a regulatory framework to ensure competition, and legal and property rights that are both clearly defined and conscientiously protected." The World Bank, *World Development Report* 1991 (Washington, D.C., Oxford University Press for the World Bank, 1991) 7.

by ruling regimes intent on managing economic liberalization in ways that minimize the political costs, and less by the interests and priorities of those institutions or individuals selected to serve as negotiating partners.

In this view, liberalization becomes merely another means to maintain the existing system. Indeed, some have defined "the main purpose of liberalization from above [as] system maintenance in a situation of acute socioeconomic crisis." Systems are maintained by "coopting wider circles of the political public, distributing responsibility for future austerity policies more broadly, directing political and religious organizations into controllable channels, and excluding all those outside the 'national consensus' defined by the regime."[20] Other accounts, in particular one recent study of economic liberalization in North Africa and the Sudan, point to the high social and economic costs it imposes on the poorest groups in these societies, and see it as little more than a device adopted by "certain sections of the bourgeoisie to maintain their predominance in the political as well as the economic sphere."[21]

Despite these perceptions, bargaining over economic policy is not entirely defined by the preferences of the ruling regime. Even in authoritarian settings, social groups both within and outside ruling coalitions influence the process. Several studies have noted the extent to which various social groups and organized interest associations have been able to exploit their positions and to

[20] Kramer, "Liberalization" (supra n. 5), 24. Waterbury makes a similar observation with regard to Egypt. Economic liberalization, in the form of economic stabilization and adjustment policies, is managed by reorganizing ruling coalitions, reshaping the constellation of actors whose interests are represented within the coalition, and creating new groups of winners and losers. To build support for liberalization, "a dominant coalition based on the military, the public sector, organized labor, and urban, white-collar interests ... is replaced by one that may still include the military but that relies more on commercial agriculture, private industrialists, and export sectors." John Waterbury, "The Political Management of Economic Adjustment and Reform," in *Fragile Coalitions* (supra n. 2), 46.

[21] David Seddon, "Riot and Rebellion in North Africa: Political Responses to Economic Crisis in Tunisia, Morocco and Sudan," in *Power and Stability in the Middle East*, ed. Berch Berberoglu (London, Zed Books, 1989) 133.

make their voices heard.[22] As the experience of Syria and other Middle Eastern states during the 1980s illustrates, however, the arrangements that have produced economic liberalization tend to resemble *social pacts* more closely than they do the Roussean *social contract* implicit in the idea of a democratic bargain: "a pact can be defined as an explicit, but not always publicly explicated or justified, agreement among a select set of actors that seeks to define (or better, to redefine) rules governing the exercise of power on the basis of mutual guarantees for the 'vital' interests of those entering into it."[23] Redefining economic rules may be entirely compatible with nondemocratic political procedures. There are few imperatives that compel authoritarian elites to adopt a democratizing strategy if their aim is simply to liberalize their economies. The legacy of the Boston Tea Party notwithstanding, taxation, in particular the adjustment costs associated with the introduction of market-oriented economic policies, is possible without representation.

Nondemocratizing Strategies of Economic Liberalization: Alternatives to the Democratic Bargain

Even where political and economic reform have occurred simultaneously, the idea of a democratic bargain fails to capture at least three approaches to economic liberalization, all of which have been adopted in different ways and to varying degrees by Middle Eastern states, and all of which undermine the notion of political and economic reform emerging through a linked process of democratic negotiation between regimes and citizens. These are (1) corporatist liberalization, or economic reform as a process of coalition management among a restricted set of institutional actors; (2) imposed liberalization, or economic reform as a defensive response to pressure from international lending agencies;

---

[22] See Joel S. Migdal, *Strong Societies and Weak States: State-Society Relations and State Capabilities in the Third World* (Princeton University Press, 1988) and Robert Bianchi, *Unruly Corporatism: Associational Life in Twentieth-Century Egypt* (New York, Oxford University Press, 1989).

[23] Guillermo O'Donnell and Philippe C. Schmitter, *Transitions from Authoritarian Rule: Tentative Conclusions About Uncertain Democracies* (Baltimore, Johns Hopkins University Press, 1986) 37.

and (3) selective liberalization, or economic reform as a process of establishing semiprivate bargains between regime elites and a limited set of private sector investors.

In each case the outcome will be a shift in the structure of mixed economies, favoring certain elements of the private sector and reducing the scope of state intervention in the economy. The outcome may also include a measure of political liberalization, particularly where international aid is linked to political reform, but it is more likely to produce economic liberalization without a significant decentralization of political power, that is, without democratization.[24] Perhaps most important, the process through which regimes introduce and pursue economic liberalization in each of these cases is marked by quite a different dynamic than that suggested by the notion of a democratic bargain. It is defined principally by the desire of authoritarian elites to limit and obscure the linkages between political and economic reform, and not by an intent to deepen such linkages and make them transparent. State-society relations may still rest on implicit, or even explicit relations of reciprocity that embrace a range of economic and political obligations. However, the nature of these relations and the uneven forms of reciprocity they entail stand quite apart from the more balanced dynamic that is said to sustain democratic bargains. Moreover, when political and economic transformations in the Middle East are explained using these categories or approaches, Syria can be understood not as an outlier distinguished by its lack of political liberalization, but as a state using one of a variety of approaches adopted by Middle Eastern (and other) states to manage economic change without provoking disruptive political change.

In the Syrian case, it clearly has not been the intent of the Asad regime to legitimate the modest disengagement of the state from the economy since the mid-1980s by increasing political participation. Instead, its objective has been to enhance the process of capital accumulation within certain non-state-controlled sectors of the economy, and thus revive the regime's capacity to extract

---

[24] See Ahmed Abdalla, "Human Rights and Elusive Democracy," *Middle East Report* 174 (January–February 1992) 6–8.

resources from Syrian citizens while minimizing the political instability that disengagement can bring about. To accomplish this, the regime has relied principally on a combined strategy of selective and corporatist liberalization.[25] It has increased the economic autonomy of certain private-sector actors, while retaining a high degree of control over much of the economy, without relinquishing political control.

This is not to suggest that Syria's economic liberalization lacks a significant political dimension: quite the opposite. Rather, the politics of economic policymaking in Syria have been dominated by a concern to insulate the regime from the political consequences of its economic mismanagement, to prevent the economic crisis from provoking genuine democratization. It has pursued a selective and corporatist approach to economic liberalization as a means for preserving the political arrangements that more sweeping economic reform might upset. This has not been an easy task; the regime has confronted important challenges in carrying it out. The Ba'thist regime's claim to legitimacy is based in large part on its redistributive and populist ideological claims; austerity budgets and policies that privilege the private sector call these into question and thus weaken the regime's legitimacy. Syria's leaders have also been forced to contend with events in Eastern Europe and the collapse of the Soviet Union; these have created pressures to extend economic liberalization into the political realm. In response, the regime has appropriated some of the rhetoric of political reform, but has employed it to reinforce existing political and economic arrangements. Selective and corporatist liberalization have thus far provided the regime with the capacity to manage a gradual process of limited economic liberalization without political liberalization. In Syria, as in a number of other countries, economic crisis is not likely to give rise to democratization.

---

[25] Steven Heydemann, "The Political Logic of Economic Rationality: Selective Stabilization in Syria," in *The Political Economy of Stabilization Measures in the Middle East* (supra n. 8).

Economic Crisis and
Economic Liberalization in Syria, 1982–1992

Opinions differ regarding the depth and length of Syria's economic crisis, but it is widely acknowledged that throughout the 1980s Syria suffered from "crippling foreign exchange shortages."[26] It ran increasing deficits in its balance of trade and its current accounts, and was unable to pay its debts to the World Bank, accumulating arrears of $210 million by 1990.[27] The most recent and best-informed survey of the Syrian economy describes the 1980s as "a lost decade for development."[28]

The sources of this crisis were several. Syria experienced a dramatic economic expansion following the 1973 Arab-Israeli war, fueling an import boom that was financed by Arab foreign aid and rising world oil prices. When oil markets declined after 1979, Syria both lost revenue directly and suffered from the declining levels of Arab financial assistance. The latter dropped from approximately $1.6 billion in 1980, to about $500 million in the early 1980s, to the point where Syria was reported by the OECD to have "paid

---

[26] This section is drawn, in slightly modified form, from Heydemann, "The Political Logic of Economic Rationality." A variety of sources have tracked Syria's economic crisis, in addition to the regular reporting in the *Middle East Economic Digest* and the Economist Intelligence Unit publications; see Eliyahu Kanovsky, "What's Behind Syria's Current Economic Problems?" Occasional Papers, Dayan Center for Middle Eastern and African Studies (Tel Aviv University, 1985); Elizabeth Longuenesse, "Syrie, secteur public industriel," *Maghreb-Machrek* 109 (July–September 1985) 5–22; Fred H. Lawson, "Liberalisation économique en Syrie et en Irak," *Maghreb-Machrek* 128 (April–June 1990) 27–52; Fred H. Lawson, "Political-Economic Trends in Ba'thi Syria: A Reinterpretation," *Orient* 29 (1988) 579–94; Gunter Meyer, "Economic Development in Syria Since 1970," in *Politics and the Economy in Syria*, ed. J. A. Allen (London, Centre of Near and Middle Eastern Studies, SOAS, 1987) 39–62.

[27] The IMF, for example, cited 1986 as a year of modest recovery for the Syrian economy, in sharp contrast to other assessments. The Fund also acknowledged that foreign exchange shortages were among the "most important factors contributing to the sluggish performance of the manufacturing sector." International Monetary Fund, *Syrian Arab Republic: Recent Economic Developments* (9 March 1988) 4, 12.

[28] Volker Perthes, "The Syrian Economy in the 1980s," *Middle East Journal* 46 (1992) 37.

back to Arab states and lending agencies $9 million more than it received" in 1988.[29] Economic slowdowns in the major Arab oil-producing states also meant lower levels of remittances from Syrian workers. After 1979, therefore, greater shares of Syria's import bill had to be financed out of domestic revenues. In addition, low rainfall led to poor harvests from 1982 to 1985, reducing foreign exchange earned from agricultural exports and cutting the supply of raw materials to the manufacturing sector. Trade and service sectors suffered accordingly. And without adequate rainfall, production levels at Syria's hydroelectric power plants declined, further hampering the manufacturing sector and leading to daily power outages in major cities.

Mismanagement and corruption exacerbated problems beyond Syria's control. The political allocation of economic benefits, the political character of major investment decisions, and the escalating cost of the regime's extensive patronage networks represented a huge drain on resources, as did inefficiencies associated with Syria's comprehensive system of price controls.[30] During the decade, Syria's economic planning apparatus unraveled. The fifth five-year plan (1981–1985) was approved, and investment decisions followed its general intent to shift public investment from industry to agriculture and services. However, the sixth five-year plan (1986–1990) has never been completed, and the importance of the

[29] Alan George, "An Economy Saved by Circumstances," *The Middle East*, December 1988, 27–28; David Butter, "Syria's Under the Counter Economy," *Middle East Economic Digest* 23 (23 February 1990) 4–5. During one period in 1986 Syria's foreign exchange reserves were reportedly as low as $10 million. Other estimates suggest much higher levels of aid during the early 1980s, but only in the wake of the Gulf War has Arab support resumed at significant levels. See Kais Firro, "The Syrian Economy Under the Assad Regime," in *Syria under Assad*, ed. Moshe Maoz and Avner Yaniv (New York, St. Martin's Press, 1986) 62.

[30] See Volker Perthes, "The Bourgeoisie and the Ba'th: A Look at Syria's Upper Class," *Middle East Report* 170 (May–June 1991) 31–37. According to Yahya Sadowski, "Cadres, Guns, and Money: The Eighth Regional Congress of the Syrian Ba'th," *MERIP Reports*, no. 134 (July–August 1985) 7, Asad made "massive use of patronage" during his struggle against the Muslim Brotherhood to reinforce his popular standing and was unable to curb it after the conflict ended in 1982.

planning bureaucracy has undergone a steady decline.[31] Military spending also contributed significantly to the crisis. After 1976, the cost of Syria's military presence in Lebanon rose from $450 million a year to almost $1 billion a year, while other military spending grew from $900 million a year in 1976 to $1.9 billion a year in 1983.[32]

The Political Logic of Syrian Liberalization

The cumulative impact of these circumstances necessitated Syria's gradual move towards economic liberalization after 1981. But the logic underlying the Ba'th regime's approach was determined less by an interest in enhancing economic efficiency or a generic commitment to markets than by the imperatives of regime survival. By the early 1980s, the economic crisis, particularly Syria's lack of foreign exchange, threatened to undermine the continued flow of resources needed to satisfy both the regime's own rapacity and the demands of its clients. It seemed likely to cause serious strains in, if not the breakdown of, the regime's ability to satisfy its fiscal commitments to the general population in terms of subsidized food, welfare programs, health care schemes, and so on. Perhaps more important, the crisis undermined the ability of the regime to sustain the extensive patronage networks it relies on so heavily for its support. Both circumstances could have provoked a serious political crisis. Though resilient and flexible in many respects,

---

[31] According to a former member of the parliamentary economic implementation committee (a group of experts who provided technical guidance and oversight of proposed projects), Syria has had no effective planning process for at least a decade, and the relation between the five-year plans and economic policy became increasingly tenuous during this time. He described plans for large-scale construction projects presented to the committee with no budgets, no rationales, and only the skimpiest of details. Whereas, prior to the 1980s, committee members had felt able to challenge such proposals, it became increasingly apparent that their role was to approve the projects presented to them without question. Interview, Damascus, 12 August 1991.

[32] Kanovsky, "What's Behind" (supra n. 26), 6; and Patrick Clawson, *Unaffordable Ambitions: Syria's Military Build-Up and Economic Crisis*, Policy Papers, no. 17 (Washington, D.C., Washington Institute for Near East Policy, 1989) 7. Clawson does not indicate whether this figure includes the cost of Syria's presence in Lebanon. I assume it does not.

systems of rule in which legitimacy is purchased and compliance bartered in exchange for employment, privileged access to goods, or welfare benefits, are singularly vulnerable to shifts in economic performance.

Other factors added to the pressure for economic restructuring and helped shape Syria's response to its economic crisis. These include the ideological, military-strategic, and economic-structural setting within which the crisis took place. Even patronage-based authoritarian regimes rely on ruling formulas in their search for legitimacy, and accord their ideological principles more than rhetorical attention. When, as noted above, this formula is of a transformational nature and is built around a set of radically populist and redistributive norms, economic crisis becomes a serious ideological issue. The capacity of the regime to fulfill its populist commitments is an important measure of its legitimacy. When the state is entangled in (multiple) open-ended military conflicts, as Syria has been, burdens itself with crippling levels of military spending, and employs an ideology of national security and mass military mobilization as elements of its ruling formula, its ability to balance military and domestic political commitments during a period of economic decline is severely diminished. Issues of "guns or butter," or perhaps "guns or cadres," become concerns that threaten not just the political fortunes of one set of elites but the structure of the political system as a whole.[33] Under these conditions, economic liberalization becomes a crucial component of the logic of authoritarian political survival, even while political imperatives determine the scope of reforms, the target of reforms, and, to an extent, the timing of reforms.

At the same time, and perhaps most importantly, the Syrian regime has pursued liberalization in a highly selective fashion. Rather than embark at one time on a full-fledged program of economic liberalization, with its attendant political risks, the Syrian government has managed economic reform as an inherently political process. This process has taken the form of mobilizing the economic participation of sectors previously excluded from the regime's ruling coalition, notably the private commercial,

---

[33] Yahya Sadowski, "Cadres, Guns, and Money" (supra n. 30), 3–8.

agricultural, and light manufacturing sectors, in order to generate the resources needed to satisfy the demands of politically important coalition members based in inefficient public sector industries, the ruling Ba'th party, the rigidly corporatized trade unions, the state bureaucracy, the military, and the security services. Beginning in 1982 and continuing until the present, elements of the private sector with a high capacity to generate foreign exchange through export and trade, and with low capacity to organize in opposition to the regime, have benefited from a gradually deepening process of liberalization and rationalization of their activities. At the same time, the public industrial and state-bureaucratic sectors, which are more important to the regime as sources of patronage and which therefore represent a greater source of potential political instability, have been insulated from the demands of economic liberalization.[34]

By the end of the 1980s, Syria's "liberalized" sectors had become an important source of capital accumulation for the regime as a whole. Between 1985 and 1989, production in the private and joint sectors rose from S£42.6 billion to S£111 billion. Capital formation in these sectors increased from S£6,519 million to S£15,229 million during these years. Between 1986 and 1989 private sector commodity exports rose from S£3,373 million to S£16,189 million, reaching S£19,782 million in the first ten months of 1990, the most recent figures currently available.[35] In 1989 Syria announced its first trade surplus in thirty years, to the skepticism of some observers, and credited the impressive activity of the private sector and newly formed joint-sector agricultural enterprises for making the surplus possible.[36]

---

[34] On the political character of Syria's public sector see Jean Hannoyer and Michel Seurat, *Etat et secteur public industriel en Syrie* (Beirut, CERMOC, 1979), and Jean Leca, "Social Structure and Political Stability: Comparative Evidence from the Algerian, Syrian, and Iraqi Cases," in *Beyond Coercion: The Durability of the Arab State*, ed. Adeed Dawisha and I. William Zartman (New York, Croom Helm, 1988) 164–202.

[35] These figures are from the Ittihad Ghuraf al-Tijara al-Suriya (Federation of Syrian Chambers of Commerce), *Al-taqrir al-sanawi 1990* (Annual report 1990) 15.

[36] David Butter, "Syria's Under The Counter Economy" (supra n. 29), 4–5.

These sectors now provide, at least in part, the resources needed to sustain Syria's authoritarian system of rule. Throughout the implementation of this strategy, moreover, the regime's coercive capacity has remained much in evidence, both to ensure that the beneficiaries of liberalization do not attempt to use their economic gains to challenge the regime, and to suppress the political pressures that arise from those social groups and classes at the core of the regime's ruling coalition (or patronage system) whose interests are most damaged by the effects of selective liberalization and by competition from those sectors that have benefited from it.

Selective Liberalization and Syrian Business Associations

As a result of Syria's selective and corporatist approach to economic liberalization, private sector businessmen once identified as a significant threat to the economic and political control of the regime, and thoroughly marginalized as a result, have become an increasingly important component of the regime's economic strategy, and have achieved a measure of political clout as well.[37] This transformation in the character of business-state relations has been particularly evident in the post-1980s renaissance of the Syrian chambers of commerce and chambers of industry.

Syria's chambers of commerce were formed in the late nineteenth century as one of many manifestations of Syria's growing integration into the world economy and the increasing importance of European-style forms of business organization.[38] Under the French

---

[37] Fred H. Lawson, "Political-Economic Trends" (supra n. 26), 590. Lawson records the regime's efforts to keep the activities of private-sector capitalists in check during the late 1970s and early 1980s. He argues that 1981 through 1985 witnessed a "reassertion of state control" and clampdown on private sector mobilization, following the liberalizing trend of the early 1970s. What he regards as a new centralizing effort, however, is interpreted here as the initiation of selective stabilization policies in which attempts to increase foreign exchange earnings and domestic revenues are compatible with policies seeking to mobilize private sector participation in the economy.

[38] The first Syrian Chamber of Commerce was formed in Aleppo in 1880, followed by the opening of a Damascus chamber in 1895. The chambers of industry arrived in Syria much later; the first was formed in Damascus in 1945. Currently, there are thirteen chambers of commerce in Syria, with Damascus as the seat of the largest and most influential branch. The chambers coordinate

Mandate, and increasingly during the 1946–1958 independence period, the chambers acquired significant influence as representatives of the emergent Syrian business community. Among the most visible symbols of this status was Khalid al-ʿAzm, regarded as one of Syria's most progressive industrialists. As the first president of the Damascus Chamber of Industry, founder of the Syrian Cement Company, a member of one of the country's most influential families, and a regular member of the Syrian government throughout the 1946–1958 period, al-ʿAzm held the posts of Minister of National Economy and Minister of Industry on and off during these years. Both within the government and within the bureaucracy, the chambers were formal participants in the process of designing Syria's post-independence economic institutions, in debates over economic policy, and thus in the political conflicts that led to the collapse of independent Syria and the formation of the United Arab Republic in 1958.

During the union, Syrian chambers were largely stripped of their influence. With Nasser's endorsement, they were reorganized along highly corporatist lines and placed under direct ministerial supervision. The chambers were transformed from wholly autonomous and influential associations that played a central role in defining Syria's economic priorities into semiofficial administrative agencies, whose functions consisted largely of supervising the compliance of their members with state regulations. By the time the Baʿth seized power in March 1963, the chambers had essentially been excluded from a role in economic policymaking, and their formal role as the mediators of business interests was basically confined to representing employers on the labor-management arbitration boards. After 1963, no members of the chambers could be found in the country's parliament, and certainly not in the successive Baʿthist governments. By the early 1970s, a Syrian economist noted in a semiofficial study that the chambers of commerce no longer had a meaningful place in the country's political economy,

---

their activities through a Federation of Syrian Chambers of Commerce, also located in Damascus. In Damascus and Aleppo, chambers of commerce and chambers of industry operate as independent organizations; in other cities, the two operate jointly.

and were badly in need of reform in keeping with the new realities of Syrian socialism.[39]

This situation changed little during the first decade of Asad's rule, despite the limited economic opening that followed his rise to power in 1970. Though Syria's private sector had high hopes that Asad's "corrective movement" and the economic reforms of the early 1970s presaged a more sustained improvement in its fortunes, its gains were quite limited, and the chambers remained marginal to the politics of economic policymaking.[40] It was not until the severe economic crisis of the 1980s that the relationship between the state and the private sector underwent more substantive change, creating the conditions for the revival of the chambers.

Driven by the collapse of its foreign exchange reserves and its growing reliance on domestic sources of capital, the regime has sought to enhance the capacity of the private sector to generate capital through manufacturing, agriculture, trade, and particularly exports, and more generally to relegitimate the role of the private sector in the Syrian economy. In August 1983 the government began to permit private-sector businessmen to use up to half of their export earnings to finance the import of goods to be used in production. Additional new measures passed in late 1984 eased access to credit for private-sector importers, once the regime possessed sufficient foreign exchange to make possible a limited resumption of imports. These policies had an immediate and striking effect. From 1985 to 1986 the private sector's share of imports rose from 16 to 25 percent, and of exports from 8 percent to 30 percent in the same period.[41]

Mobilizing the private sector became a more explicit element of the regime's economic policies in 1985 and subsequent years,

[39] Yahya Arudki, *Al-iqtisad al-suri al-hadith*, vol. 2 (Damascus, Wizarat al-Thaqafa, 1974) 269.

[40] For an example of the (officially endorsed) optimism shown by the private sector to Asad's early reforms see Antoine Guine, *La Syrie nouvelle: exposé sur l'ouverture économique en Syrie suivi d'un bilan politique et économique des réalisations du régime du President Hafez El-Assad* (Damascus, n.p., 1975).

[41] IMF, "Syrian Arab Republic" (supra n. 27), 46. The following paragraphs draw in part on this document.

particularly in areas that showed high probability of generating foreign exchange and expanding exports. Continuing changes begun in the early 1980s, broader flexibility was given to Syrian residents in the summer and fall of 1985 to import goods to be used in industrial production for which the public sector had previously held an import monopoly, and access to credit facilities to finance such imports was eased. These regulations also permitted private-sector importers to use their own foreign exchange to pay for imported goods.[42] In March 1987 the government expanded the categories of businessmen eligible to retain up to half of their foreign exchange earnings to finance their own imports. And in April 1987, it increased the maximum amount of foreign exchange that could be retained from 50 to 75 percent of earnings for the import of certain categories of items.

Beyond specific import-export reforms, the regime created new categories of activities permitted to the private sector. In February 1986, it introduced Legislative Decree No. 10. The decree provided for the creation of joint stock companies in agriculture and tourism with a minimum 25 percent share held by the state. By 1989, eleven new joint-sector agricultural enterprises had been approved. Firms created under this decree receive highly privileged treatment: they are not bound by the constraints of the five-year development plans; are not required to sell their products to the state; are exempt from import and export restrictions and taxes; are able to hold foreign currency accounts within Syria, transfer foreign exchange out of the country, and exchange 70 percent of their foreign currency into Syrian pounds at the market rate.[43] Subsequent legislation exempted fruits and vegetables—which became the leading crops grown by joint-sector agricultural ventures—from taxes on agricultural products and facilitated their export. By 1991, Syria's joint-sector farms had become leading suppliers of these crops to the

---

[42] These reforms greatly increased demand for foreign exchange and put the Syrian pound under considerable pressure. As a result, in January and February 1986 the regime launched a major crackdown against illegal currency transactions, arresting hundreds of money changers.

[43] Hans Hopfinger, "Capitalist Agro-Business in a Socialist Country? Syria's New Shareholding Corporations as an Example" (unpublished paper, 1990).

Arab Gulf states, and important contributors to Syria's economic recovery.[44]

These changes have helped restore the chambers of commerce and industry as the leading representative associations of the private sector, and to a more meaningful place in the process of economic policymaking. The chambers have assisted the regime in its efforts to relegitimate the private sector's participation in the economy, offering steady support for liberalization throughout the 1980s. In the process, the chambers revived and expanded their role as advocates of the private sector in debates over economic policy, and began once again to be regarded as useful sources of advice and guidance on the management of economic affairs. In 1981, for example, at the outset of the economic crisis the government formed a Committee for the Guidance of Imports and Exports, including as members the prime minister and other ministers, as well as the presidents of the Damascus Chambers of Commerce and Industry. A decade later, a senior employee of the Damascus Chamber of Commerce singled out the chamber's representation on this committee as a symbol of the private sector's growing influence. "Whether we agree or disagree with [the committee's] decisions," he said, "we are there in the room and they consult us on every step."[45]

Moreover, a review of Damascus Chamber of Commerce annual reports for the years 1984 through 1989 shows that during the 1980s it developed the apparatus and tactics of a modern lobbying group, with a research department preparing scores of memoranda on various issues for the use of the cabinet; regular meetings between association officials and government ministers; and a journal serving as an outlet for association views on current economic developments (as well as a forum for expressing

[44] One source noted that Syria had replaced Eastern Europe as the source of vegetables and fruit to the Gulf states. He indicated that the biggest problem facing growers was how to respond to the explosion of demand: public-sector transport facilities were inadequate. He said the chambers of commerce were considering approaching the government to establish a joint-sector transport company to accommodate the demand for agricultural goods. Interview, Executive Director, Federation of Syrian Chambers of Commerce, 31 July 1991.

[45] Interview, 10 August 1991.

regular and effusive support for Hafiz al-Asad). Through these channels, and through personal ties between leading chamber officials and the regime, the chambers have very adeptly exploited their corporatist links to the government to try to broaden the range of activity open to the private sector, to expand the guarantees offered by the state to private business, and to expand the scope of existing liberalization decrees. In an interview in 1988, a chamber official credited the chambers with securing government approval for a joint sector in agriculture, and indicated that the primary concern of the chambers was to expand the joint sector into industry, something that they have so far been unable to do. Chamber memoranda focus on expanding the categories of goods exempted from import and export regulations and tariffs, enhancing credit facilities, reducing taxes, and, in general, the kind of everyday concerns that one would expect of any business association.

As these examples show, Syria's policy of selective liberalization produced substantive changes both in the organization of the economy and in the character of business-state relations. Like the private sector more generally, the chambers are now taken more seriously than at any time since 1963, and they have exploited liberalization to carve out for themselves a more autonomous, and more significant, role in debates over economic policy. In perhaps the most dramatic example of their revival, two members of the Damascus Chamber of Commerce and one of the Aleppo Chamber of Commerce were elected in parliamentary elections of May 1990, the first clearly defined "representatives of business" to serve in parliament since 1963.[46] As one prominent business leader, successful politician, and senior official of the Damascus Chamber of Commerce remarked of Syria's private sector in the 1990s, "it has no boundaries."[47]

[46] See Volker Perthes, "Syria's Parliamentary Elections of 1990: A Renewed base for an Old Regime" (unpublished paper, 1990).

[47] Interview, Badia Fallaha, Vice President of the Damascus Chamber of Commerce and member of parliament (one of two from the DCC elected in May 1990) 8 August 1991.

Confining the Private Sector:
The Economic and Political Limits of Liberalization

Despite this sentiment, regime policies continue to restrict the private sector within distinct boundaries. The regime has carefully preserved the privileged position of "national" economic sectors, including petroleum and mining, banking, agricultural processing, cement, glass, and paper manufacturing, and so on. In these sectors, where workers are heavily unionized, the number of workers per firm is the highest in Syria, employment serves political and patronage functions, and the regime has sought to cultivate its political base along highly clientalist lines, rationalization and liberalization have been scrupulously avoided. No set of decrees has been passed encouraging private-sector investment in heavy industry similar to those that have facilitated private investment in trade, light manufacturing for export, agriculture, tourism, and services (and for many reasons it is not clear the private sector would pursue such opportunities were they available). Nor has privatization of inefficient state-owned industries been raised as a strategy, unlike the case of Egypt or many other states.[48]

The regime has also been careful to contain the private sector in political terms. The chambers remain under the tightly guided auspices of the state; liberalization has not loosened the corporatist bonds that ensure the regime against the emergence of an independent and adversarial business community.

Insulating politically important sectors from the demands of liberalization, however, has not entirely insulated them from its effects. Economic liberalization has brought significant adjustment costs. Employees of the state have watched their fixed salaries lose considerable ground over the past decade to inflation and to the withdrawal or reduction of many state subsidies.[49]

---

[48] Ibrahim Helmy Abdel-Rahman and Mohammed Sultan Abu Ali, "Role of the Public and Private Sectors with Special Reference to Privatization: The Case of Egypt," in *Privatization and Structural Adjustment in the Arab Countries*, ed. Said El-Naggar (Washington, D.C., IMF, 1989) 141–81 .

[49] The price of flat bread has risen 600 percent in recent years, from about one-half a Syrian pound per kilo to S£3 a kilo. The black market in tea, sugar, and rice has all but disappeared and these goods are now widely available, but they have become increasingly unaffordable for most Syrians.

Midlevel bureaucrats may earn as little as $60 to $80 a month, university professors $110 a month, and pensioners about $50 a month.[50] Popular dissatisfaction with the consequences of liberalization is fueled by many sources. Growing discrepancies between public- and private-sector salaries; continued high inflation; elimination of subsidies on basic commodities such as sugar, tea, and rice; the perception that government policies now favor a "parasitic," "speculative" private sector; and the apparent retreat of the regime from its longstanding populist commitments, have generated serious concern among a variety of groups, including the General Federation of Trade Unions, conservative factions within the Ba'th party, and the much less politically significant Communist party.[51]

These impacts have caused the regime to devote significant attention to coalition maintenance, but with a distinctive dynamic, one shaped by its corporatist and selective approach to liberalization. Unlike the problems of coalition management associated with full-blown economic stabilization programs, where regime elites

---

Basic pharmaceuticals are now more widely available, but even those produced by state-owned enterprises cost between S£20 to S£50, enormously expensive for the vast majority of people, whose monthly salaries might range from S£1800 to S£3500.

[50] These figures are based on the official incentive exchange rate, introduced in mid-1991 as part of Syria's exchange rate reform process, of S£42 to the dollar. This rate was sufficiently close to the true (i.e., black market) rate to persuade many who had previously used the black market to shift their transactions to the state-owned banks.

[51] See, for example, al-Ittihad al-'Am lil-'Ummal fi al-Qutr al-'Arabi al-Suri [General Federation of Syrian Trade Unions], "Mu'tamr al-ibda' al-watani wa'l-i'timad 'ala al-dhat: al-taqrir al-'am" (Conference on national innovation and self-sufficiency: final report) (Damascus 1987). The document notes the efforts of union leaders to preserve the primacy of the public sector in the face of growing challenges from the private sector in terms of salary, productivity, and quality of management. Later, during the parliamentary debate surrounding the 1991 introduction of the Legislative Decree encouraging private investment, Communist party deputies challenged the law as a retreat from the nationalist and populist principles that have guided the Syrian economy. The statement of Communist Prime Minister Mahmoud Daoud was reproduced in the newspaper of the Bakhdash faction of the Communist party, *Nidal al-sha'b*, no. 469 (early March 1991). See also a followup report in *Nidal al-sha'b*, no. 470 (late March 1991) 1–2.

seek to balance the costs of restructuring among all members of the dominant coalition, and to ensure that some core set of coalition members remain committed to the process at all times, the Syrian regime has a different but equally difficult task.[52] It must simultaneously persuade the private sector of its sincerity and commitment to reform, without which it would abstain from investing, while persuading its clients and beneficiaries that their position is secure, that they will be protected from the demands of liberalization, and that economic reform will not interrupt their privileges and benefits.

This requirement has forced the regime to sacrifice coherence in its economic rhetoric to the preservation of flexibility in its economic policies. In early March 1990, the Minister of Economy and Foreign Trade, Muhammad Imadi, told the Kuwaiti paper *Al-Anba'*: "the Syrian Government's economic plan sought to support the private sector. It increased its contribution to exports by 300 percent between 1988 and 1989 and allowed it to retain 75 percent of its overall revenues from exports in foreign currency to finance its imports."[53] A week later, Prime Minister Mahmoud Zu'bi spoke to the annual congress of the Damascus Worker's Federation, emphasizing "that the public sector will be the principal factor in the national economy and that the government views the private and mixed sectors as complementary to the public sector."[54] These mixed messages, and policies to match, have become a familiar part of the regime's approach to managing economic reform.

Rather than trying to persuade its clients to support liberalization, therefore, the regime seeks to reassure them of their relative immunity from its requirements and its costs. The regime has not undertaken the political challenge of constructing a grand coalition in support of liberalization, but has in essence cultivated two distinct coalitions, one economic and liberalizing, the other political and populist, and has adjusted the incentives and benefits

---

[52] John Waterbury, "The Political Management of Economic Adjustment and Reform," in *Fragile Coalitions* (supra n. 2), 39–56.

[53] Foreign Broadcast Information Service (FBIS), *Daily Report: Near East and South Asia*, 15 March 1990, 40.

[54] Ibid., 20 March 1990, 31.

it provides to each depending on the role defined for it. In this sense, liberalization has not brought about a general renegotiation of the populist coalition that has helped to sustain the regime for three decades. It has instead produced a much more limited set of semiprivate bargains, or narrow and exclusive pacts. General austerity measures have been introduced, but in a piecemeal fashion. The regime has called on Syrians to reduce consumption and assist in "achieving economic self-reliance," but continues to identify itself as the provider of social welfare. Regime clients have been reassured, but have been made aware, as well, that resources are limited and that they bear the leading responsibility for the country's economic development.[55] Prices paid to farmers for their crops by state purchasing agencies have been raised. To mobilize private-sector participation, local and foreign businessmen have been granted guarantees protecting their activities within defined economic sectors. Syria's capitalists have been accorded a limited degree of political recognition, and have benefited from a consultative role in shaping economic policies that affect their areas of interest.[56]

This strategy is not risk-free. The adjustment costs of liberalization on the general population are hard to contain and, as noted above, can spill over into politically important sectors: austerity programs are felt most sharply by salaried workers in the public sector and the state bureaucracy. Even though business groups currently go out of their way to show support for the regime and for the ruling party, it may be difficult to prevent private-sector representatives from acquiring a greater measure of political power than the regime intends, and using their positions to support more far-ranging reforms. Moreover, the private sector simply may not

[55] Prime Minister Mahmud Zu'bi's address to parliament on 28 December 1986. Translated in BBC Summary of World Broadcasts, *Weekly Economic Report* art 4: *Middle East, Africa, Latin America* (12 January 1987) ME/W0008 A1/6–10.

[56] As noted above, representatives of the Chamber of Commerce and Chamber of Industry sit on the Committee for the Supervision of Exports and Imports (Lajnat Tarshid al-Istirad wa'l-Tasdir), which is chaired by the Prime Minister and also includes the Minister of Economic and Foreign Trade, the Minister of Supply and Internal Trade, and the Deputy Prime Minister for Economic Affairs.

be able to satisfy the consumption demands of those groups at the core of the ruling coalition, postponing, but not resolving, the need for more substantive structural adjustments. As Waterbury has argued with regard to Egypt,

> The external resources that might have gone into structural adjustment itself and the attendant remaking of the dominant coalition were used instead to sustain the consumption of the existing coalition, and to add to it at least one new member: private-sector interests in imports and banking. At the close of the 1980s, this formula no longer appears economically sustainable. Rents have declined while the claims of coalition partners have expanded, but the productive structure of the Egyptian economy has not been significantly altered.[57]

Syria's strategy has differed from Egypt's in important ways. The regime has made some effort to curb the demands of its supporters, the private sector has become a net contributor to the regime's resources and not simply an additional burden, and the macroeconomic and legal frameworks of the Syrian economy have been altered in meaningful ways to promote substantially higher levels of private-sector activity. These choices have raised the costs and potential risks of the path chosen by Syria's leaders, but they are also less destabilizing than a more systematic approach to economic liberalization.

Prospects for Democratization in Syria

Given the relative success with which Syria has pursued a selective and limited strategy of economic liberalization in Syria, is there a possibility that the expansion of economic reforms might at some future point lead to a substantive political opening? Is it possible the Syrian regime will move from a strategy of selective liberalization to implement a "democratic bargain" of some form as it seeks to expand the role of the private sector? Is it likely, rather than simply possible, that Syria's private sector, through its business associations or otherwise, will mobilize in opposition to the regime and in support of democratic reforms?

---

[57] Waterbury, "Political Management," 49.

For many observers of Syria, the moment when the prospects for some form of political liberalization seemed greatest occurred in late 1989 and early 1990, following the collapse of socialist regimes in Eastern Europe, and in particular the fall of Nicolae Ceaușescu in Romania. Syrian businessmen were among those arguing that the transformation of the international political system caused by the events in Eastern Europe had created new opportunities for domestic political changes. In one unusually public example, expatriate Syrian businessman Omran Adaham wrote an open letter to President Asad making precisely this kind of argument, though it is worth pointing out that Adaham adopted the approach of a loyal opposition, calling for the reform of the current regime, and not its replacement.

Far from setting off a chain-reaction in Syria, however, the events in Eastern Europe and the then Soviet Union after 1989 have provoked a fascinating and largely defensive response from Syria's rulers. Very little of this reaction has centered on the relationship between the economic and political crises of socialism, but some aspects of the regime's response are worth recalling because of the insights they provide into the ways the regime has used the demise of the Second World to redefine and relegitimate its own economic and political strategies.

In several speeches and interviews during the course of 1990, Asad and a few other senior officials offered an unapologetic and even innovative justification for the nature and form of Syrian political life, rejecting in particular the notion that what happened in Eastern Europe was necessary or inevitable in Syria. President Asad characterized Western-style democracy, for example, as corrupt and too individualistic. He claims that Syria has been practicing democracy since the "corrective revolution" of 1970 that brought him to power. He argues that Syria is an example of tolerant pluralism, pointing to the presence of a mixed economy with private, joint, and public sectors as one proof of this, and to the existence of the National Political Front "coalition" government as another. In his remarks, Asad also emphasizes Syria's distinctiveness: "Syria is not a duplicate of other states." It has its own view of democracy, socialism, and freedom. What is appropriate for other states is not appropriate for Syria, and Syria must determine independently what kinds of political arrangements are best suited for it. This position, in which Asad does not criticize changes in other states but rejects them for Syria, is aimed not only at silencing domestic critics but at maintaining sound relations with the states that have emerged from the collapse of the Soviet Union and with the states of Eastern Europe, despite the dramatic changes they have undergone.

Among the most interesting of Asad's reflections are his comments on freedom. Taking an approach that is almost Hobbesian, Asad carefully distinguishes between freedom and anarchy, and emphasizes the central role of the state in ensuring that freedom does not overwhelm order. In his 1990 revolution day address he noted that "restricting freedom tarnishes it, but regulating its practice makes it brighter. Restricting freedom means dwarfing it, but regulating its practice means developing it and making it healthy.... Freedom and its regulations belong side by side. They do not live apart.... Like everything in this universe, freedom needs order."

Considering Asad's disregard for the practice of freedom, it would be easy to dismiss these thoughts. However, Asad's attention to such topics as pluralism and freedom in a speech marking Syria's most important political anniversary indicates how seriously the Syrian regime is challenged by local reactions to democratization in Eastern Europe and the demise of the Soviet Union. Despite the regime's readiness to make some changes in the system of rule, which are partly but not entirely cosmetic, Asad's speeches are clearly intended to establish the boundaries beyond which reforms will not be considered or are likely to be taken as threats to the security of the state.

Thus, despite the seemingly enthusiastic response to the elections in May, Syrians realize that the underlying goal of recent changes is to reinforce an authoritarian system of rule and not to initiate a process of meaningful political transformation, even one guided from the top. In fact, by the summer of 1990, and certainly by 1991, the popular expectation that the shocks of late 1989 and early 1990 might provoke reforms had given way to resigned disappointment that nothing much had happened, that a Ba'th party congress scheduled, in part, to discuss the events in Europe would not be held, that the regime had weathered the shocks, and that Asad himself remained firmly in control.

Syria's economic fortunes over the past two years have contributed to the reduction of pressures on the regime. By 1989, partly as a result of liberalization measures but principally because of increasing oil exports, Syria's economy showed tentative signs of recovering from the 1981–1989 crisis, even prior to the resumption of large-scale Arab support following the Gulf War. In 1990, the government announced its second annual trade surplus in a row. Syria's foreign exchange position remains difficult, but it is much improved from the period in 1986 when the IMF reported reserve levels of only $10 million. These improvements have not dissuaded the regime from moving forward with its selective approach to economic liberalization. The May 1991 decrees promoting foreign and local private-sector investment represented a significant expansion of the guarantees and privileges the regime has extended to the private sector. However, they have also provided the regime with the resources it requires to preserve political stability and to manage the process of economic liberalization without engaging in political liberalization. For the foreseeable future, Syria seems likely to remain an example of the resilience of authoritarianism in the face of economic crisis.

State, Legitimacy, and Democratization in the Maghreb

ABDELBAKI HERMASSI

IS the Arab State condemned to remain a diminished state, permanently suffering from a legitimacy deficit? Does the absence of sufficient legitimacy result from a recurrent structural lack of moral justification, from a political experience of noncorrespondence between the political entity and the community of which it is a member?

Historically, the Arab state had to find its justification in its being linked to the Islamic ecumenical grouping; once decolonization got under way, the ecumenical grouping of Islam shrank simply to a religious community. It is now the Arab corpus that is the main unit of reference and identification; it is with reference to the Arab whole that the public interest is seen and the general will defined. Abdallah Laroui notes that the state organization is merely "the transitional instrument that has to be used to bring into being a human type that alone is judged to be worthy of the legitimate ambition of the Arabs. Like the nostalgia for the caliphate (which it replaces), the utopia of the union does instead of a theory of the lawful state; in this very way it prevents a serious grasp of the real state."[1]

Even with the strengthening of the state apparatus and territorial sovereignties, in the absence of a theory of the state, the modern Arab state lacks legitimacy. Salafism and unionism deny states any possibility of legitimatization because they see in them the main obstacle to the achieving of a wider entity, one that

---

[1] Abdallah Laroui, *Islam et modernité* (Paris, La Decouverte, 1987) 44.

would better satisfy hearts and spirits—in a word, a charismatic community. The same goes for modern ideologies; both liberalism and Marxism tend to present existing states not as legitimate in their own right, but as instruments of a class or of a constellation of classes pursuing immediate material interests. At the very moment when the state is becoming stronger in material terms, it cannot win the loyalty of its citizens because of an ideological heritage that is both negative and impossible to circumvent.

This kind of approach to the question of state legitimacy, while generally valid for the whole Arab world, must nonetheless take account of a certain number of regional specificities. The particular cases of the Maghreb states are notable, if only because there the twin sources of state delegitimatization spring mainly from Berberism and Islamism.

State capabilities also affect the bases of legitimacy. How able the state is to carry out certain duties and offer well-defined services expected by its inhabitants will, beyond any shadow of a doubt, affect the state's legitimacy, just as it will that of the regime and that of its government. In answering people's needs to identify with a group or a community, the state creates a basis for what we may call external legitimacy. But there is also an internal legitimacy of the regime, ensuring peace, protecting members from outside and domestic dangers, and maintaining at least a minimum of welfare and a certain standard of living.

Where the state fails to perform these tasks, one can find all sorts of reactions—the dissatisfied may protest to attract the attention of the authorities, or they may transfer their loyalty to revolutionary movements or to ethnic groups. They may sink into cynicism or alienation, interspersed from time to time with riots, terrorist acts, or other expressions of discontent.[2]

The Maghreb state has always tried to define its legitimacy in black-and-white terms: one indivisible nation, Arab language, Islamic faith. Such a position almost by definition excludes the expression of conflicting interests or the affirming of ethnic or religious diversity. Thus, instead of laying down general values susceptible of normative and situational adaptation, the call for

[2] John H. Herz, "Legitimacy, Can we Retrieve It?" *Comparative Politics*, April 1978, 317–43.

legitimacy tends to stiffen into a rigid formula, unable to accommodate differences.

We may claim at the outset the impossibility of legitimizing the Maghreb state through the Islamist or Arab utopia. These competing conceptions of political order would deprive the state of any form of loyalty and leave it only the language of force. "The local State equips, teaches, employs and organizes ... but these achievements do not bring it loyalty or create a consensus around it, particularly since its propaganda endlessly repeats that the State only represents a state along the road to the great unitary Arab State."[3] These utopias would convey an ideology at odds with the tasks the state performs in its existing boundaries.

When assessing state-building in the Maghreb, it is important to draw a distinction between the Maghreb states—which are widely accepted as frameworks of political reference—and the Maghreb regimes—which are going through a fairly severe legitimacy crisis. This distinction may help account for both the conflicts and resistance that the government's action (or inaction) provokes and the true limits of the various levels of anti-establishment activity.

The Maghreb of the last fifty years has enshrined nationalism as the dominant ideology. It was nationalism that enabled it to withstand the long night of colonialism; it was the triumph of nationalism that led it to build up the state system and set in place ambitious projects of economic development. Unlike the Arab East, where the ideology of Pan-Arab unity triumphed, it was the idea of a territorially limited national state and nationalism that emerged triumphant. This happened in the 1930s, when the national elites succeeded in downgrading Salafi reformism and elbowing out the supporters of liberalism and socialism. Moreover, none of the political parties that embraced the national movement presented a Pan-Arab platform. The Tangiers Congress, meeting with the dominant theme of the unity of the Greater Arab Maghreb, merely consecrated the independent territorial state, a position already enjoyed by Morocco and Tunisia, and one that had to be won for Algeria.

[3] Abdallah Laroui, *Mafhoum al-Dawla* (Casablanca, Arab Cultural Center, 1981) 169.

It is not that the nationalists let slip opportunities for mobilizing religious feeling or activating the sense of Arab solidarity. The striking fact remains, however, that these issues were subordinated to one major cause—that of serving the political communities that were taking shape in Tunisia and Morocco and Algeria, which were seen almost as nations in themselves. We shall have the chance to see that the ambiguity between local nationalism and wider Arab nationalism persisted. But the fact remains that Maghrebis have an attitude to the national state that is not constitutively negative. The idea, widespread in the Arab East, of a state that is nothing but the artificial creation of a colonialism that splintered up entities into states, is one that does not correspond to the experience of most Maghrebis. Even though the regimes in power have had to face a series of crises reflecting the painful birth of civil society, the idea of a national state has not been directly challenged.

Why were Maghrebi states more broadly accepted than those in the Arab East? Among the reasons are a history of relatively powerful political centers (this tradition was greatly strengthened by the colonial impact), the fact that the Maghreb was profoundly Islamized but not completely Arabized, and the Maghreb's geopolitical position, including its role as a cultural boundary. The result of all this has been that the Islamic (or, if one prefers, the Arab-Muslim) connotation is more likely to prevail over ideological and militant Arabism. It is in the light of these influences that one starts to understand how lasting, distinct political entities, based on a deep sense of collective identity, have historically taken shape.

And what has become of the regimes at the end of over a quarter century of independent existence? First, we must understand that everything, or nearly everything—the legacy from the past, the rapid erosion of traditional society—has helped place the state at the center of the processes of national integration and socioeconomic development. What the people expected from independence and independent government was that it give access to everything the colonial system had withheld—security, jobs, social mobility, and dignity. The converging of these expectations with the demands of state-building constituted the substance of the national project as it presented itself over the last few decades. Ideally, the formula strove towards the taking over of society by the state. As

it was not possible to count on the spontaneous functioning of social forces to realize so ambitious a project, the idea was that the
society had to be transformed. Whether it was a plausible reason
or an excuse, this postulate allowed the existing social institutions
to be neutralized and replaced by more or less corporate structures
for the purpose of providing a framework for society within the
state apparatus.

The degree to which the state could take over rested on a whole
series of considerations: the class structure, the degree of social
and political mobilization, and, particularly, each state's predisposition. Morocco was from the outset liberal; Algeria enlisted the
state in a vast project of industrialization; and Tunisia vacillated
(as it still does) between bureaucratic and liberal capitalism.

But despite differences of approach, the enlisting of the state
produced results that were everywhere dramatically visible. Since
independence, the infrastructure of each state has doubled or
tripled; societies have been profoundly shaken and transformed
to the point of becoming unrecognizable under the weight of a
series of development plans; a new class of private and state
entrepreneurs has been born; a broad, replenished working class
is starting to test its strength.

Yet popular support for the state's ambitious project could not
last forever. Disenchantment with development policies became
obvious in the late 1970s, as increasingly did the fact that the
political formula and the very program of the national liberation
movement seemed to have exhausted their potential.

It is true that in the past signs of discontent had always existed,
but the governments of the first years of independence enjoyed a
considerable margin of maneuver. People were ready to have faith
and accept measures of austerity and hardship in the hope of a
better future, if not for themselves then for their children. It was
only when certain outcomes of the development policy, such as the
widening of old gaps and the creation of new disparities, started
to become visible that discontent took on crisis proportions and
that the national consensus was challenged.

In society, the crisis has taken the form of an increasingly
marked intolerance of inequality. This intolerance first showed
itself in the working-class union milieu, where there was a record
number of strikes, both legal and illegal. Worse still was the

bursting in on the political scene of the rejects, those whom growth had excluded. Class consciousness and corporate-based and sector-based interests have become more pronounced, to the detriment of national unity. Above and beyond the objective disparities between income brackets, what has made awareness of the gaps between the various social categories more acute has been the behavior of the nouveaux riches. From Ibn Khaldun to Veblen it has been clear that the nouveaux riches display luxury and novelty, leading to social disintegration. Ostentatious consumption produces hostility and envy in the popular classes and despair among the young, particularly the students. With the proliferation of educational degrees, the student masses have lost all hope of achieving a status similar to that which preceding generations of graduates attained.

Increasingly, success and mobility are seen as linked to favoritism, patronage, and regionalism rather than to hard work and competence. The politicians themselves, to paraphrase Max Weber, do little to dispel the impression that they live *from* rather than *for* politics. The result is that Maghreb states are far from the takeover of society by the state that was seen at the start of independence. Indeed, these states are far closer to the privatizing of the state. Certainly, the "state" never really drowned the "private," even in its most authoritarian phases. What is distinctive about the present situation is, on the one hand, the attempt by pressure groups to monopolize the state and, on the other, the appearance of resistance and protest that can no longer be accommodated within the existing framework.

What people now call national disenchantment does not exclusively concern class conflicts; the challenges of the left and unions to specific policies are aimed at the social and political arrangements themselves. The essential preoccupation of the leading elites has been with economic and social development—"how to catch up with the West." In the past, the opposition attacked the means, the state-centered framework, rather than the ultimate ends. In contrast, the new opposition has been concerned with considerations of identity and justice, the state-centered framework, and is almost indifferent to the problems of development and efficiency.

In the past there was a more or less explicit social pact by which citizens abdicated their political rights in favor of the government, which, in return, guaranteed them social rights. It was in the name of this pact that the people granted a quarter of a century of obedience to the political slogan of the day: "One man, one party, one plan." The 1970s and 1980s were years of social and cultural clashes. By the 1990s the state was showing increasing signs of withdrawal and disengagement; it is the whole political system that will be convulsed.

After years when the number of strikes increased dramatically among the workers, a cycle of riots began: urban riots in Morocco in 1981 and Tunisia in 1984, and the Algerian explosion of October 1988. In most cases, these came in reaction to the state's retreat from certain sectors of social life as a result of adjustments ordered by the International Monetary Fund. There was thus a weakening of the distributive capacity of the state, hurting the lower classes. At the same time, these adjustments led to a closer association between the rulers and the nouveaux riches.

The protest is, in part, against the class nature of the state and the dwindling of its scope. But there is also protest against the state's cultural policy and its identification with the worldly nouveaux riches. The reaction to the cultural orientation of the state can be seen in the reemergence of a Berber cultural claim, very well described (as regards Algeria) by Mohamed Harbi.

Harbi tells how the Kabyle cadres, when independence dawned, felt great bitterness at being excluded from political power, while other groups, even those less committed on the battlefield, benefited from the fruits of Kabyle action. The successive presidents of Algeria were aware of these Kabyle reservations, but they believed they could overcome them treating Kabylia in an economically and socially preferential way. At the same time, haunted by the fear of any Kabyle separatism, they prevented all demonstrations of Berber identity. Supported by the desire to assert the authority of the state and to create a uniform society, Arabization was originally thought of as a social control operation. The aim of state leaders was less the solution of the cultural question than the orchestration of the voice of the people, but their policies served to show all the erring ways of the state as primary employer and sole cultural entrepreneur.

Administrative Arabization, with its daily harassments in the courts, in traffic checks, and in schools, provoked tensions and bad feelings. A tendency to reject the Arabic language, hitherto unknown in Kabylia, gradually grew up. The signs of cultural unrest continued to increase. In Paris in 1967 the Berber academy was born, which took up all the excesses and ideological simplifications of Arab Islamism. In 1973 the Algerian government took another step towards cultural repression by abolishing the chair in Berber held by the writer Mouloud Mammeri. Assertion of cultural identity left the university benches and went out into the street. It was shown by exclusive use of Berber and French in a number of cafes, hotels, and restaurants and even in some administrations in Algiers (Popular Communal Assembly and Wylaya). Everything became a pretext for refusing the arbitrary decisions of the state. Under the cover of sport, the J.S.K. Tizi-Ouzou football club served as a rallying point and attracted increasingly anti-authority crowds. In May 1977 at Algiers stadium, in the presence of Boumedienne, the cultural demand became explicit.

> The explosion of Tizi-Ouzou in 1980 was aimed at the absolutist state and posed the problem of democracy and the right to be different for all Algerians. A form of national integration that denied diversity compromised the unity of Algeria, a unity that no Kabyle questions today.[4]

Even on an economic level, the national state saw itself deprived of its monopoly. It was the entrepreneurs and the business people in the private sector and especially the informal sector who were going to gain in status at the expense of the cadres and the educated elites. This phenomenon is well described by Moncef Bouchrara, talking about what he calls the rampant industrialization in Tunisia.

The vast majority of entrepreneurs in the informal sector and even the big entrepreneurs have not finished their schooling (that is, they are mainly monolingual in Arabic). Nevertheless, they have shown an extraordinary spirit of enterprise. But this enterprise is only partly based on individual initiatives, ingenuity, and motivation. It depends, too, on the mobilization and strategies of traditional basic groups such as family, clan, village, and regional

[4] Mohamed Harbi, "Nationalisme algérien et identité berbère," *Peuples Méditerranéens*, April–June 1980, 31–38.

communities. (For example, the political and institutional role of private entrepreneurs: Makhtar Zarrouk, Abdelwaheb Ben Ayed, Haj Soula, and the emergence of Sfax, the areas of the Cap Bon, and Sidi Bou Zid). It is an "ethno-entrepreneurial class."

This ethno-entrepreneurial class, from Sfax, Djerba, Metouia, and Khiari, is founded on cultural resources. Today, three-quarters of the commercial and industrial businesses created in Tunis belong to people who come from the south of Tunisia—from Sfax to Djerba, including Metouia and Matmata. This class's activities reach to Europe, as migrants create enterprises across networks of economic specialization and ethnic solidarity. For the last ten years, across the Maghreb, it has been at the forefront of economic growth. It has given birth to thousands of illegal and unauthorized markets. Trabendo, Souk Lybia, and la Rue Zarkoun are just so many places of exchange and negotiation, just so many means for people to organize things at a societal level that they cannot do at the state level.

The crisis of authoritarian legitimacy, along with the difficulties of the state in taking a central position on the socioeconomic level, foretells a certain autonomization of civil societies. In this respect, we can see three vectors of change.

First and foremost is the formation of political parties, even if these parties continue to experience difficulties in building up a social basis of their own in order to get away from their club status and have a real say on the political scene. Then there are the human rights organizations. More numerous and more active in the Maghreb than in the Machrek, these groups make up a growing opposition. Even when used by the powers that be, they show a sensitivity to the law and serve as an embryo of public opinion. Finally, there are women. Excluded from society and from power in certain Arab countries, suffering under the weight of discriminatory legislation in most Arab states, everywhere subject to what Stuart Mill called the despotism of custom, Arab women have been the rejects of social development. In several Arab countries, they have demonstrated their disagreement when discriminatory legislation has been adopted. In addition to defending statutory interests, the Arab woman's protest has the value of an example to society as a whole. She is asking for her autonomy, in fact. In practice, it is not a question of knowing—as certain people would have it—whether religion or the law grants these rights to women, but of knowing what women think and do with the rights that are granted.

It is, however, essential to note here that the emergence of a civil society and the birth of free public opinion continue to meet serious obstacles. What can be confirmed is that different elements in society see themselves less and less in terms of the vertical, monolithic organization of the party-state. The state is trying to disengage itself from society, without giving up its political monopoly.

Maghreb states have readjusted their economic policies in response to national and international pressures. But they believed they could do this without turning the local political configuration upside down. Economic liberalization (*infitah*) could be accompanied by the maintenance of political hegemony: what Clifford Geertz calls authoritarian liberalism, or the emergence of a combination between "this Smithian idea of how to get rich and this Hobbesian idea of how to rule."[5]

It is in this context that we should situate the rise in power of the Islamist movement. Islamism was inconceivable as long as the national state still operated, in fact and in belief, as a welfare state. It was only when the population felt abandoned to bare market principles, and when the party-states reacted to the advances of the civil society and to the erosion of their authority by a reinforcement of their monopoly, that Islamism erupted onto the scene. It was with the dismantling of the national union, the Tunisian General Workers' Union (UGTT—Union Générale des Travailleurs Tunisiens) in 1978, which represented the most important social counterpower, that the Tunisian regime signed its defeat; in Algeria, it was the riots of 1988 and the murderous scale of repression that consecrated the end of populism and the beginning of political anomie.[6]

The Islamist movement presented itself as the appointed beneficiary and sole legitimate inheritor, bringing the legitimacy crisis to its paroxysm. One has to acknowledge the skill of this movement

[5] Comment in plenary session, in *Daedalus*, Winter 1989, 238.
[6] Abdelkader Djeghloul, "L'Algérie en état d'anomie politique," *Le Monde Diplomatique*, March 1990.

in exploiting the two themes to which the Maghreb population was very sensitive, namely, justice and identity. It is because the political parties did not identify this kind of concern that they did not capture the aspirations of the people. The IMF-induced reforms carried out by the government provoked serious resistance; the move from a distributive economy to an economy regulated by the price system and competition inevitably creates apprehension.

Throughout the Maghreb, those who were excluded from economic growth and those who lost out in the structural adjustment found a voice in the Islamist associations, which set out to improve conditions of daily life: employment, housing, transport. Weaving social protest with a moral and religious discourse denouncing inequality and injustice, corruption and complacency, the Islamists quickly became the leading opposition. They knew the language that transforms the humiliating daily battle to find food into a general struggle against a political regime held up as responsible for the frustrations of every moment.

With the exhaustion of official nationalism as well as the left-wing ideologies, Islam rapidly became a pole of mobilization; an instrument of training; a field for political autonomization, cultural possibilities, and economic development. Does the Islamist component carry demands for fundamental modification of the political system?

This is François Burgat's thesis; he sees a new wave of nationalism in contemporary Islamism. Doubtless, he argues, Islamist mobilization is owing in part to the weakening of the regimes in place. Doubtless it also contains an "extremist" section. But Islamism is really pursuing in a more global way the exploitation of an old nationalist dynamism.[7]

It restores to the dominated the possibility of expressing themselves in their own language. By enabling them to act and express themselves politically in the categories of their culture, it restores historical continuity to the collective imagination, which the colonial parenthesis had interrupted This lexical and syntactic break with Western political terminology is deeply felt by the countries

[7] François Burgat, "Des fellaghas aux intégristes," *Le Monde*, 3 June 1991.

of the North. The response of the French right reminds us of its reaction towards those known as fellaghas; as for the left, stuck in their literal attachment to the symbols of secularism, it is still suffering from the possibility "that one day someone might dare to write a piece of history in a different vocabulary to the one it has forged. But in fact, the birth of a new Islamist political generation is no less or more hostile to France and no less or more incapable of adopting democratic behavior than these fellaghas, whom it supports today, were in their time."[8]

However, the image of Islamism that is most often taken up by those in power and in the media is that of accumulated frustrations, a sign of dead ends rather than a medium of transformation. This interpretation is almost perfectly illustrated in the writings of Gilles Kepel. The democratic aspirations of young people, in this view, have been blocked by those who have grabbed power and wealth since independence, and who are today attempting to pass on privilege to their children. Those children have been educated in Europe, in the United states, or in Western educational institutions on the spot, while the majority only has the right to monolingual education, putting it at a disadvantage on the labor market, which in turn feeds frustration even more.

> During the last fifteen years, this democratic frustration among the young has mainly been expressed through the only channel open to it: the reislamization movements.... [T]hese movements have sought to fill the function left vacant by oulamas that have been weakened or taken into the public service. Expressing themselves "in the name of God," interpreting as they please the sacred texts that are all their militants (the literate ones) read, they denounced in the same breath the "impiety of those in power and the social injustice suffered by a younger generation denied a future."[9]

Kepel argues that reislamization "from the top," the conquest of the state following the example of the Khomeinist strategy, began to run out of steam in the 1980s. The new movements of reislamization "from the bottom" had no revolutionary ambition. Instead, they offered palliatives to the shortcomings of

---

[8] Burgat, "Des fellaghas aux intégristes," 2.

[9] Gilles Kepel, "Impasses arabes," Le Monde, 7 March 1991.

the state in all the social domains (education, health, youth training, unemployment, etc.). They sought to create a sort of countersociety around the network of mosques that obeyed the commands of the sacred texts to the letter in daily life. These "from the bottom" movements, unlike their predecessors, were endowed with a real popular base and profited both from the leniency of the established authorities, who saw them as a distraction from the radical and political forms of reislamization, and from considerable subsidies, particularly from Saudi Arabia and Kuwait.

Thus there is a countersociety that can be tolerated up to a certain point, but that invariably, at one time or another, poses the question of its access to the political system and that more often than not is blocked. Cornered in this impasse are the youth who have been tempted by violent solutions or the search for distractions, even temporary ones, such as the recent support for the adventure of the Iraqi regime. Unless the West manages to finds solutions to the structural economic problems of the Middle East, "the political language of revolutionary Islam," says Kepel, "will inevitably become the bellicose speech of a South looking for revenge."[10]

How can one deal with Islam? The failure of the Maghreb regimes in terms of satisfying material needs and offering hope to the urban youth does not necessarily put them on a collision course with the Islamists. What I and Remy Leveau, among others, are arguing is for inclusion of the Islamists in a more democratic setting. A democratic state and Islamists could have distinct and complementary functional roles.

Leveau suggests a parallel between the role played by the Islamists in the contemporary Maghreb and Arab societies and the role of the communist parties in Europe in the 1930s; the two movements effectively offer those who have been disappointed by economic growth and modernization a "somewhere else." This alternative allows them to dream, while at the same time accepting compromises that will reinforce the system for the time being, allowing the states to make a certain number of concessions to the latest challengers.

[10] Kepel, "Impasses arabes."

Leveau writes,

If the Islamist movements still appear in the collective imagination
as a sort of counterstate, a more realistic perception should attempt
to analyze what their role could be in a democratic setup. The
sudden changes that have taken place in the Maghreb since the
removal of Bourguiba in November 1987 allow us, perhaps for
the first time, to envisage democratization as a realistic strategy
for the state apparatus to consolidate its power while running
fewer risks than in maintaining a facade of absolutism that puts
it at a disadvantage in the competition with the Islamists. This
supposes on the one hand that the Islamist movements are granted
recognition and that in return they agree to participate in an
institutional interaction that will legitimize the state and whose
objective will in fact be protection against the seizure of power. For
this, the various participants have to trust one another, especially
in the transition phase, and the Islamist leaders, if they are not
thinking of taking all the power for the moment by submitting
themselves to the decisions of universal suffrage, as is foreseeable,
have to have the hope of participating in an institutional setup
where they have some influence.[11]

I have quoted this text in full, because it is a text that, while
presenting the political problem confronting the Maghreb and the
Arab world, also includes all the apriorisms and constraints that
prevent easy or rapid solutions. Given the accumulated vulnera-
bilities of states in pursuit of legitimacy, is it possible for them
to concede a "forum function" of defending those excluded from
growth to their Islamist challengers? And are the Islamists, who
have for so long claimed to be the exclusive representatives of the
community, capable of coming out of anti-establishment activity
and agreeing to be one party among many? All the signs indicate
that the process of learning democracy will be long and difficult.

In reality, political openness has started badly. Since the early
1980s, the regimes began to envisage or to introduce a multiparty
system not as an end in itself, but rather as the price of a certain
disengagement of the state from society and as a compensation for
getting the different social partners to accept economic reforms.

[11] Remy Leveau, "Eléments de reflexion sur l'Etat au Maghreb," in *Change-
ments politiques au Maghreb*, ed. Camau Michel (Paris, CNRS, 1991) 269–80.

Even in the Algerian experience—where the regime invested the most in the democratic wager—from the outset, the experience was an opening manipulated by Chadli's team, which wanted to remain in power, and by part of the FLN, which wanted to participate in a new government dominated by the Islamists. In fact, the stake in the October 1988 crisis and the ensuing "openness" was not initially the setting up of a transition to democracy. This after all, was not what workers and young rioters were demanding. As Abdelkader Djeghloul saw so clearly, Chadli's team sought the "eviction of the old guard," whether populist or FLN, which represented an obstacle to liberal economic reforms. By winning the "Indian wrestling," in some way they played the sorcerer's apprentice: they did indeed liberate forces over which they had less and less control.[12]

Elsewhere, political liberalization took place on a basis of antagonism between the most acculturated elites and the Islamist counterelites, an antagonism that took the form of a real cultural schism. If the elites as a whole became hostile to those in power, it remains that both the elites and the middle classes saw in the rise of Islamism a serious threat to their status, their vision of the world, and their way of life. This growing split was noticed in the universities, in the union struggles, and in the great debates about subjects as diverse as the status of women, the Gulf crisis, and the nature of civil society. Gradually, the competition between the two poles became an almost limitless struggle for hegemony rather than an accommodation within a democratic setting.

In fact, all the camps have hegemonic ideas and have difficulty imagining sharing power with their rivals. One side "inhibits" the political system as a whole by trying to impose religious formulations on contemporary problems. By reducing all the things that don't work in society to their religious dimension—their nonconformity to divine prescriptions—the Islamists doom to failure the efforts of all those—political parties, intellectuals—who would undertake to bring partial solutions to the problems being faced. It is this disqualification, whether real or potential, of the government and above all of the cosmopolitan intelligentsia that finally forces

[12] Djeghloul, "L'Algérie en état d'anomie politique."

the latter to favor an alliance with the government. This alliance does not, of course, acknowledge itself as such, since it is made paradoxically in the name of defending civil society.

It is this very logic that led the urban elites and the middle classes to prefer the authoritarian solution to the risks of democratization. Rarely, writes Jean Daniel, speaking of Algeria, has a bid for power against a democratic process delighted so many democrats.[13] Rarely has action against Islamism reassured so many Muslims. Rarely has such a large number of civilians felt themselves so protected by a military putsch. As soon as the cancellation of the second round of the general elections in Algeria was announced, the Tunisians, the Moroccans, the Egyptians, and in Algeria the women and the Kabyles, like all those who regretted having abstained in the first round and thereby having played into the hands of the Islamic Salvation Front, breathed again. France as well. Both the internal antagonisms and the pressures of the problems posed mean that democracy is not for this time. It is to be feared that the traumas caused by the delays and frustrations may discredit the authorities and reinstate the traditional divorce between the state and society. Because one political formula is dead and a new formula is taking a long time to appear, it is not time for instant recipes and results. Rather, it is time for reflection on the means, the ways, and the cost of transition.

[13] *Nouvel Observateur*, just the week after the coup.

Civil Society in Israel

JOEL S. MIGDAL

HOPES for the blossoming of democracy in the Middle East cannot rest simply on changes within the state organization itself. Just as important as reforms in the procedures of the state and in the means to select key political leaders is a transformation within the broader society.[1] The growth of civil society is the mortar and bricks of any possible democratic project in the Middle East.[2] This paper looks at the Israeli case to explore the burgeoning of civil society and how that has affected state-society relations. Has the remarkable growth of civil society in Israel since the mid-1960s strengthened the democratic state? And, if it has not (as I will argue), why not?

What is "civil society" and how does it differ from "society"? In a narrow sense, civil society is the autonomous and inclusive public life beyond the close control of the state. Even as it includes groups with wildly different interests and goals, it has at its core a common agreement among its members over the constitution of the collective moral order, about the construction of

I would like to thank Uri Ben-Eliezer, Ellis Goldberg, Baruch Kimmerling, and Yael Yishai for their lengthy and thoughtful comments and criticisms of an earlier draft of this paper.

[1] This point, indeed, has been a truism in political science. See, for example, Gabriel A. Almond and Sidney Verba, *The Civic Culture* (Princeton University Press, 1963).

[2] Bendix, et al., note that "the independence of private associations is a synonym for civil society" and that for civil society to exist a "consensus" is required between state and society. "Reflections on Modern Western States and Civil Societies," *Research in Political Sociology* 3 (1987) 14–15.

society as a whole. One could think of it as a kind of uncontrolled common discourse. Of course, this does not signify people simply walking in lockstep. But it does mean some sharing of norms and values about how to resolve conflicts and clashing interests, how to organize power and authority, how people should behave towards one another in the public sphere, what property rights should entail, and what the boundaries of the society should encompass. The boundaries question involves not only the physical political boundaries of the state (a question of no mean importance in the Middle East) but also the equally crucial issue of who should be considered a rightful member of the society and thereby receive its benefits and rights. For example, transient visitors within the physical boundaries—or, in most societies, guest workers—are not considered to be such members.

Civil society assumes, too, some concurrence about the rightful existence of institutions other than the state organization that themselves promote, and operate within, the rules of this moral order. Local PTA's, charity groups, churches, businesses, and social clubs, for example, may be considered by the members of civil society as appropriately operating in the context of society's moral order. Even if an element of exclusiveness resides in these organizations (the Episcopal Church is only for Episcopalians, the PTA is not for childless couples), these institutions help create and reinforce both the inclusive norms and the boundaries of the larger moral order within which they operate. In short, there is both a passive and an active dimension to civil society: passive, in the acceptance of a certain order, and active, in its volitional element, which creates, maintains, and reproduces the moral order through institutions and individual behavior. The term "society" is broader than civil society because it can include, too, individuals and groups who reject that order (do not accept the passive dimension) and those who may accept it but do not participate in institutions or engage in public behavior to strengthen the order (there is no volition among them). Broader society, to be sure, may also contain a volitional element—organizations prescribing certain behavior, but not directed towards the acceptance and strengthening of civil society's outline of how society should be construc1ted; society, as opposed to civil society, may lack the inclusive dimensions normatively and institutionally binding its parts in a common framework.

Societies in the Middle East for the most part have, to date, still not hammered out strong, inclusive civil societies; both the passive and active dimensions of civil society have been extremely weak. The understanding of the moral order and of the construction of society is still highly fragmented, and institutions to press specific interests and points of view within the context of that moral order are still largely feeble. But can we assume that the growth of civil society, as it has occurred in Israel, will necessarily lead to the strengthening of democracy in the Middle East? I will propose here that the relationship between the emergence of civil society and a democratic state may be more complex in the Middle East than general writings on civil society would lead us to believe.

Theories have most often portrayed civil society as bolstering the state, enhancing its legitimacy and its ability to coordinate the diverse tendencies in society. The case of Israel, in contrast, indicates a variant pattern of state–civil society relations. Here, civil society grew alongside broad societal recognition of the legitimacy of the Israeli state, as most of the earlier theories would have expected, but civil society in this instance had a long-term corrosive effect on the state's ability to channel the diverse currents in society. To explain this anomalous effect of civil society, I will argue that we need to reject the undifferentiated portraits of civil society common to most of the literature. By breaking down civil society's active or volitional side institutionally, we can see how the particular patterns of growth of different parts of civil society can have a determining effect on state-society relations.

In the classical views presented by both Hegel and Gramsci, civil society emerged as an abutment to the state; it strengthened the predominance and hold of the governing organization by affirming it as the appropriate body to make and enforce society's rules.[3] In Hegel's version, it is the common agreement in society

---

[3] Hegel put forth the notion of civil society as one that emerges from the interdependence of individuals, their conflicts and their needs for cooperation. Those needs give rise to the state; and it is the law, the principle of rightness, that links civil society to the state. G. W. F. Hegel, *Philosophy of Right* (Oxford, The Clarendon Press, 1942) 122–23, 134–35. Marx reacted to

about the state as an ideal good that forms the backbone of civil society. Gramsci, in contrast, sees the cultural elements that will make up civil society as molded through the power of the state to accept a hegemonic dominance of a particular set of ideas supporting the state. In both theories, civil society supports the state's rule through a normative consensus in civil society. Such an understanding of the role of civil society does not contradict current (mostly Weberian) interpretations of the state. Even if the state's ultimate position rests on the possible use of violence in order to have its way, its day-to-day successes (and thus its long-term prospects) depend on voluntary compliance with its dictates even when the likelihood of violent retribution by arms of the state seems very small. Civil society from such a perspective helps insure those successes by reinforcing the notions that the state is the proper organization to make most rules, that other organizations can make some rules and these will complement those of the state, and that the state's ability to maintain and defend a framework of rules, directly or indirectly, works to further the interests of those in civil society. In short, widely accepted theories in the

---

Hegel's conception, arguing that the state is merely the mechanism to defend privileged propertied interests in civil society. He understood civil society in a material sense, the expression of particular property rights. Gramsci noted that besides the educative agencies of the state helping maintain hegemony, there are, "in reality, a multitude of other so-called private initiatives and activities [that] tend to the same end—initiatives and activities that form the apparatus of the political and cultural hegemony of the ruling classes." This, for Gramsci, is civil society. Antonio Gramsci, *Selections from the Prison Notebooks* (International Publishers, New York, 1971) 258. Stepan wrote, "Following Gramsci, we stress that an important requirement for hegemony is a rough congruence between the dominant values of civil society and those of political society." Alfred Stepan, *The State and Society: Peru in Comparative Perspective* (Princeton University Press, 1978) 97. Whereas Hegel believed that society created the demand for the state, others, including Stepan, have argued that the state can create civil society. Otto Hintze alluded to this mutuality of the state and civil society and the role of the state in creating its own civil society, using the term "nationalities" instead of civil society: "The European peoples have only gradually developed their nationalities; they are not a simple product of nature but are themselves a product of the creation of states." Otto Hintze, "The Formation of States and Constitutional Development: A Study in History and Politics," in *The Historical Essays of Otto Hintze*, ed. Felix Gilbert (New York, Oxford University Press, 1975) 161.

social sciences see the state and civil society as mutually reinforcing through their common support of an ideology expressing the legitimacy of state rule.

In the last decade or so of Communist rule in Eastern Europe, a somewhat different understanding of civil society came into fashion, which is worth noting here, as well. It, too, does not fit the Israeli case very neatly.[4] In East Europe, civil society came to be understood as the antagonist of the state, quite unlike most of the associations that grew up in Israeli society. East European civil society expressed an alternative understanding about the norms and procedures for public life. As in the earlier interpretations of civil society, the emphasis in the Communist states was on the role civil society plays in presenting a coherent image of what is befitting in the public sphere. But now the autonomy of civil society pits its notions against the unacceptable actions (and ideology) of the state and party. Rather than bolstering the idea of the state's rightful dominance, civil society hastens its downfall by chipping away at any widely held conception that the state's overpowering role is proper. Civil society, in these instances, offers a parallel moral order to that presented by the state, as well as alternative sets of practices.

The argument in this paper rests on the premise that we need not think of civil society and the state only in terms of two sprawling institutional complexes, bearing on their shoulders some gargantuan notions—whether complementary or contradictory—of what is the proper way to order public life, much as Atlas bore the entire world on his shoulders. The relationship of state and civil society may not be best revealed by focusing on encompassing, coherent ideologies, whether reinforcing or conflicting, that support or bring into question the ultimate right of the state to rule. Focusing studies of civil society exclusively on questions of legitimacy, consensus, and hegemony (the passive dimension) may draw attention away from important cases in which the state's right to rule is not widely questioned but where the growth of civil

---

[4] See, for example, Andrew Arato, "Empire vs. Civil Society: Poland 1981–82," *Telos* 14, no. 50 (1981–82) 19–48. For a critique, see Zbigniew Rau, "Some Thoughts on Civil Society in Eastern Europe and the Lockean Contractarian Approach," *Political Studies* 35 (1987) 573–92.

society's institutions (the active or volitional dimension), nonetheless, dramatically affects the overall distribution of power. States may be enthusiastically cheered as the proper governing organizations, quite unlike the East European cases, while still finding that their ability to control society, to formulate policies, and to implement those policies may erode steadily, all in the context of a burgeoning civil society.

The organizations in civil society, at the same time, may find their autonomy and leverage increasing, but in an environment in which the overall framework that could reconcile and resolve their disparate interests, cultural perspectives, and views (i.e., the state) is atrophying. In these circumstances, the growth of civil society may be self-limiting, since civil society depends on a commonly accepted set of rules—a single discourse—for the interaction of different civil associations. The argument here, then, is that the state's ability to rule effectively may erode as civil society expands, even where the organizations in civil society overtly legitimate the state, and this erosion, in turn, may make civil society become increasingly uncivil. The widening realm of autonomous action among the groups in civil society may rob the state of key levers in controlling the population and deprive civil associations of the common language they need to coexist. The key to understanding the effects of civil society upon the state, as we shall see, is to identify the varying growth of different components of civil society; those components have very different effects on the nexus of state–civil society relations.

In the British-ruled mandate for Palestine, the unceasing clash of Jews and Arabs, coupled with a colonial system that encouraged institutional bifurcation, prevented the sprouting of a countrywide civil society encompassing both peoples. And, even within the social boundaries of each communal group, the imperatives of the struggle, the need to mobilize people and resources as extensively as possible, and the challenge of organizing within a colonial framework, focused attention on each side's central political organizations. This period was crucial for both sides in the development of relations between politics and society. For Jews and Arabs alike, key groups scrambled to build central political organizations to confront the British and each other even before the societies themselves gelled in the context of the new,

British-imposed boundaries. There was little room for the nurturing of autonomous civil organizations in either the Jewish or Arab communities, as political organizations demanded dominant control over the ordering of social life.

After the establishment of the Israeli state, the pattern of limited autonomy for civil organizations among its population (now including an Arab minority in addition to the Jews) continued, partly because of the persisting central role of the state in war mobilization and because of the previous pattern of state-society relations that had been established. Even as Israel was inundated with diverse newcomers, the emphasis was on state-directed "immigrant absorption" rather than on the promotion of a civil society that could bridge the vast cultural differences, especially those between Jews of European origin and those of North African and Asian origins. The state sought, too, to control and isolate what its leaders saw as the potentially subversive Arab minority, rather than fostering civil ties between it and the Jewish population. It is still difficult to read how far society has come in developing participatory civic life outside the control of the Israeli state organization. As late as 1988, Gadi Wolfsfeld could describe his book *The Politics of Provocation* as the first study of political participation in Israel, indicating that the notion of initiative from society in the public realm was still quite limited.[5]

The legacy of the relations between politics and society during the period of the mandate and the *yishuv* (the Jewish community in pre-1948 Israel) had a deep impact on everyday life after independence. The key institutions in the prestate period were the fledgling organizations that would eventually make up the larger organizational complex of the state as well as the political parties, which were closely linked through personnel, function, and patronage to those other organizations. In Israel's first twenty years or so, public life was appropriated almost entirely by professional politicians—staffing the state and what Gramsci called political society, the political parties. The preponderance of initiative did move towards the state from the political parties, which still remained key (but diminishing) links among elements in the larger

[5] Gadi Wolfsfeld, *The Politics of Provocation: Participation and Protest in Israel* (Albany, N.Y., State University of New York Press, 1988).

society, but the pattern of leaving ordinary citizens on the outside looking in did not change substantially. A variety of works found the Israeli public standing on the sidelines with little sense that it could help shape the future of the society.[6] Not surprisingly, Israel had the largest public sector of any democracy in the world and devoted record proportions of its GNP to public services.[7] Israelis were inveterate political junkies, to be sure, stuffing themselves with information about public life in the form of news broadcasts, newspapers, and (loud) political discussions, but their initiatives in trying to shape the political and social landscape were paltry. As Wolfsfeld noted, "The high level of psychological involvement in politics can be traced to the obtrusiveness of political decisions into everyday life. Decisions about prices, salaries, reserve duty, and war are all made by a highly centralized government. Keeping abreast of politics in Israel is simply a necessity of life."[8]

If an event had a public dimension to it, the state or political parties saw it as their prerogative, indeed their duty, to lead the society in response. From health issues to charity drives, it was the government's and parties' initiatives that set the agenda and defined the extent and mode of public participation. In one book, the author began by saying, "A typical response of an Israeli to a proposed study of interest group development in Israel is, 'But how can you study interest groups? There aren't any.'"[9] Even the sphere of market relations was dominated by the large state enterprises and the heavy regulation of commercial activities by the state.

But, indeed, over time there came to be a multitude of autonomous social groups, and the market slowly came to develop a set of relations outside the direct control or oversight of the state.

---

[6] See, for example, Alan Arian, *Consensus in Israel* (New York, General Learning Press, 1971); E. Etzioni-Halevy, *Political Culture in Israel* (New York, Praeger, 1977); and Itzhak Galnoor, *Steering the Polity: Political Communication in Israel* (Beverly Hills, Calif., Sage, 1982)

[7] Brenda Danet, *Pulling Strings: Biculturalism in Israeli Bureaucracy* (Albany, N.Y., State University of New York Press, 1989) 14.

[8] Wolfsfeld, *The Politics of Participation*, 15.

[9] Marcia Drezon-Tepler, *Interest Groups and Political Change in Israel* (Albany, N.Y., State University of New York Press, 1990) 1.

Various culture groups began to develop public practices (some with political overtones, some without) that became important motifs of the society. Moroccan Jews, for example, developed a set of pilgrimages and public celebrations that drew participation beyond their own culture group. As Drezon-Tepler and others have demonstrated, a public life beyond the controlling organizations of the state and the political parties began to reach a critical mass about two decades after independence. Following the 1973 War, civic organizations and activities seemed to mushroom. Many activities came to be centered in new formal associations; others took place through much less tightly organized groups or were not organized at all, but simply indicated similar civic behavior by people not formally linked to one another. The private sector produced an increasing share of national wealth, and government's hand in industrial and commercial relations seemed to lighten a bit (particularly with growing pressure from Israel's main international creditors). Various culture groups, ranging from religious factions to ethnic communities, organized to assert specific definitions of what the practices and beliefs of society as a whole should be.

All these represent heightened activity in society carving out autonomous realms of civic action, as well as increased contestation over what the content of state-society relations should rightly be. In a paper of this size, it is impossible to look at all these components of society. Here, we will examine five different categories of those carving out an autonomous civic life, which differ in their relationship to the dominant political organization and in the degree to which they aggregate public actions (see the accompanying table). Their differing strengths stem from the particular legacy of earlier relations between politics and society and, as we shall see, have had a particular effect upon the contemporary state. We can term these six types (1) fellow-travelers, (2) patriots, (3) do-gooders, (4) complainers, (5) protesters, and (6) interest brokers, as seen in the following table.

FORMS OF CIVIC LIFE

	Adversarial to State	Supportive to State or Nonpolitical
Aggregative	Protesters (Complainers) (Interest Brokers)	World Population Do-Gooders Fellow-Travelers
Nonaggregative	Complainers	Patriots

Fellow-travelers are seemingly the least interesting from the perspective of those concerned about the creation of autonomous associations that form the backbone of civil society. Many of these groups are nominally independent of the government but were originally organized (or at least inspired or influenced greatly) by political parties and government agencies. Most prominent here is the Histadrut, which is laced into party politics and government funding at every turn. A mainstay of its social power lies in its sprawling health maintenance organization, which is heavily subsidized by government revenues. But dozens of others exist as well, from some of the immigrant associations funded by the Ministry of Immigration and Welfare to an organization such as the Association on Behalf of the Soldiers (funded by the Ministry of Defense), which among other tasks has collected gum and pencils for soldiers at the front. Government or party funding is probably not an unflawed indicator of which organizations are fellow-travelers, since so many groups receive subsidies of one sort or another, even those that have established a modicum of independence. But for some, funding has limited the organization to promoting established public or party policies or to public education campaigns. One example is an environmental group, the Council for a Beautiful Israel, which was founded by a Knesset member in 1968. "Manned by professionals: architects, educators, lawyers, and other public figures ... it was content to launch educational campaigns in schools, factories, gas stations, and the other institutions that were presumably conducive to raising environmental consciousness."[10] Nonetheless, even the limited autonomy of fellow-travelers creates an important volitional dimension in society outside the direct

[10] Yael Yishai, *Land of Paradoxes: Interest Politics in Israel* (Albany, N.Y., State University of New York Press, 1991) 81.

control of the state—that autonomous space has, on occasion, opened the way for yet more autonomy. The Histadrut is a case in point. It has increasingly gone head to head with government officials on key industrial and labor issues—both with the Likud in power and, more surprisingly, with the Labor party in control.

In contrast to the fellow-travelers, the other five categories have, indeed, worked to carve out a broad swathe of public space not dominated by the professional politicians of the state or the parties. Their efforts in forging a true civil society have been much more telling. Patriots, the second category, have not been organized into associations at all but nonetheless have participated in a civic life quite supportive of the state. They have come together for memorial services for soldiers killed in Israel's wars or in loose friendship groups to help define the civic religion and other common civic practices outside the direct control of the state. During the 1982 Lebanon War, thousands of them assembled for progovernment rallies. They turn out to vote (Israel has one of the highest turnout rates for any democratic country where voting is not compulsory) and religiously tune into the national news broadcast nightly on state television. These sorts of activities, and the core of beliefs that sustain them, cannot be overestimated. They helped forge a common public space, with deeply shared values, for Jews coming from seventy different countries, with different languages, cultures, and religious practices.

While the effects of their actions have been complementary to those of the state, patriots have also placed severe limits on the expansion of civil society. For one, patriots, by definition, do not build formal organized groups, which have the most sustaining effects on the growth of an autonomous civil society. And, what is even more important, a good share of the civic practices they have constructed have excluded the Arab population (almost a fifth of Israel's citizens are Arab). Once the Palestinians in the occupied territories were added to the population as well, the practices of patriots became increasingly exclusive (or what Kimmerling has referred to as primordial rather than civil).[11]

---

[11] Baruch Kimmerling, "Between the Primordial and the Civil Definitions of the Collective Identity: Eretz Israel or the State of Israel?" in *Comparative*

Do-gooders, the third category, have operated on both sides of the civil society–state divide. At times, they have intersected with issues of public policy, acting much the same as standard interest or lobbying groups. But a prime motivation for organizing, as well, is to change values and practices in society, and not always to seek direct intervention of the state. Organizations such as the Society for Prevention of Smoking, the Heart Society, and the Cancer Society have aimed their messages at the Israeli public as well as at the institutions of the state. Yishai has made the point that, while they often appear to have a nonpolitical air about them, such do-gooder associations can become the tail that wags the dog.[12] The Heart Society, for example, has made a number of important decisions about appropriation of its resources that have established the parameters for the state's own health policy.

These sorts of groups, too, should not be underestimated in the creation of civil society in many liberal democracies. They have established a public domain parallel and often complementary to the state's realm, weaving diverse elements of society together in a broad variety of civic practices. Several very strong organizations of this sort have emerged in Israel, but many others have been among the weakest associations. Too often, the line between do-gooders and fellow-travelers has been blurred by government and party officials. Do-gooders have slipped into being fronts for, or have been co-opted by, the state or the political parties. Whereas in liberal democracies, such as the United States, do-gooders have gained an important toehold in creating an autonomous social realm, in Israel all but a select few have found themselves standing on a very slippery slope.

Complainers, the fourth category, are not unique to Israel. In Western societies first, and then in others, there has been a burgeoning of ombudsmen, consumer complaint columns in the newspapers, radio call-in shows, whistle-blowing organizations, and more.[13] "Their appearance," writes Brenda Danet,

---

Social Dynamics: Essays in Honor of S. N. Eisenstadt, ed. Erik Cohen, Moshe Lissak, and Uri Almagor (Boulder, Westview Press, 1985) 262–83.

[12] Yael Yishai, personal correspondence, 8 March 1992.

[13] See Walter Gellhorn, *Ombudsmen and Others* (Cambridge, Mass., Harvard University Press, 1966), as well as his *When Americans Complain* (Cambridge,

"is a response to the call for greater accountability of public institutions, and for at least partial redress of the tremendous imbalance of power between individual citizens and these huge institutions."[14] Some of these organizations, such as the ombudsman, are centered in the state itself, acting as an internal check on the practices of government agencies. Others are autonomous of the state. In either case, they promote independent and safe means for voicing grievances, often (but not always) directed against the state itself, as well as being autonomous channels for influencing the behavior of the state.

In Israel, the government established the office of the ombudsman in 1971, one of the earliest moves in this direction outside Scandinavia. Additional municipal, army, and police ombudsmen followed. Israelis also developed consumer organizations, a television show to air private complaints, and much more. These sorts of organizations expanded the domain of civil society, if not by binding people together socially (complaints are frequently individualistic in nature), then by limiting the domain of the state. For civil society to flourish, it needs arenas of social life relatively free from the overpowering control and influence of the state. Complainers acting through formal channels legitimize limiting the boundaries of state action and thereby open public space to other civic discourses and practices. They create independent channels of political and social communication.

But complaining in Israel, as in the case of the patriots, is marked by a tension in terms of the expansion of civil society. Despite the growth of complaint-handling organizations, many grievances go through channels that exclude portions of the public. These mechanisms are based on all sorts of particularism—familism, friendship groups, old army ties, and much more.[15] These bases of association only exacerbate the tension between the two competing forms of social identity in the collectivity

Mass., Harvard University Press, 1966), and the volumes of the International Ombudsman Institute, Ombudsman and Other Complaint-Handling Systems Survey (Edmonton, Alberta, Law Center, University of Alberta).

[14] Danet, *Pulling Strings*, 1.

[15] This is the subject of Danet's excellent book *Pulling Strings*.

based on civil and more particularistic sentiments.[16] Kinship and friendship ties serve not only to stratify Jews in terms of in-groups and out-groups, they accentuate the tremendously diffi-cult time Arab citizens in Israel have had in entering the corri-dors of Israeli civic life. With the addition of the occupied territo-ries, the tendency to limit access of certain groups (Palestinians, above all) to the activities that would normally be thought of as properly in the realm of civil society has restricted the ex-pansion of civil society all the more. In short, the differing abil-ities to have one's complaint heard and acted upon based on kin-ship and friendship group membership have retarded the knit-ting together of civil society. The independent channels of polit-ical and social communication have divided society rather than integrating it. The result is different playing rules for different groups, a situation antithetical to the flourishing of civil soci-ety. While complainers have enhanced the chances for civil society to flourish by helping to institutionalize the limits of state prac-tices, at the same time they have often voiced their grievances within exclusive, rather than broadly civic, channels of commu-nication.

The fifth category, protesters, burst onto the Israeli scene in the 1970s. The first instance was a set of protests against poverty and government social-welfare policy staged by youths from poor neighborhoods calling themselves the Black Panthers. Their some-times violent demonstrations took the government aback, causing leading officials both to try and co-opt some of the Panthers' leaders and to delegitimize them. Few Israelis will forget Prime Minister Golda Meir's dismissal of the protesters as "bad boys." Another protest, this time in the form of a vigil, and much more sedate than those of the Black Panthers, rose directly out of the 1973 War. Even while the war continued to rage, a young scien-tist, Motti Ashkenazi, stood silently with his placard in front of the Knesset building day after day. His demonstration was aimed at the political leadership, especially Defense Minister Moshe Dayan and Prime Minister Meir, whom Ashkenazi identified as the cul-prits responsible for the deaths of his fellow army reservists in

[16] See Kimmerling, "Between the Primordial and the Civil Definitions of the Collective Identity."

Egypt's surprise attack at the Suez Canal. Ashkenazi's protests were electrifying. Hundreds of other soldiers joined him in his vigil, which finally did serve as catalysts to force the resignation of the two political leaders.

Like complainers, protesters seek responsiveness and accountability by checking the state's practices. But unlike much complaining, protesting is a form of collective action. Ashkenazi succeeded when others joined his cause, even if not in a formal organizational setting. Protesting goes beyond complaining by channeling dissatisfaction and forging ties among those objecting. It mobilizes political participation in a public realm outside the customary state channels, including those of the established political parties.

Throughout the 1970s, political protest gained ground as an accepted (if not always acceptable) form of citizen-initiated social action. In 1976, for example, Arab citizens organized a highly visible protest called Land Day, which later came to be commemorated annually. Important new groups, fighting against the ever-present seduction of joining the fray of party politics, emerged during the decade. Gush Emunim and Peace Now, the two most prominent ones, had a major impact in debates about the future of Israeli society and politics. But they certainly were not the only protesting groups. Throughout the 1970s, new protest groups formed and the number of demonstrations kept rising. The increase in the number of protests continued into the 1980s, especially during the 1982 War in Lebanon, after which the number seemed to level off. One count of protests found the number running over 150 per year in the first half of the 1980s.[17] And their impact, both among those in groups such as Gush Emunim and Peace Now and those protesting other issues entirely, was not insubstantial. As Wolfsfeld wrote, "Citizens who would have been shut out of the political process a few years ago are getting a real chance to be heard."[18]

But, like complainers and patriots, protesters have had a problematical effect on the development of civil society. Protesters

[17] Wolfsfeld, *The Politics of Provocation*, 17.
[18] Ibid., 19.

awakened the citizenry to the need to take the initiative on public questions, often through organizations that go on to have a lasting effect on state-society relations. Too often, however, protests, like the actions of patriots, do little to create long-lasting ties in civil society, as a kind of permanent space outside the realm of the state. Moreover, when they are violent (which is relatively uncommon in Israel, although violence is more prevalent than in the past) they can undercut the building of a common framework of rules, so necessary for civil society. In fact, protests in Israel seemed increasingly to polarize the society about its overall social identity.

Perhaps the oldest form of autonomous associational life in Israel is found in our last category, the interest brokers. The prototype of an interest group in Israel is the Manufacturers Association, whose origins predate the state.[19] From 1921 through the post-independence years, the association aimed to represent employers and to promote the interests of industrialists. "Its relatively high annual budget, ... a well-staffed organization, and the expertise of its administrative workers," wrote Yishai, "have contributed to the association's efficiency. A wide membership and a cohesive organizational structure also constitute major assets."[20]

But for all the success of the Manufacturers Association, it was not typical of interest brokers in Israel. Through most of its life it was genuinely autonomous, remaining fairly free of party or government control (although it did have especially close relations with the General Zionists party at some points). The resources that it represented also set it apart in enabling it to have a substantial effect on government policy. Israeli interest groups, on the whole, have not found the same kind of nurturing environment as have such groups in, say, the United States. Like do-gooders, interest brokers have found themselves either co-opted by the state or smothered by it. Many of Israel's professional associations, for example, have been emasculated by their incorporation into the Histadrut, with its close ties to party and state. Where such cooptation has not been possible, the state has, at times, moved to

---

[19] Drezon-Tepler, *Interest Groups and Political Change in Israel*, 47ff.
[20] Yishai, *Land of Paradoxes*, 69.

nip in the bud the independence of interest groups. As Yishai put it, "the state is manipulative, its authority extending octopus-like over interest groups."[21] In 1980, the passing of the Associations Law enabled the state to delve into the records and affairs of interest groups as a form (or, at least, a threat) of intimidation. Yishai comments,

> by enacting this law, the state attempted to grasp the rope at each end, i.e., to ensure the freedom of association and to control the group arena. The absence of a similar law in many other democracies, however, highlights the prominence of the state in the Israeli context. The state was authorized by its early founders to overcome the divisions that beset the Jewish people in the Diaspora.... The state was thus ordained to rise above all sectional differences.[22]

Israeli civil society, then, has been shaky in precisely those areas where a number of Western liberal democracies' civil societies have been strongest. Do-gooders and interest brokers in Israel have remained weak, stymied in their efforts to create a space for durable autonomous associations and institutionalized social relations beyond the realm of the state. Because these sorts of associations have been co-opted or smothered by the state, the arenas of public life have been dominated by the state along with informal groups based on particularistic personal ties. The enfeeblement of that part of civil society made up of aggregating, inclusive, and highly institutionalized associations has been a legacy of the all-encompassing role of the state and the key parties before and immediately after independence, as well as of the enduring Arab-Israeli conflict. In the struggles to define the character of social relations in the broad public realm, interest brokers and do-gooders have not been as evident as in other democracies. The playing field has been dominated by the state. Uri Ben-Eliezer

---

[21] Ibid., 335.

[22] Ibid., 335–36. Bendix, et al., do note that "civil society comprises only a segment of the population." Those not in civil society tend to be marginal sorts—those abandoned by their parents, homeless people who do not participated in the market, illegal immigrants, etc. "Reflections on Modern Western States and Civil Societies," 23.

described the preeminence of the state in terms of the legacy from the period of the yishuv:

> In contrast to the development of American society, people in Israel, particularly during the pre-state period, were organized in various social frameworks that did not necessarily give expression to the free will of their members. What indeed is the meaning of freedom of choice when receiving the documents necessary to even enter Palestine required a particular political affiliation; when the allocation of jobs through the labor exchange was governed by membership in a political party; and when receipt of medical services was conditional on membership in the trade union?[23]

State-society relations, however, have not remained static since the period of the yishuv. From that time on, patriots have played a key role in supporting the creation of what Liebman and Don-Yehiya have described as Israel's civil religion, as well as in creating modes of appropriate daily behavior in the public realm.[24] Civil society did burgeon in the 1970s and 1980s. But the forms that civil society took in Israel at that time, complainers and protesters, have given Israel's state-society relations a special cast. Complaining often tends to be individualistic and nonaggregative. When people's complaints are addressed or the immediate issue passes, the complainers withdraw from the public realm. While protesting tends to be more aggregative, it too tends to bring people into civic arenas, where key questions of public behavior are being struggled over, for relatively short bursts of activity. Even groups such as Peace Now, which have been on the scene for well over a decade, have seen their visibility and prominence wax and wane depending on whether the time was conducive to launch protests (as it was during the war in Lebanon). The kinds of civic groups with staying power in such arenas, do-gooders and interest brokers, have been relatively weak in Israel.

[23] Uri Ben-Eliezer, "Testing for Democracy in Israel," in *Critical Essays on Israeli Society, Politics, and Culture*, Books on Israel, vol. 2, ed. Ian S. Lustick and Barry Rubin (Albany, N.Y., State University of New York Press, 1991) 77.

[24] Charles Liebman and Eliezer Don-Yehiya, *Civil Religion in Israel* (Berkeley and Los Angeles, University of California Press, 1983).

Complainers and protesters, to be sure, have helped forge elements of public life outside the control of the state, and they have had an impact on the struggles about the shape of society. But both of these groups have set the civil society on an adversarial course with the state, while accepting the state as the proper address to direct complaints. Rather than creating arenas—public spaces—where the state is largely absent or at least negligible in the struggles over the establishment of the norms and patterns of daily behavior, these forms of civil society have had a dual effect. First, they have further accentuated the centrality of the state in many realms of life through their entreaties and protests aimed at government officials. It is not the appropriateness of the state's role in handling all these issues that they have questioned but how well the state has performed its role. The effect of complaining and protesting has been to put a tremendous burden on the state to make things right, while at the same time challenging the state in the way it has handled issues up until now. State accountability has moved to the center of the state-society nexus, while it has overburdened the state with more responsibility to make things right than it can deliver on. In Israel, the outcome was to erode the legitimacy of the state during the 1970s and early 1980s. Levels of discontent with government rose from the 10 to 20 percent range in the late 1960s to as high as 70 to 80 percent for the decade after the 1973 War.[25]

The prominence of protesters and complainers, as against do-gooders and interest brokers, has had a second effect on state-society relations: underscoring the exclusive particularism within the population. Complainers have used connections and pull to voice their grievances, and even protesters, some scholars have suggested, have relied "on primary relations and networks of families, friends and friends of friends as a basis for mobilization."[26] We have already commented on how this sort of fragmentation makes the creation of an inclusive civic life all the more difficult to institutionalize. It has had another effect, as well. Through their emphasis on back channels, complainers have further accentuated

---

[25] Wolfsfeld, *The Politics of Provocation*, 14.
[26] Uri Ben-Eliezer, "The Meaning of Political Participation in a Non-Liberal Democracy: The Example of Israel" (mimeo), 28–29.

the heavy demands on the state to service multiple, particularistic fragments of the society. Certainly, this phenomenon is common to all democracies, but because these demands come in the absence of highly institutionalized civic associations that agree on the rules of the game, the upshot has been grave difficulty in state leaders' sorting out priorities and taking initiative in highest priority areas. In a self-reinforcing process, with the state frozen in this regard, the public all the more has resorted to back channels to gain state responsiveness, lending further divisiveness to social relations.

The growth of civil society is not simply a black or white question of whether it exists or not; the strength or weakness of different pillars of civil society, stemming from the environment in which it developed, is bound to have a profound effect on the nature of the state and its relationship to its citizens. Civil society cannot simply be analyzed as an undifferentiated institutional complex. In Israel, as we have seen, the prominence of nonaggregative elements of civil society (complainers and patriots) as well as ones with an adversarial relationship to the state (protesters and complainers) has overburdened the state. The paralysis of the state, in turn, has undermined its role as the framework for establishing universality among civil associations. With little direction from the state, public associations and behavior have inched increasingly towards particularism and exclusivism. Pull and connections have continued to dominate over broad and inclusive civic sorts of public participation. And the definition of society has rested on narrowly religious and ethnic criteria over more broadly civic ones.

PART 3
Practical Politics

Prospects and Difficulties of
Democratization in the Middle East

BÜLENT ECEVİT

I FIND it risky to be categorical about qualifications or impediments for democracy. The assumption that societies conditioned to a totalitarian way of life over a long period cannot easily adapt to democracy is not always valid, in view of the smooth transition to democracy of Germany and Italy after the Second World War, or of Spain and Portugal more recently. The German and Italian peoples' previous submission to totalitarian rule, on the other hand, indicates that a high level of education or a rich intellectual heritage is not necessarily a guarantee for democracy. The assertion that democracy cannot be imposed from outside is challenged by the example of post–World War Japan. That democracy is the preserve and privilege of Christian Western societies with a high level of development is refuted by the examples of Turkey and India. Exceptionally multiracial, multireligious, multicultural, and restive India also challenges the argument that democracy cannot function and survive in a society reft with deep cleavages and conflicts, and the example of Turkey also refutes the assumption that democracy and Islam are incompatible. Nor can the difficulties encountered in democratization by most Latin American countries be attributed to Latin American character. Except for an interruption during the Pinochet rule, which was prodded from outside, Chile has had a quite long tradition of democracy, and Costa Rica, although surrounded by rather undemocratic and unstable societies of similar origin, has had a sound tradition of sophisticated democracy. I have cited these cases as a response to the arguments of apologizers for the lack or failure of democracy in some countries.

I believe two conflicting trends universally exist in the human subconscious, namely, aspiration for freedom and revulsion from freedom—or, to use an expression of Erich Fromm, "fear of freedom." And, for the emergence of an atmosphere conducive to democratization, a conscious collective effort or the shock effect of a societal tremor may be needed for the supremacy of the aspiration for freedom over revulsion from freedom. Obviously, there are certain cultural, legislative, institutional, or structural prerequisites for the successful implementation of democracy, but I am convinced that these can be acquired in any society if the political will, or the necessity for such acquisition, effectively emerges. But, of course, the pace and process of acquiring such prerequisites and of adapting to the rules of democracy may vary from one society to another. In particular, the evolution of democratic culture may prove to be more difficult for some societies than for others.

Transition to democracy from a theocratic dictatorship may be more strenuous than transition to democracy from a secular dictatorship. Or, transition to democracy from communist totalitarian regimes may prove to be more arduous than transition to democracy from right-wing authoritarian or totalitarian regimes. Such regimes usually have an economic infrastructure that is easily adaptable to democracy—they enjoy the benefit of varying degrees of experience with the market economy and private entrepreneurship, and this, in turn, may prevent serious economic setbacks and deep social unrest during the course of transition to democracy. Communist regimes, however, do not provide for such an infrastructure. Consequently, countries that are now trying to replace communist dictatorships with democracy may face greater difficulties in transforming their economies, and these may breed doubts, for an interim period, about the economic and social rewards of democracy.

People under communist dictatorships have been accustomed to certain social amenities such as very low prices for basic goods and services, low rents, and comprehensive social security, including guaranteed employment or income. Yet they are bound to forgo such amenities during the initial stage of transition to market economy, and democracy cannot function without some degree of market economy and without diminishment of the state sector. This may generate disillusionment with democracy, as confirmed by the emergence of nostalgic pro-communist demonstrations in Moscow recently. But the working people may enjoy better social benefits and higher incomes than before during the course of transition from right-wing dictatorship to democracy, since market economy functions increasingly in favor of the working people under a democratized regime. Hence, it would not be prudent to expect or to force East European countries and the former members of the Soviet Union to achieve transition to democracy as quickly as Spain or Portugal or as post–World War II Germany and Italy.

It would also not be realistic to expect each newcomer to the fold of democratic nations to duplicate exactly the democratic models of the West. The national characteristics, cultural heritage, and specific conditions of each society may inevitably be reflected in the structuring of its own democracy.

In other words, democracy should not be regarded as a ready-made suit to fit all societies. Democracy should rather be tailored according to the nature of each different society. For instance, as Joshua Muravchik wrote in a recent article, "what the Japanese have is Japanese-style democracy rather than American-style democracy" and "this is exactly what they ought to have,"[1] even though democracy was introduced to Japan by Americans. There is no stereotype even for Western democracy, as can be seen from the differences among the democratic systems and institutions of the United States, the United Kingdom, and the Nordic countries. There are, however, certain basic requirements of democracy that no nation aspiring to it may ignore or dilute— such as respect for human rights and the rule of law, freedom of expression and association, competing parties, freely and periodically elected governments, and effective checks on power.

The Situation and Prospects in the Middle East

Democratic movements and representative governments can hardly be said to exist in the Middle East, and it is difficult to talk

[1] "Dialogue," U.S. Information Office, Washington, D.C., 21 April 1991.

or write about something that does not exist. One can, however, speculate about why something does not exist and how it could be made to exist. And this is what I shall try to do. Of course, democratic Turkey is an exception in the Middle East, but Turkey is only partially a Middle Eastern country. It has more extensive cultural, political, and economic ties with Europe and America, and now with parts of Asia, than with the Middle East. Israel, certainly, is another exception, but it is an isolated case in the Middle East. Besides, Israeli democracy has the same deficiency as ancient Athenian "democracy"—it is a democracy that does not apply equally to all sections of the population.

The picture in the rest of the Middle East is rather bleak from the angle of democracy. Winds of democratization have been blowing all over the world in the last decade, from the Philippines to Latin America, from the Soviet Union to South Africa, from Central Asia to Eastern Europe. Yet not a leaf has been stirred by these winds in the Middle East—neither in the Arabic countries of the region nor in Iran. It is as if the Middle East is out of this world and out of touch with the times—not only because the region has not moved with the global winds of freedom, human rights, and democracy, but also because of the anachronistic sociopolitical systems of some of the regional countries. Slight signs of change are discernible in Iran after Khomeini's death, but it is not yet clear what these signs will yield.

The picture is certainly not uniform in the Middle Eastern Arabic world. Saudi Arabia and the other Arabic Gulf countries are ruled by dynastic families with practically unchecked powers, and they abide by archaic traditions in spite of the steadily growing numbers of their Western educated elites or technocrats. There seems to be some movement in Yemen toward modernization and democratization. Iraq and Syria are modernistic societies in many respects, but their political regimes remain despotic, although they are not ruled by dynastic families. Egypt has always been a dynamic Arabic society, but existing trends of modernization and democratization have been hindered in that country by strong fundamentalist and conservative forces. Lebanon is a tragic case—a relatively modernized society in which democracy could flourish in spite of its semifeudal structure, if it were not for its factionalism and interminable internal conflicts spurred from outside. Jordan seems to be quite prone to democratization. It is an extensively educated, modernized, and rather open society, largely influenced by English culture and living under the benevolent authoritarianism of an enlightened monarchy. But its intended transition to democracy is hampered by the continuing uncertainty of the future of the Palestinians who constitute at least half the population of Jordan and, more recently, by the momentum that Islamic fundamentalism has been gaining in the country.

In my view, the greatest obstacle in the way of modernization and more extensive democratization in the Middle East is the group of anachronistic regimes of the Gulf region centered around Saudi Arabia. Their anachronism, their immunity to change, is an anomaly, because the Middle East is not a peripheral region of the rapidly changing world. On the contrary, it is a vitally important part of the modern world and, with its immense oil reserves, it is, in a sense, the hub of international economy and politics. So much so that the slightest turbulence in the Middle East stirs the whole world into action—even into military action, as has been seen on the occasion of the recent Gulf Crisis. There is no other region of the world in which nonregional powers are so actively and so permanently involved.

Such close involvement and interaction with the rest of the world, particularly with the most developed, most modernistic, and most democratic countries of the world, should theoretically infuse the Middle Eastern atmosphere with strong currents of change, modernization, and democratization. But this has not been the case, because some countries, particularly the United States and the West European countries in general, have based their interests in the Middle East on the perpetuation of the most anachronistic and despotic regimes of the region. While they claim to encourage the spreading of human rights, freedom, and democracy around the world, they lend their support to the most anachronistic and despotic regimes of the Middle East. While they are very sensitive to violations of human rights even in nascent small countries detached from the rest of the world, they close their eyes to flagrant violations of human rights in the pro-Western oil-rich countries of the Middle East.

Robbers can be punished by cutting off their hands in some of these countries. Women accused of adultery may be stoned to death. Unveiled women may be jailed. If such cruel and archaic ways of punishment were to be exercised in most other countries, including those Middle Eastern countries that are not as pro-Western, the West would indignantly react, but in the case of the Gulf countries of Arabia they do not. During the recent Gulf crisis, the religious police of Saudi Arabia raided the home of a Western diplomat and roughly arrested the ladies and gentlemen attending a normal farewell party. The reactions of the victims of this outrageous intrusion to a private home were diplomatically hushed and no protests came from any of the Western allies—not even from the Western media.

In a recent address to the United Nations Commission on Human Rights, American Ambassador Kenneth Blackwell rebuked "those nations that continue to buck the trend" of respect for human rights, mentioning Cuba, North Korea, and Burma, and asked the Commission to "expose their human rights violations,"[2] but he made no mention of those despotic Middle Eastern countries where archaic forms of human rights violations are still committed in the name of "justice." Western powers seem to be satisfied with the non-Westernized but pro-Western anachronistic regimes of the Middle East, because they obviously fear that the forces to be generated by democratization and change may threaten their own vested interests in the Gulf region. Yet their unqualified support for such regimes may prove to be a liability rather than an asset for the West in the near future. The increasing popular reaction against the corrupt and oppressive rules of the submissively pro-Western, obsolete regimes of the Middle East now tends to rally behind a new form of Islamic fundamentalism, in the absence of organized and effective secular opposition. This new fundamentalism may be militantly anti-Western, in contrast to the fundamentalism of the existing ruling classes. It may become the Sunni version of Iranian Shi'ite fundamentalism; we may even witness instances of tactical cooperation between the militant Sunni and Shi'ite fundamentalist movements. Although sectarian religious differences in the Islamic world of the Middle East are so sharp as to cause frequent political and even military

---

[2] "USIS Wireless File," Ankara, Turkey, 30 January 1992.

conflicts, political expediency may temporarily mitigate these differences.

I believe it is in the interest of not only the peoples of the Middle East but the whole world, including particularly the West, that every encouragement should be given to lay the groundwork for a sound process of modernization and democratization in this vitally important region. Otherwise, the increasing tension between the realities of the current world and the anachronism of the sociopolitical systems of the Gulf countries, the contrast between the spreading of democratic values around the world and the persistence of archaic despotism in large parts of the Middle East, coupled with the brewing popular reaction to this region's despotic and corrupt regimes' increased dependency on the West, are bound to lead, sooner or later, to cataclysmic explosions that may upset the whole world much more violently than the recent Gulf crisis.

Potential forces of modernization, secularization, and democratization are not lacking in and around the Middle East. Turkey has proven during the republican period that secularism and democracy are compatible with Islam and can infuse an Islamic society with great dynamism. The newly emerging independent Turkic states of Central Asia and the Caucasus, which are bound to have a marked impact on all the Islamic world including the Middle East, are determined to follow the same path as Turkey in this regard. There are also sizeable groups of Western-educated elites in all the Middle Eastern countries, most of whom would be ready and willing to give wholehearted support to modernization, secularization, and democratization in their homelands, once the pressures of despotic or fundamentalist forces on them begin to be reduced.

Palestinians could be a very important agent of change in the Middle East if they had their own independent state. I am confident that the great majority of Palestinians, including the PLO leadership, would be willing to adhere to an equitable arrangement of cohabitation or confederation with Israel. I believe those Israelis or Jews who consider the Palestinian movement as an extension or cutting edge of the so-called "Arab nationalism" and as a threat on their statehood and security are mistaken. The Palestinians have acquired over long years of isolation and suffering a sense, even a consciousness, of a separate national identity of their own. They have often witnessed the betrayal of their cause by several Arab countries. They have been pushed around in the Gulf countries, which have immensely benefited from their managerial, scientific, and technocratic acumen, while depriving them of citizenship rights. Palestinians attach great importance to education, but many Arab countries have been niggardly even about schooling possibilities for the children of Palestinian instructors whom they employ in their own schools and universities.

Several Arab countries have been a greater obstacle than Israel, in my view, to the establishment of a geographically based Palestinian state. Palestinian leaders may not be in a position to admit this publicly, but it has been my experience that in private conversations they are apt to acknowledge it. In fact, they have been increasingly frank about their disillusionment with many Arab countries in recent years.

Why should certain Arab countries want to obstruct the establishment of a Palestinian state? Why do they persist in presenting the Palestinian case as an Arab rather than simply a Palestinian cause, thereby constantly adding fuel to Israeli suspicions and intransigence, while they keep betraying the Palestinian cause? The answer that I can suggest is this: the Palestinians have adapted, to a remarkable degree, to democratic ways of self-rule and decision-making, through the efforts of the PLO leadership to maintain the unity of their national movement amidst the diversity of ideologies, strategies, and religions. They must also have been inspired by the democratic institutions of the Israeli regime, even though they have been discriminated against and have suffered under that regime in the occupied territories. They are highly educated and modernized and, because of the active and influential position of many Christian Palestinians in the PLO, they cannot afford to present their cause as "Islamic." Therefore, if a geographically based Palestinian state is to be founded, it would have to be a modernistic, democratic, and secular state. Leaders of all the Middle Eastern Arab nations must be aware of this. Yet they do not want a dynamic Arab state to emerge in their midst that would be an effective agent of modernization, secularization, and democratization in the whole region, since this would upset not only the anachronistic and despotic regimes of the Gulf countries but would also prod the more modernistic dictatorships of the Middle East to democratize. This, I believe, is the main reason why many Arab countries of the region have tacitly but persistently obstructed the emergence of a Palestinian state.

Although the Turks do not belong to the Arab world and are only partially Middle Eastern, Turkey also seems to be a deep cause of concern for most of the Middle Eastern Arab countries, particularly for those with anachronistic, despotic, and fundamentalist regimes like Saudi Arabia, and also for Iran. Turkey is a deep cause of concern for them, not because they suspect Turkey of having irredentist tendencies to revive the Ottoman Empire—they know that no such idea exists in Turkey. The main reason they are concerned is that republican Turkey has been the only Islamic society to have embarked upon a radical course of modernization and democratization; and, although until early in this century the Turks were regarded as the leading force and banner-bearers of Islam, Turkey has become in the republican period the only Islamic society with a thoroughly secular regime.

Contrary to the assertion of many Islamic theologians and politicians that Islam is not compatible with secularism and the Western form of democracy, republican Turkey has proven that Islam is compatible with secularism, with democracy, and with a Western way of life. The fundamentalist Islamic regimes of the Middle East are, therefore, afraid that Turkey may be an enticing example to their own peoples, thereby threatening the dogmatic precepts of their archaic and despotic sociopolitical systems.

Saudi Arabia and Iran have therefore been spending huge sums to destabilize Turkey's secular and democratic regime—mostly with the earnings of their speculative activities in Turkey—to indoctrinate young minds and to support fundamentalist activities, not only in Turkey but also among the Turks in West Europe. Although it does not mention Turkey, a recent article in *The Guardian*, entitled "Militant Islam's Saudi Paymasters," gives extensive information about the Saudi efforts to inculcate minds in many Islamic countries with their own brand of Islamic fundamentalism.[3] According to the same article, "'it is

---

[3] *The Guardian*, 29 February 1992, 5.

an unbelievable irony,' says Shireen Hunter, Deputy Director of Middle East Studies at the Center for Strategic and International Studies in Washington, 'that the West blames only Iran for the rise of fundamentalism.'" Encouraged by the West's delusion that Saudi fundamentalism could be an effective bulwark against communism, against Iranian Shi'ite fundamentalism, against the anti-Western postures of certain Islamic countries, or against opposition movements that might threaten friendly regimes in such countries, the Saudis have been spreading their own obsolete and retardant concept of fundamentalism with tacit Western support.

Yet the West is now alarmed by the fruits of this campaign, as in the case of Algeria recently. A strategic mistake of the Algerian administration, in my view, has been the allowing of free elections without first allowing and encouraging a proper multiparty system including strongly based secularist options. The same mistake has been made in Jordan. Such negligence of the rules of a convincingly pluralistic democracy pushes most of the discontented, including many secular-minded individuals, to rally behind the fundamentalist opposition. As King Hussein of Jordan said in his interesting CNN interview on March 15, "extremism," whether it be fundamentalist or not, "is born out of despair and anger." And I believe the best way to check and prevent fundamentalism, or any other kind of extremism, is to open all channels of democratic expression for the people to air their despair or discontent peacefully, and to search for rational solutions to their problems.

I had an interesting experience in Amman early last year. I was talking with an enlightened Jordanian journalist, and asked him how Islamic fundamentalists had come to be so strongly represented after the elections in the parliament of a modernistic country like Jordan. He said, "I am a Christian, but even I voted for the Islamic fundamentalists." Astounded, I asked him the reason, and he explained: "Because there was no other organized opposition."

An opportunity for a modest but possibly effective beginning of democratization has been missed in the Middle East after the Gulf War. I had two long conversations with President Saddam Hussein in Baghdad, shortly before and shortly after the Gulf War. During our conversation before the war I tried to sound him, not only about his ideas with regard to a peaceful solution to the crisis but also with regard to democratization. He certainly did not seem to be interested in democratization at that time. On the contrary, he argued that even countries with a deep-rooted democratic tradition had to suspend democracy during periods of crisis—which is not true.

But in our second conversation, soon after the war, he talked extensively about the merits of democracy and about his plans for democratization. I did not think, of course, that he had developed a sudden love for democracy, but he had obviously become convinced that he could satisfy the Kurdish opposition, prevent Western interference in Iraq's internal affairs, and avoid the partition of the country only by taking convincing steps in the path of democratization. In fact he started a dialogue in Baghdad to that effect with opposition leaders, giving them de facto official recognition. However, he seems to have given up this plan after the creation of a so-called "safe haven" in Northern Iraq by the Allies. An explosive authority vacuum has been created there, and an anarchic form of Kurdish autonomy has been virtually established under Western protection. He obviously saw no practical use any more in carrying out his democratization plan under the circumstances. In other words, he was not given a chance to have the seriousness of his intention tested.

I suspect that possibly Saudi Arabia may have convinced the Allies to refrain from giving such a chance to Saddam Hussein since, if democratization had started in Iraq, even in a modest way and degree, this might lead to a stronger Shi'ite political movement in the south of Iraq, and that would be discomforting for Saudi Arabia. Besides, pressures within and on Kuwait for democratization would increase, with its chain reactions on Saudi Arabia and the rest of the Gulf region. Yet the Saudi rulers seem to be determined to avoid taking any real steps in the way of democracy. Instead, they try to present an appointed small council of loyal and royal dignitaries as a "democratic institution," and expect their Western allies to applaud them on that account.

The Turkish Case

As I said earlier, republican Turkey is the only predominantly Islamic society that has officially and effectively adopted laicism and has embarked upon a radical course of modernization and democracy. Republican Turkey has been built through the combination of comprehensive modernization, secularization, democratization, and the assertion of Turkish national identity. These are the four indispensable and interdependent pillars on which the new Turkish state and sovereignty rest.

Islamic fundamentalists of the Middle East renounce and attack all these pillars. They renounce Turkey's modernization movement because this contrasts sharply with the archaic values and way of life that the fundamentalist or theocratic states of the region stick to. They renounce Turkey's secularization and democratization because they consider them a threat to the ideological foundations of the anachronistic regimes of the region. Arabic fundamentalists and theologians in general claim that Islam is transnational and, therefore, incompatible with the concept of national identity. But the Arabs themselves have always been ardently nationalistic and have claimed to be the select race of Islam. They have used the alleged transnationalism of Islam as a cloak for their claim to a dominant position in the Islamic world. They therefore brand the concept of Turkish national identity, which has gained pace with the republic, as anathema. In fact, a high-ranking Saudi dignitary visiting Turkey as the head of the Faisal establishment in 1985 openly suggested that the "obstacle of nationalism would have to be eliminated" before Saudi Arabia could consider further cooperation with Turkey.[4] Those Arabs who preached transnationalism were happy with the Ottoman regime in this regard because, particularly since the mid-fifteenth century, that regime did everything to suppress Turkish national identity.

At this point, I would like to dwell briefly on the historical background of the Turkish people's difficulties and advantages in adapting to democracy.

To start with, I must try to explain why a state established by Turks should try to suppress Turkish national identity. This was not because of the assertion that Islam was transnational. I would suggest two other reasons. With the spreading of the Ottoman Empire to large parts of Europe, and particularly after the conquest of Istanbul, the sultans considered it politically expedient

---

[4] Teoman Erel, *Milliyet*, 1 April 1985, 5.

to stress the multinational character of their domain. That, in my view, was one of the reasons why they chose to suppress Turkish national identity and to obliterate the Turkish origins of the empire. Secondly, the Turks, as the founding people of the empire, were freeborn members of the state and, in this capacity, they were the only people who could legitimately and effectively limit the powers of the sultan. In fact, certain dynastic Turkish families who had played leading roles in the foundation and flourishing of the empire could sometimes rule over the sultans. For instance, Grand Vizier Chandarli Halil Pasha was able, on one occasion, to dethrone Mehmet II and replace him with the former sultan, Murat II, Mehmet's father. Murat was a gifted statesman and commander, but he had retired to private life because he was bored with the constraints of power. Halil Pasha was still grand vizier when Mehmet II returned to the throne. But, as an ambitious ruler, Mehmet could not accept sharing power with the experienced grand vizier and had him executed after conquering Istanbul. Mehmet the Conqueror replaced him with a renegade, Zaganos Pasha, who was of either Greek or Serbian origin. For more than two centuries after that all the grand viziers and most of the viziers or high-ranking officials and officers were recruited from among Christian-born renegades of European origin.

For even a longer period, the permanent army—the so-called Janissary corps, labeled by Europeans "the terrible Turk"—consisted entirely of renegades of non-Turkish European origin. Although their children would acquire the status of freeborn Turks, the renegades were technically slaves of the sultan, with hardly any indemnity for life and property. So, in the Turkish sector of the Ottoman Empire, the people were free but deprived of political power and of any possibility of participation, while slaves were in ruling positions. This strange arrangement ensured for the sultans practically unlimited power. The slave system ended with the reforms initiated after the first quarter of the nineteenth century, and Turks began to be recruited into the administration and the army, but, in effect, the alienation of the administration and the people continued and the unchecked powers of the sultans remained intact to a large degree.

Even linguistic and cultural barriers were erected between the Turks and the administration. From the mid-fifteenth century, an artificial official language called "Ottoman" was created. It was a concoction of three unrelated languages: Arabic, Persian, and Turkish, ensuring that the free Turks could not even converse with the centers of power and the educated elite. Arabic and Persian cultures, which were quite rich and creative originally but had become stagnant in time, completely replaced Turkish culture among the elite, guaranteeing that the Ottoman system could remain immune to change for a long time. The Turkish people were also largely deprived of educational possibilities and their economy was left very underdeveloped. In fact, Turkey remained a most neglected region of the rich empire, so that the Turks would remain deprived of economic as well as political power.

A different policy was followed with regard to other parts and communities of the empire. They were allowed to be ruled largely in accordance with their own traditions and systems—provided that they remained loyal to the sultan. So, particularly the European regions of the empire had the opportunity of keeping up with the changing world, while the Turkish center of the empire was left behind the times. In other words, although it was the pivotal element of a large and prosperous empire, Turkey remained completely uninfluenced, until the nineteenth century, by the changes taking place at the rim of the Ottoman domain, and by the changes that it indirectly caused in the rest of the world. This paradox may perhaps best be described by a phrase from T. S. Eliot's *Four Quartets*—Turkey was "at the still point of the turning world."

Even in the nineteenth century, the pace of change was rather slow. The Ottoman regime was strictly theocratic for the Turks. The Turks were supposed to be ruled in accordance with Shari'a, the canonical law of Islam, and in compliance with the precepts of the Islamic holy book, the Koran. They could obtain and read the Bible in Turkish, but the Koran was never allowed to be printed or translated into Turkish, through the Ottoman period. The Turkish versions of the Koran that had existed before were also banned. Most Turkish villages were left without mosques or properly educated preachers. The Muslim Turks had to wait till the establishment of the secular Turkish Republic, early in this century, in order to have access to their own holy book, to be able to read and understand it in their own language, to have mosques built in all the villages, and to have educated preachers in those mosques.

This paradox of the theocratic Ottoman regime was still another basic feature of the state policy of preventing the Turks from participating in politics and checking the powers of the sultan. If the people could read and understand their own holy book, and could study and discuss their religion with the help of educated preachers, they could begin to question the official interpretations of the Koran and of the Shari'a, and to challenge the legitimacy of power as exercised by the sultan. To prevent this, the people had to be kept utterly ignorant of their religion. So, apart from administrative, linguistic, and cultural barriers, a religious barrier was also installed between the theocratic state and the people, between the ruler and the ruled, in the Turkish domain of the empire. Thus, the inalienable freedom that the Ottoman Turk was born with was rendered totally ineffective in politics.

This strange Ottoman heritage could be considered as a big obstacle in the way of democratization. Yet among more than twenty states that were born out of the ashes of the defunct Ottoman Empire, only Turkey and Greece were able to embark on democratization. Hopefully the other Balkan countries also may now be able to democratize their regimes, but long after Turkey and Greece.

How was Turkey able to adapt to democracy so quickly in spite of its historical impediments, and so easily to replace a theocratic regime with a secular one and prove that Islam could be compatible with secularism and democracy? Certainly the radical reforms Atatürk initiated have greatly contributed to this revolutionary transformation. But I believe certain elements of Turkish culture and some features of the Ottoman system have also facilitated it. In fact, the first seeds of democratization were sown during the period of decline and reform of the Ottoman Empire. A constitution was promulgated and a parliament was established, even if in rudimentary form, in 1876. This first Ottoman parliament, certainly, was based on limited suffrage and had rather restricted powers; besides, it was suspended after a short period. But this first Turkish experience in constitutional and parliamentary government should be judged on the basis of its performance and spirit rather than its structure and prerogatives. It must also be remembered that parliamentary democracy was far from being perfect at that time in most European countries.

A British historian, Edmund Ollier, evaluated the first Ottoman Turkish parliament in the following words, in a book written during the Ottoman period:

In Turkey the popular sentiment found expression through the national Parliament; and the members of that body were not disposed to endorse everything that the Government had done, but exercised their right of criticism as freely as if constitutional forms had been of long standing in the dominions of the Sultan.... That experiment had been tried under the most difficult circumstances conceivable—in the midst of foreign war [the Russo-Turkish War] and domestic revolution, and it is not surprising that it had met with a harsh and sudden interruption.

But it must be recollected to the credit of the Turkish character that the Ottoman Parliament had not been in all respects a failure. It would not have been surprising if a people so entirely unaccustomed to legislative forms had shown a complete incapacity to adopt them, and had simply registered the decrees of the executive power. But the Chamber of Deputies at Constantinople had acted in no such manner. It had shown spirit, energy, independence, and debating faculty; it had made itself felt in the councils of the nation; and had proved how true a germ of hope for Turkey dwells in those forms of liberty that have been the salvation of the West. If the jarring elements of Turkish society are ever to be organized to harmonious ends, it must be in the arena of free debate, and although the prorogation of the Chamber may have been a necessary evil in that moment of supreme agony, it is only by the resumption of constitutional law and the rights of popular election that Turkey can ever inherit a new life, or acquire an interest in the future age.[5]

The first Ottoman Turkish parliament was prorogated on account of a war, but the first non-Ottoman or anti-Ottoman Turkish parliament, "the Grand National Assembly of Turkey," was established on account of a war. Atatürk decided in 1920, at the early stage of the War of Liberation he had launched against great

[5] Edmund Ollier, in *Cassell's Illustrated History of the Russo-Turkish War*, vol. 2 (London, Cassell, Petter, Galpin, & Co.) 5, 75.

odds against the strongest powers of the world in occupation of the country, that this assembly could only succeed to the extent that it represented the will and rallied the active support of the nation. He considered this assembly necessary in order to be able to legitimize the liberation movement against the religious and political authority of the sultan, as well as in the eyes of the international community.

During the course of the war, the Grand National Assembly enjoyed immense power and freedom. Even the details of war strategy and tactics could be extensively debated, and Atatürk himself could be freely questioned and criticized as commander in chief. It was an unbridled forum of debate, and had full authority over the government and the army. It confirmed the British historian's conviction that Turkey could "inherit a new life" and "acquire an interest in the future" only through constitutional parliamentary democracy. The performance of the Turkish Grand National Assembly confirmed the Turkish people's propensity for democratic rules and forms, in spite of the heritage of centuries-long despotic theocratic rule. This propensity for democratization may largely have been acquired through the Turkish people's exclusion for centuries from positions of influence in the theocratic despotic system of the Ottoman Empire, and thanks to their severance from the artificial and stagnant official culture and the religious dogmatism of the regime. It can be said that a compound of "civil society" was allocated to the Turkish people in which they could think and talk and believe as they wished, provided that they did not try to interfere in state affairs or participate in politics and try to check the power of the sultan. It was as if the state had made a tacit agreement with the freeborn Turks of the empire: "Keep away from my business and I shall keep my ears closed to what you think or say." As a result, the Turkish people enjoyed incomparably greater freedom of thinking, conviction, and expression than the ruling and elite classes of the system.

For centuries under Ottoman rule, the educated and the elite did not have access to any forum where they could freely converse and discuss, but there were plenty of coffeehouses, in every corner of the country, where the common people, not the rulers but the ruled—the great majority that was excluded from state affairs and politics—could gather at any hour of the day to talk and to discuss matters of interest to their hearts' content. At the same time, the liberty enjoyed by shadow-players or puppet-players was unparalleled.

The traditional Turkish shadow play called the "Karagöz" is regarded nowadays as children's entertainment. But during the Ottoman period it was a very serious and important institution for adults. Two main characters dominated the Turkish shadow play scenarios: Karagöz, who represented the despised and cast-off but outspoken and witty, obstinate, and clever Turk who was uninfluenced by Ottoman culture and by the establishment—in other words, the people—and Hadjivat, the elite, alienated from the people, who had been enslaved by the system. Hadjivat's flowery Ottoman language is unintelligible to Karagöz—the people—his values are strange to Karagöz, and his personality rather shallow. In every scenario Karagöz heaps upon Hadjivat his rebellion against the system and ridicules the ostentation of the alienated Ottoman elite. The French poet Gerard de Nerval has this to say about Karagöz:

> He always belongs to the opposition. He is either the scoffer of the middle classes or a man of the people whose common sense finds something to criticize in the acts of the authorities. Karagöz is allowed freedom of speech, he always defies the rod, the saber and the rope.[6]

Another foreign observer, Louis Enault adds:

> In Turkey, a country ruled by an absolute monarchy and a totalitarian regime, Karagöz is a character who never deludes himself or is never lulled into a sense of security by shutting his eyes to the evils that surround him. On the contrary a Karagöz show is a risqué revue, as fearless as a militant newspaper.... Karagöz heaps judgement on the Grand Vizier and sentences him to prison. His barbs prove disquieting to foreign ambassadors; he lashed out at the Allied Admirals of the Black Sea fleet and the generals of the Crimea armies at the time of the Turkish-Russian war. His

[6] Gerard de Nerval, *Voyage en Orient*, vol. 1 (Paris 1861) 201. See Metin And, *Karagöz: Turkish Shadow Theatre* (Ankara, Dost Yayınları, 1975) 53, 67–68, for this and the following quotes.

public is delighted and the government indulgently allows his brash outspokenness.[7]

And an English observer says that Karagöz is "often witty, at times seditious, neither sparing the Sultan nor his ministers."[8] A French observer says:

> Karagöz defies censorship, enjoying unlimited freedom. Even the press in Europe is not so aggressive. Countries like America, England and France are much more restricted in political criticism than Turkey, which is a country ruled by an absolute monarch. Karagöz acts like some sort of unfettered press.... Even the Grand Vizier was seen to be tried in mock trial as if he were an infidel. The court, not finding his defense acceptable, sentenced him to a term of prison. If this had happened in a different country, even a single show of such seditious material would have been sufficient to promote the author's arrest and exile, whereas nothing happened to Karagöz.[9]

I have cited the examples of the traditional Turkish coffeehouse and shadow play as an endorsement of my claim that an undercurrent of popular freedom of thinking and expression balanced, in a sense, the harsh despotism of the Ottoman system. Obviously the sultans were clever enough to realize that if they tolerated the people's freedom of speech, the people, in turn, could suffer the regime's despotism more easily. This proves Hegel's claim that freedom of speech is far less dangerous than silence. He cynically says that with silence imposed by force "men have to swallow everything, while if they are permitted to argue, they have an outlet as well as some satisfaction, and in this way a thing may be pushed ahead more easily."[10] The freedom of speech that was granted as a kind of bribe to the Turks who were excluded from administration may have contributed a great deal to the ease with which the Turks could eventually adapt to democracy. Freedom of speech and expression has thus become a part of the Turkish

[7] Louis Enault, *Constantinople et la Turquie* (Paris 1861) 367.

[8] Adolphe Slade, *Records of Travels in Turkey*, vol. 2 (Paris 1855) 201.

[9] Joseph P. A. Mery, *Constantinople et la Mer Noire* (Paris 1855) 358.

[10] Karl Popper, *The Open Society and Its Enemies*, vol. 2 (London, Routledge and Kegan Paul, 1974) 310.

people's democratic culture—a kind of subculture far superior to the imitative and shallow elitist culture of the Ottoman system.

It is impossible to implement true democracy in an Islamic society unless the regime is secularized, because theocratic regimes assert, with the support of many theologians, that in Islam codes of moral conduct, the social system, and the state are inseparable from one another. In other words, it is claimed that in an Islamic society religion should be the main criterion of temporal affairs. But this concept of Islam has inevitably led to the retardation and, sometimes, even to the ossification of most Islamic societies.

I would like to make clear at this point that true Islam is not an obstacle to change. In fact, Islam was born as a revolutionary religion. Islam becomes a factor of inertia only when it is used as a power basis for state authority or for oligarchic groups, since then those oligarchic groups with vested interests in the existing system, or those rulers who do not want to forsake the religious mandate of their power, exploit religion in order to preserve and augment their interests or power and to perpetuate the system even though it may have become clearly outdated and untenable. This may be true for other religions also—but more so for Islam, since Islam is supposed to regulate the social and political life in accordance with the Shari'a, the basic religious law, which is regarded as unchangeable and uncontestable. But, in effect, in a theocratic Islamic state the rulers and the oligarchic groups, in complicity with allegedly authoritative theologians, affix all sorts of interpretations to the Shari'a to suit their own interests and objectives and ensure the perpetuation of an anachronistic system. This certainly happened under the Ottoman rule, and it is still happening under several theocratic or fundamentalist Islamic regimes in the Middle East.

Secularization is essential not only to liberate the people from bondage to obsolete and despotic regimes, but also to liberate Islam from the exploitation of rulers and oligarchic interest groups. It is also essential for democratization in an Islamic society, because, under a theocratic regime, the country is supposed to be ruled according to the will of God, and how can the will of the people, which is a basic element of democracy, contest the "will of God"? An Iranian militant fundamentalist political movement calls itself the "Hizbullah"—the "Party of God." How can a party of the people challenge the authority of a so-called "Party of God"?

Republican Turkey has effectively demonstrated that secularism, that is, the separation of the domains of religion and of the state and politics, is possible, and that it gives great dynamism to the society while restoring religion to its proper function in human life. Turkish secularism has also proven that it does not weaken religious feelings among the people. On the contrary, the people of secularist Turkey are more sincerely and more consciously attached to Islam than people in any theocratic or fundamentalist country, because their attachment to religion does not owe to the coercion of a despotic regime, but comes from the heart. Thus Turkish secularism has initiated what may be regarded as a "reformation" in Islam—restoring religion to its original purity.

The Turkish people's exclusion from the sphere of influence of the dogmatic and distortive teachings of the theocratic Ottoman regime has facilitated Turkish society's transition to secularism. During the centuries of Ottoman rule, most of the people outside the ruling or elite classes continued to evolve and enrich their own concept of religion and religious culture in the Turkish Sufi tradition they had brought with them from Central Asia and that had been perpetuated, in pure and intelligible Turkish, in the verses and songs of gifted folk poets. Normally, in a theocratic regime, religion evokes fear of God, and fear of God breeds fear of change, fear of freedom, and unquestioning submission to authority. But the Turkish Islamic Sufi tradition, as perpetuated in folk poetry, inspires love of God, and love of God is reflected on the human being. This, in turn, breeds tolerance and freedom. This cultural tradition, I believe, has greatly facilitated the Turkish people's easy adaptation to secularism and democracy.

It is indicative that, while the Iranian Shi'ite movement is very dogmatic, the Turkish branch of Shi'a, called the "Bektashi Alevi" movement, is distinctly tolerant and open to change, and inspires freedom of thought. Therefore, the Khomeini form of fundamentalism has had no influence at all on the Turkish Alevis. The Alevis and the majority of the Sunnis in Turkey can largely resolve their differences through their common moral attachment to the poet philosophers of Turkish folklore who keep the Turkish Islamic Sufi tradition alive.

In my recent visit to the Turkic republics of Central Asia and the Caucasus, I saw numerous statues of the great leaders of that tradition, who were revered as the symbols of their culture and identity, and the walls in some main squares or streets were inscribed with verses quoted from them. It was obvious that even decades of communist atheism could not suppress or obliterate that tradition. And now the same tradition seems to ensure these newly independent peoples' transition to a secular democratic regime, no matter how much Iran or Saudi Arabia may try to lure them to their own obsolete model. One of the main reasons why these Turkish peoples of Central Asia or the Caucasus now regard Turkey as a model is modern Turkey's attachment to secularism and democracy, and our common Sufi cultural heritage may provide for a stronger bond between us than geopolitical interests.

Women's Emancipation and Equality

Last but not least, I would like to dwell upon the function of women in democratization. The participatory culture of democracy starts at home. In order for new generations to grow up in a democratic atmosphere there must be democracy at home, and the emancipation and equality of women is the prerequisite of democracy at home. Lack of democracy at home would render half the population in any country unable to participate in the political life and decision-making processes. Besides, a male child who grows up in a nondemocratic family atmosphere, where there is patriarchal despotism, tends either to be a despot himself or to submit to despotism in mature life.

One of the major obstacles in the way of democratization in the fundamentalist countries of the Middle East is the lack of freedom and equality of women. Freedom and equality of women do not always ensure democracy, but I believe that the chances of sound democracy are very slight in a country where women are not emancipated and are not free and equal. And secularization is essential, in an Islamic country, for the emancipation of women.

Women in republican Turkey obtained freedom and equality in the early 1930s in a fuller sense than in several Western countries of the same period, simultaneously with Turkey's transition to a secular regime. And these two factors, namely, secularism and the emancipation and equality of women, have jointly helped open the way for democracy in Turkey.

I felt I noticed a faint but encouraging sign of women's emancipation, which could also spark off the flame of secularization and democratization in the Middle East, when the ladies of some prominent Saudi families broke the rules for a few days during the Gulf crisis and insisted in driving their own cars at the risk of imprisonment. I prayed that the emancipated women of democratic countries would effectively demonstrate their solidarity with those Saudi women and encourage them to take more radical steps in the way of emancipation, secularization, and democratization. But my prayers were not heard. I believe, however, the Middle East, being such a vitally important part of the world, cannot for too long resist the winds of democratization that are being felt over all the rest of the world.

American Policy toward Democratic Political Movements in the Middle East

WILLIAM B. QUANDT

A T a time when democratic political movements seem to be gaining ground in many parts of the world, the Middle East appears to be a notable exception. Is this because the United States is throwing its weight behind the status quo, a status quo built around authoritarian political regimes of various sorts? Or is the reason that something in Middle East political culture is hostile to democratic politics?[1] Or is the answer some combination of the two?

It is true that until recently the United States had not attached great importance to supporting democracy in the Middle East. Elsewhere, in Latin American and in East Asia, democratic movements have been given much greater encouragement from Washington, and success stories of democratic transformations are fairly widespread. Why has the Middle East been the exception?

It is unfair to say that American policy has been consistently hostile to democratic movements per se in the Middle East. After all, both Turkey and Israel have been among the closest friends of the United States and both have been relatively democratic in their political practices. In an earlier period, Lebanon as well enjoyed a measure of support from Washington, at least in part because of its commitment to democratic processes. Offsetting

---

[1] This is the view of Elie Kedourie, *Democracy and Arab Political Culture* (Washington, D.C.: The Washington Institute for Near East Policy, 1992). For Kedourie, Islam and democratic political values are incompatible.

these examples of American support for democracy in the Middle East, however, are many more cases where official American policy seemed to stand directly in opposition to populist, antiestablishment political forces. Most dramatic was the American intervention in Iran in 1953 in support of the Shah against the Mossadegh government, which was at least popular, if not necessarily democratic. In subsequent years, Washington provided massive support for the Shah, particularly through arms sales in the 1970s. In addition to Iran, other monarchies in the Middle East, such as Saudi Arabia, Jordan, and Morocco, have all enjoyed support from Washington.

Not only have monarchical regimes generally found favor in official circles in Washington, but also Arab dictatorships such as those of Saddam Hussein in the 1980s and Hafiz al-Asad of Syria have been on fairly good terms with the United States at various times over the years. How can an American policy support for democracy be reconciled with such obvious exceptions to the rule?

The answer to this question seems quite straightforward. At the times the United States has supported nondemocratic regimes in the Middle East, the reasons have usually been one of the following: oil was at stake, Israel was involved, or Soviet bids for influence in the Middle East were being countered. These three concerns—oil, Israel, and the Soviet Union—were the driving forces behind American Middle East policy throughout most of the period from the 1950s through the 1980s. Democratization was viewed, at best, as a secondary objective. The United States, on balance, was willing to deal with existing political regimes when their foreign policy orientations served one or more of these three core interests. While not apologizing for this narrowly constructed approach to the Middle East, one can nonetheless note that most other countries adopted very much the same policies as did the United States. (For example, the Soviet Union was regularly prepared to sacrifice the interests of indigenous communist parties if it served Moscow's interest to deal with one regime or another in the Middle East.)

With the end of the Cold War, conditions may now exist in which the old paradigm that governed American policy can be successfully challenged. There is no longer any reason to support nondemocratic regimes in the Middle East simply because they stood on the American side during the Cold War. Still, the United States will have an interest in maintaining access to Middle Eastern oil and in promoting Arab-Israeli peace as part of its broader commitment to Israel's security and well-being. How will these two interests be affected by the growth of democratic political movements in the region?

On the face of it, there is no reason to believe that democratic governments in the Middle East, whether in the Persian Gulf or in North Africa, would be less willing to sell oil than the petro-oligarchs of today. So oil supply is unlikely to be jeopardized by the mere existence of democratic governments, assuming they were somehow to come into existence. The question then is not so much whether the United States could live comfortably with a Middle East in which popularly elected governments controlled the oil spigots. To that question the answer is certainly yes. The proper question is, how can one envisage a transition from the existing situation in the Middle East today, where nondemocratic regimes control the flow of oil, to one in which more open, participatory democracies have assumed responsibility for the management of this unique resource.

Insofar as strategic analysts think about this question in Washington, the question arises, "Why rock the boat?" The Saudis are indeed far from being a model of Western-style democracy, but they are also far from being the most repressive regime in the region. And if King Fahd were to be replaced, not by a Saudi Thomas Jefferson but rather by a Saudi Khomeini or a Saudi Saddam Hussein, democracy would be even more remote than it is today.

The key value for the United States with respect to access to oil supplies is stability and predictability. Few in the West want to gamble with the consequences of radical political upheavals in the Gulf region. Although it is true that Iran managed to resume oil production on a large scale after its revolution, one should not trivialize the cost to the world economy of the upheavals that accompanied the downfall of the Shah and the rise of Khomeini. For much of 1978 through 1979, very little oil from Iran was exported. And then after 1980, Iranian oil supplies were restricted as a result of the long Iran-Iraq war.

The total cost to the world of these disruptions to Iran's oil supplies is certainly measured in the tens of billions of dollars. If the same kind of upheaval were to affect Saudi oil supplies in the 1990s, the United States, and all of the rest of the world, would go through a very difficult economic recession. So, even if one can be relatively sanguine about the behavior of any stable government with respect to its oil resources, it is much more difficult to be optimistic that prolonged political upheaval could take place in a country like Saudi Arabia, or in other large oil producers, without creating serious disruptions to the world economy.

Even though democratization inevitably entails some risk of instability, there is no basic reason for the United States to be so cautious about discussing democratic political change in the Arab world or elsewhere in the Middle East region. It is quite possible for the United States to lend support to cautious moves in the direction of political participation, such as those envisaged in some Gulf states, without worrying too much about the nervous reactions of the regime in Saudi Arabia. The United States has been very hesitant to use the word democracy in discussing policies and objectives in the Middle East, and this has been noted by aspiring democrats in the region with some dismay.[2] In our general policy statements, and certainly in our private discussions with regimes in the region, there is no reason not to place emphasis on the importance that we attach to democratic political values, respect for human rights, and the important links we see between opening up economic systems and political systems as a basis for long-term growth and stability in the region. Even if some regimes react negatively to this kind of discourse, oil will continue to flow. American interests are not incompatible with American principles.

Concerning our other major interest in the Middle East, namely, Israel and the Arab-Israeli peace process, our preference in the past has been to deal with any regime, such as that of Anwar Sadat of Egypt, that was willing to negotiate a settlement with Israel. If Hafiz al-Asad of Syria, or Yassir Arafat of the PLO, or King Hussein of Jordan were to emulate Sadat, they would win

---

[2] A noteworthy exception is a speech on 2 June 1992 by Assistant Secretary for Near Eastern Affairs Edward P. Djerijian, Meridian International Center, Washington, D.C.

a degree of American support whether or not they upheld democratic principles. Yet in the long run a lasting Arab-Israeli peace is more likely if some degree of democratization does take place in the Arab world, and particularly in the countries surrounding Israel. So even here, our long-term interests are perfectly compatible with support for democratic movements. Nonetheless, there is an understandable hesitation to push for democracy in a country like Jordan or in Syria, when there is little chance that American efforts will be rewarded and when the risks of derailing the fragile peace process are fairly substantial.

It is worth looking at a recent Middle East case where neither oil nor Israel was a major consideration for American policy. In late 1991 and early 1992, Algeria scheduled elections for its national assembly. The United States had encouraged the process of political and economic liberalization in Algeria, although not at a particularly high level. After the results of the first round of elections in late December 1991, it was clear that the Islamic movement, the Front Islamique du Salut (FIS), was on its way to an electoral victory. Somewhat surprisingly, there was not much reaction in Washington to the possibility that an Islamic state in North Africa might soon emerge. By contrast, several European countries, especially France, and Algeria's immediate neighbors, Tunisia and Morocco, showed strong signs of anxiety.

When in mid-January 1992 the Algerian authorities decided to suspend the second round of elections rather than risk a victory by the Islamic movement, the United States reacted mildly. But it is simply not the case that Washington was somehow behind the Algerian decision to abort the electoral process. After initially indicating its belief that Algeria had acted according to its own constitutional provisions, the State Department corrected itself and took a decidedly neutral posture on whether or not the suspension of the elections had been justified. No doubt many in Washington would have felt somewhat uneasy if the FIS had in fact come to power.[3] Few believed that the leaders of the Islamic movement were model democrats. At the same time, however, the United States seemed prepared to maintain normal relations

---

[3] Djerijian (supra n. 2) noted: "While we believe in the principle of 'one person, one vote,' we do not support 'one person, one vote, one time.'"

with Algeria under whatever circumstances might emerge from the political test of wills between a nondemocratic, one-party nationalist regime and a prospective Islamic regime. This is an issue that will no doubt arise again in the future. Based on the Algerian case, we can expect the United States to be prepared to deal with Islamic movements that come to power through elections in a normal manner.

In the coming years, it is quite likely that the United States will face a wide range of political experimentation in the Middle East. Existing regimes have failed to win popular support in most parts of the region. Pressures for political change exist. Democratization is now widely discussed, if little practiced. Islamic movements may well try to use elections to come to power, without intending to play by democratic rules once they have consolidated their power. All of this will pose dilemmas for Washington, but none of them seem to be unmanageable. Not all of the uncertainties that accompany political change in the Middle East necessarily will pose significant threats to American national interests. What then should be done by the United State to prepare itself for a period of political transformation in a region where major interests continue to exist?

First, the United States should extend the range of its political contacts in key countries. In the past, American officials were often prohibited from meeting with opposition figures, for fear of offending friendly regimes. Some of this hesitation to meet with or talk to opposition leaders still exists. Looking to the future, the United States needs to be better informed about possible successor leaders in key Middle Eastern states, and should have no hesitation to establish normal communications and contacts with a variety of political groupings, if for no other reason than to learn more about the programs and personalities that make up these movements.

Second, the United States should reconsider its traditional stance toward political change in the Middle East. In the past, we have spoken of stability as a supreme objective in the Middle East, and yet emphasis on stability can lead to support for regimes that have lost support from their own people and that have ceased to be viable partners for the United States as it pursues its own policies in the region. We should accept the inevitability of political change, and should stress that the important point is that change should be brought about through peaceful means rather than through violence and revolution. We should place greater emphasis in our public statements on the need for respect for human rights, for political freedoms, and for broadening opportunities for political participation within Middle Eastern states. Along with our conventional emphasis on the Arab-Israeli peace process, our concern for controlling weapons of mass destruction, and our commitment to encouraging economic reforms, an emphasis on democratization, liberalization, and human rights would appeal to many in the Middle East who are now convinced that the United States will back any regime, regardless of its policies toward its own people, if only that regime agrees to support American foreign policy objectives. During the Cold War, such a stance may have made sense for Washington, but it is increasingly obsolete.

If regimes in the Middle East do take steps in the direction of political reform—opening up their political systems, allowing freedom of expression, respecting the rule of law, holding free elections—then the United States should demonstrate in its actions and in its words that it supports and will encourage the continuation of these efforts.[4] Countries such as Turkey, Egypt, Jordan, and Yemen are all struggling to introduce elements of democratization into their political life, and the United States has a strong interest in seeing that these processes succeed and continue. In some cases, this will require the continuation of aid programs that no longer enjoy much popular support in the United States. But by linking in the American public mind the provision of economic support for countries moving toward democracy, a constituency for continued assistance could still be maintained.

In order to encourage democratic political change in the Middle East, the United States should continue to promote the Arab-Israeli peace process. The absence of a solution to the Arab-Israeli conflict has been used for years by various Arab regimes as an excuse for maintaining harsh dictatorial rule. If the Arab-Israeli

---

[4] Djerijian (supra n. 2) put it well: "Those who are prepared to take specific steps toward free elections, creating independent judiciaries, promoting the rule of law, reducing restrictions on the press, respecting the rights of minorities, and guaranteeing individual rights, will find us ready to recognize and support their efforts."

conflict were on its way toward a solution, and if an emerging Jordanian-Palestinian confederation were to adopt broadly democratic principles of government, it would be increasingly difficult for Arab dictators to justify the continued repression that they have relied on for so many years. In brief, one of the benefits of success in Arab-Israeli peace talks may well be to strengthen moderate and democratic political forces in the region. Palestinians are among the best placed of Arabs to inject democratic principles into their political institutions. They, after all, have suffered from the lack of democracy in the region and have gone further in accepting pluralism within their own political movement than have most Arab regimes.

With the end of the Middle East Cold-War era, the United States has an opportunity to place greater emphasis on issues of human rights in its relations with countries of the Middle East. Both in public and in private, American officials should take a tough stand whenever flagrant abuses of human rights can be demonstrated. This should be done even when it risks embarrassing friendly countries, as it almost certainly will on occasions.

With respect to the growing strength of Islamic movements in the Middle East, the United States should avoid overreacting to the specter of a monolithic Islamic threat. Islamic movements will manifest themselves in a variety of ways, often as a result of quite specific circumstances in different countries. In some cases, the United States should have no intrinsic difficulty in dealing with these Islamic movements. On other occasions, there will be objective conflicts of interest and of policy, and it will do no good to bend over backwards and pretend that these do not exist. In brief, the United States should treat Islamic movements as complex, multifaceted phenomena, and not as a monolithic threat. We should take our stand with respect to Islamic movements and governments on a case-by-case basis. And we should remember that it makes little sense to lump all political currents that call themselves Islamic together, just as it would make little sense to lump all political movements that identify themselves as democratic or as Christian under the same label.

Finally, the United States is likely to have an opportunity in the near future to influence the political transformation of Iraq. At some point, Saddam Hussein will certainly be removed from power. When that happens, the United States and its Western allies will have considerable influence over the transition. Any new Iraqi regime will need generous support from the outside world. It will need a relaxation of the economic embargo. It will need to export its oil. It will need relief from demands for repayment of debt and reparations. Decisions on each of these measures can be related to the democratic political performance of the new regime. In this sense, the United States has a chance to demonstrate that its war against Iraq was not simply for oil, but was also designed to bring an end to aggressive dictatorships and to open the way for democratic political participation.

If the United States is to inject a concern for democratization into its Middle East policy, several considerations must be borne in mind. First, a policy of active support for democratization abroad is incompatible with a sharp turn toward isolationism in the United States. If we choose to disengage from world affairs, if we turn our gaze exclusively inward, we will have little time or energy for encouraging constructive political change abroad.

Assuming that we can avoid the extreme of isolationism, we must also be wary of the other extreme of American triumphalism. The fact that the United States won the Cold War does not mean that it can impose its views and its values everywhere in the world. To assume that "markets and democracy" can be exported according to a single model, and be made to work universally, is a sign of naïveté. We will not be able to force our version of democracy onto an area that has had little experience of its own with pluralistic politics. Nor can we create democratic movements where they do not exist. The point is not to have "Made in the USA" democracies sprouting up throughout the Middle East. The point is rather to encourage political movements in the region that represent indigenous forces for constructive political change, that respect human rights, that respect political freedoms, and that respect diversity. On occasions, such movements will create political systems that do not resemble classical democratic experiments elsewhere. But they may represent considerable progress beyond the authoritarian regimes of the recent past.

With an eye toward our own past, we would do well to show patience with countries struggling to adopt democratic methods of governance. We, after all, did not immediately find a workable constitutional formula; we began with a very restrictive franchise; we fought a civil war before adding the principle of equality to the rights protected by the government. And this all took a full two generations to accomplish. How much more difficult will it be for poor countries to democratize in the era of instant communications, galloping population growth, and rapid urbanization?

In conclusion, the United States should be prepared to cooperate with other major powers in promoting political and economic change in the Middle East. The United States today is preoccupied with its own economic illnesses. American public opinion polls show little support for continued foreign assistance. And without economic clout, the United States cannot expect to wield great influence over political evolution in the Middle East. Therefore, the United States will need partners who can contribute some of their own economic resources to a strategy for encouraging change in the Middle East. Europe and Japan are the obvious candidates, since they share with the United States democratic political systems, and they enjoy economic prosperity that allows them to contribute a share of their wealth to the construction of a new political and economic order in a region of the world that continues to be of vital importance to them as well as to us.

Voices of Opposition

The International Committee for a Free Iraq

CHIBLI MALLAT

T
HE International Committee for a Free Iraq, which includes Iraqis and non-Iraqis, is based on a new concept of international relations, as the Iraqi patrons are committed to human rights after the present dictatorship is brought to an end. The committee seeks the establishment of independent bodies that will supervise the road of Iraq to democracy after the end of the present dictatorship, through independently monitored free elections and the protection of human rights.

This study and the chapter "Obstacles to Democratization in Iraq" below are dedicated to Ahmad Chalabi, Edward Mortimer, and David Gore-Booth. Ahmad Chalabi has been the moving force behind the efforts to rally the Iraqi opposition behind an achievable democratic programme, and is the elected coordinator of the Iraqi National Congress, which met in Vienna 16 to 19 June 1992, and then in Salaheddin (northern Iraq) in October 1992. Edward Mortimer is a distinguished author and columnist with the *Financial Times*, and was the first in the West to open up the channels of contacts between Iraqi oppositional figures and the British Foreign Office, whose Middle East undersecretary the Honourable David Gore-Booth was key to British policy adopting enlightened positions throughout the Gulf crisis. I have coordinated with Ahmad Chalabi and Edward Mortimer the work of the International Committee for a Free Iraq, which has opened up for me avenues for addressing the case of Iraq in practical ways that books do not generally permit. Some of this experience is included in these chapters. Much as I have benefited from discussions with Ahmad Chalabi, Edward Mortimer, and David Gore-Booth, the reflections included in this chapter only engage my responsibility. This dedication of these studies to them is but a sign of gratitude for the new horizons that I believe they have opened for the people of Iraq and the Middle East.

The committee was founded in London in the Spring of 1991. It came out publicly for the first time on 21 June 1991, at the House of Commons, in the presence of several Iraqi and international patrons.[1] Although the ICFI includes some fifty Iraqis of all political hues, ethnic and religious origins, and ages, it is not equipped to operate as an Iraqi oppositional front, because it also includes several non-Iraqi members.[2] The ICFI has therefore served as a mini-think-tank: on the international side, it presents ideas and offers positions that are disseminated through various channels and eventually reach decision-making circles in significant states. This process is helped by prominent and influential patrons, who belong to the nonexecutive branch of government and therefore do not face possible conflicts of interest. On the Iraqi side, the ICFI has worked essentially for the unification of the Iraqi opposition on a democratic platform.

The first problem faced by the ICFI was a mindset. As acknowledged by two senior congressional aides, it was difficult to conceive of democracy for Iraq, as Iraqis were not perceived to be sufficiently "mature" for such a form of government.[3] This is corroborated in a reply by Richard Haass, of the National Security Council dealing with Iraq, to the charge of the laxity of the United States government during the Iraqi popular revolt in March and April 1991. For Haass, it was impossible to imagine occupying

---

[1] The meeting took the form of a press conference that was addressed by the three international coordinators, Edward Mortimer, Ahmad Chalabi, and myself, and by Hoshyar Zebari (the representative in London of the Kurdish Front), David Owen, the former U.K. Foreign Minister and David Howell, Chairman of the House of Commons Select Committee on Foreign Affairs. The launch of the ICFI in the United States took place on 1 October 1991 in the Senate Building in Washington, when the three coordinators spoke, as well as Senator Claiborne Pell, Chairman of the Senate Foreign Relations Committee, Senators Paul Simon and John MacCain, and Congressman Stephen Solarz.

[2] See program and list of patrons in the International Committee for a Free Iraq *Newsletter* 2 (London, May 1992).

[3] Peter Galbraith, on the staff of the Foreign Relations Committee and Michael Van Dusen, senior aides to the U.S. Senate and House of Representatives Foreign Relations committees respectively, in meetings with Iraqi oppositional figures in London.

Iraq and leaving it soon afterwards with eighteen million Iraqis reading the *Federalist Papers*.[4]

Although this mindset remains, all the major leaders of the Western world, including President Bush, are on record demanding "democracy" in Baghdad. Indeed, the fact that Hussein remains in power is clearly the greatest thorn in the Allied "victory." This clear negation of "victory" was not so evident in March 1991 (when the first preparations for the creation of the committee started), and it is to the credit of the ICFI that it made enough of an impact on the media and on chanceries to impose, at the London G-7 meeting in the early summer of 1991, the "democracy" clause of the final declaration.

The ICFI also succeeded in helping the emergence of resolutions 706 and 712. It was anticipated, soon after the end of the war, that a major issue would have to be addressed in relation to sanctions against Iraq. The conundrum was clear and simple. Remove sanctions, and the Iraqi government is allowed a breathing *political* space essentially through allowing renewed oil revenues to help it reestablish its repressive networks. Allow sanctions to remain, and the Iraqi people will be the main victims of the resulting suffering. The narrow way forward was to demand that the resumption of oil sales be supervized by an international body. This monitoring would make sure that the money was earmarked for the welfare of Iraqi citizens and that the Iraqi government would not benefit. This proposal was put forward by the ICFI on 15 July 1991. The main gist of the text was introduced in Resolution 706, with the proviso that a share of the revenues would go to the victims of the Iraqi invasion. A body was set up in Geneva to assess compensation and the mechanisms of the escrow account.[5]

Clearly, the target of the ICFI's work has been to redress, on the international level, the failure of established principles

---

[4] This is the way Dr. Haass explained the U.S. government's lack of trust in the proneness to democracy of Iraqis in a televised program that was organised by Richard Perle, of the American Enterprise Institute. Richard Haass was a special assistant to President Bush. Richard Perle is a former Assistant Secretary of Defense, and is a patron of the ICFI.

[5] S/RES/706 (15 August 1991).

of international law. The two key resolutions, 688 and 706 (as well as Resolution 712, with which 706 must be read) remain the most important elements in the panoply of measures separating the present Iraqi government, in law, from its victims. The two resolutions are also clearly the most annoying to Baghdad. Although the Iraqi government has accepted all other resolutions, in particular the disarmament conditions set out by Resolution 687, resolutions 688 and 706 have remained unfulfilled. As for Resolution 687, it is important, for the record, to note its negative legal impact. In the context of Middle Eastern countries that are armed to the teeth, the disarming of just one party in the shape of Iraq cannot provide lasting security. In Washington, the argument against this presentation is the readiness of officials to change Resolution 687 once the Ba'th is unseated. But disarmament clauses, compensation schemes, and boundary delimitations that attach to a state are not so easy to undo. The Security Council and Western governments would do better to introduce their "good" government conditionalities into a new Security Council resolution.

This, on the "international" side. On the domestic side, the equation is more complex, as the activities undertaken with a view to establishing democracy in Baghdad are dependent on the devastation of the country and on an opposition whose sole common denominator seems to be the hatred of its dictator, at a time when all regional powers are prowling around captive Iraqi opponents, with each country grooming the candidate it would like to inherit Iraq after the demise of Saddam Hussein.

As suggested in the chapter "Obstacles to Democratization in Iraq" in this book, avoiding the war altogether might have been possible by a concerted effort to strengthen the Iraqi opposition in its work against Saddam Hussein. This remains the necessary agendum to the outstanding problem of democracy in Iraq. For that, in the view of my reading of Iraqi modern history, the two elements (divide and rule and sectarianism) that constitute the pillar of Ba'thist policy have to be addressed so that the matrix that underlies them—the rule of law and its shadow—can be used positively in the quest for democracy.

Against the divide-and-rule strategy, it was necessary to help construct a "wall-to-wall" opposition,[6] including representatives of all generations, ethnicities, and sects. At the time of the ICFI's formation in June 1991, the great concern was the danger of a rapprochement between the Kurdish leadership and the Iraqi government, after the famous embrace of Jalal Talibani (and other Kurdish figures) and Saddam Hussein, and the danger that it would lead to an agreement that would have been disastrous to the opposition. The way I worked to undermine it was by muting the public outcry of the other groups of the opposition, so that the mistrust would not reach a point of nonreturn. Secondly, I submitted that if a serious alternative were offered to the Kurdish leadership, which had just been abandoned in the most shameful way by the West, it would help it to discontinue its desperate course with Saddam Hussein.

The alternative was provided by Poised Hammer, which was then at its beginning, with American and British soldiers crossing into Iraq from the north to implement the effective withdrawal of troops beneath the 36th Parallel. The great Kurdish fear at the time was that this policy would be abandoned quickly after the criticism leveled by public opinion against the Bush policy abated. To convince the Kurdish leadership that it was not the case, the launching of the ICFI on 21 June 1991 was an occasion for the British patrons to make a common, bipartisan appeal "to the US and British governments and to our European partners not to withdraw their forces from northern Iraq until the security of the Kurdish population has been assured, to its own satisfaction, by other means. Even if the US decides to ignore this appeal, we urge the British and other European governments to maintain their forces in northern Iraq, and if necessary to expand them to fill the gap left by US withdrawal."[7]

But the declaration was not sufficient. Serious negotiations between Baghdad and the Kurdish front continued, but a mistake of

---

[6] Formula of Allen Meizenheimer, the Iraqi desk officer in the State Department, in a telephone conversation, 12 March 1992.

[7] The statement was drafted by Edward Mortimer, and issued with the signature of the four British MP patrons. See ICFI's *Newsletter*, 1 February 1992, 5.

Saddam Hussein sealed the fate of the negotiations. The Kurds, by 21 June 1991, had been ready to accept the draft agreement hammered out with Baghdad. Mas'ud Barzani, the leader of the Kurdish Democratic party, was inclined to support it, but Jalal Talibani was more reluctant. The main problem was the ignorance of the details of the text in the West, for it had been withheld from the press. This was consistent with the dark policies of the Ba'th, but its concealment was not to the advantage of the Kurds. Furthermore, the United States State Department was encouraging an agreement between the Kurds and Saddam Hussein by assuming a neutral position through their refusal to shoulder any responsibility, whether or not the Kurds came to terms with Saddam Hussein. The Kurds could only read all this as an encouragement to sign.

Eventually, the text was leaked to the West and I was apprised of its contents, parts of which I translated for the benefit of Mrs. Ann Clwyd, founding patron of the ICFI and a Labour Member of Parliament, who has long been associated with the fight against repression in Iraq. She also distrusted the rapprochement of Kurds with Saddam Hussein. After a meeting on June 24 in the House of Commons, I conveyed to her the translation of key clauses of the draft agreement.[8]

The introduction stated that normalization would take place "on the basis of the reassurances of the leader President Mr. Saddam Hussein, God protect him, the historic architect of the 11 March 1970 Agreement." Clause 4 read:

> The Kurdistan Front declares its standing side by side with the Arab Socialist Ba'th party to confront the artificial political maneuvres in the region, which are orchestrated by foreign orders, with a view to securing the national and strategic security of Iraq.

Clause 19 prevented

> the Kurdistan Front from undertaking any cooperation with states in the region and outside except in agreement with the State of

[8] I would like to acknowledge my debt to Kamran Karadaghi, Dr. Latif Rashid, and Dr. John Foran during that critical period. Their systematic and efficient cooperation to date has been invaluable. John Foran was, to my knowledge, the first to coin the phrase "safe haven," in a cable sent to the Foreign Office from Geneva.

Iraq. Any contact with non-Iraqi parties will take place through
the National Iraqi Front and its Covenant [this is the "Front" set
up ten years ago that was being resurrected to include the Kurds
and the Ba'th].

Clause 23 stated that

> Iraq faced and continues to face dangerous threats to its national
> and strategic security, foremost the American Zionist imperialist
> menace and the ruling regime in Iran and some other regimes in
> the region. Since it is agreed that representatives of the Kurdistan
> Front are to participate in government and in decision-making, and
> in order that the national resistance to these threats be secured at
> the necessary level, the Front undertakes to support the plans and
> measures carried out by the State of Iraq to fulfill this national
> objective, whether in a military or a political form. The Front
> also undertakes to deepen popular consciousness in the direction
> of the love of Iraq and is ready to offer sacrifices to protect it, until
> martyrdom, against all its enemies.

Why did Saddam Hussein include such impossible language
into the agreement? Hussein and the Iraqi leadership apparently
thought that the military weakness of the Kurds, as well as the
refusal of Washington to be drawn in on their side, meant that
the Kurdish leadership had no choice. He was not wrong insofar as
the "safe-haven" policy was still very much in danger of imminent
collapse. Yet I think that the antiquated language of the text
was superfluous, and a mere agreement between Baghdad and the
Northerners would have dealt a fatal blow to the emergence of an
Iraqi opposition. Never would Arab Iraqis have forgiven Kurdish
Iraqis for striking a separate deal with Saddam Hussein. But the
language was also a function of the domestic shadow of the rule of
law. Saddam Hussein wanted the Kurds to commit themselves, in
writing, to a binding agreement.

John Major was duly appraised of the content of the agreement
and its language. His resolve not to go back on the safe-haven policy, which had already met with favorable public opinion despite
the "Vietnam" risks entailed, was strengthened. The declaration
of the ICFI patrons, together with the leaking of the impending
agreement between the Kurds and Saddam Hussein, secured bipartisan support for a confrontational policy (thus the importance

of Ann Clwyd's intervention as Labour MP) and impressed British foreign policy in a way that brought it to bear enough pressure on the United States to delay withdrawal from northern Iraq. A few precious weeks were gained, which allowed the routed Kurdish leadership to reconsider and gave it some confidence in increased Western commitment to prevent new bloodshed in Kurdistan.

In October 1991, the large Kurdish city of Suleymaniyya, which lay beneath the 36th parallel and was hence outside the safe-haven ambit, fell into Kurdish hands almost without a fight. The Iraqi army was demoralized and collapsed rapidly after popular tension rose in the city. By then, Poised Hammer had also become a success with the United States administration, and the prohibition of Iraqi flights over the whole of Iraqi Kurdistan ensured the region effective protection from Saddam Hussein. In that context, the Kurdish-Baghdad agreement, which would have dramatically split the opposition, had become unnecessary—and burdensome—for the Kurds.

The fear of Kurdish collapse remained in case Poised Hammer (now more popular as Provide Comfort) was threatened, and the "liberation" of the whole of Iraq was still not in the cards because of the failure of Arabs and Kurds opposed to Saddam Hussein to rally in a serious opposition. It was therefore necessary for the opposition to regroup around a program that would be effective domestically and internationally, and constitionally plausible. Only through a clear and satisfactory program spelling out rights and duties ethnically and otherwise could the rule of law emerge from the shadow. Such a text was also an essential requirement against the divide-and-rule policy of the regime.

It was also vital to bridge sectarianism, which antedates the present government. As is evident to all observers of Iraqi history in the twentieth century, Iraqi religious communities and ethnic groups were trapped in the logic of the nation-state.[9] The only resolution would be a proper constitutional framework—and this ideal constitution was still missing.

---

[9] See the remarkable study of Pierre-Jean Luizard, "L'improbable démocratie en Iraq: le piège de l'Etat-Nation," *Egypte-Monde Arabe* (Cairo) 4 (1990) 47–89, which develops the history of this point over the century with great scholarship.

Throughout the winter of 1992, ICFI patrons embarked on a series of seminars and conferences addressing these issues, notably a two-day conference on "Constitutional Frameworks in Iraq," held in London from 11 to 13 February 1992. Elsewhere in the world, Iraqis were also meeting to discuss related human rights issues, with a focus on Charter 91, which had been drafted by Kan'an Makkiyye after several discussions and seminars in London and in the United States. Emphasis on human rights had also been undertaken in a systematic manner by the Organization for Human Rights in Iraq, whose President, Dr. Saheb al-Hakim, and his main aide, Ghanem Jawad, tirelessly put forward the human rights dimension of the Iraqi crisis in exhibits and "tribunals" held all over the globe. A major point of satisfaction emerged with the release of the report of the United Nations Special Rapporteur on Human Rights, Max van der Stoel (a former Dutch foreign minister) on 18 February 1992. In his view, "this exceptionally grave situation demands an exceptional response.... Confronted with such an intolerable situation, [the UN Commission should not] confine itself to condemnation alone.... Specifically, the Special Rapporteur recommends the sending to Iraq of a team of human rights monitors who would remain in Iraq until the human rights situation has drastically improved."[10]

All these efforts were important, both from the educational and from the political point of view. But they were not decisive. It was the organizational side of the Iraqi opposition that mattered most, and the focus of the ICFI work was, from April 1992 onwards, threefold, as was indicated in a press release dated 22 April:

> While supporting the principles of elections [in Iraqi Kurdistan], the ICFI stresses that these elections, which have been in great part the result of the ICFI's support for safe havens in the North of the country, must offer hope for a democratic way forward for all Iraqis. It welcomes in this context the idea of the formation of a joint delegation comprising the leadership of historic Iraq, Kurds and Arabs, Sunnis and Shi'is, as well as the other national and religious communities whose coexistence is the backbone of freedom

[10] Max van der Stoel, *Report on the Situation of Human Rights in Iraq, Prepared ... in Accordance with Commission Resolution* 1991/74, UN Doc. E/CN/1992/31 ("Conclusions").

in a future Iraq. This delegation will be visiting major capitals of the world in order to coordinate the international efforts towards fulfilling the democratic agenda in Baghdad. The visit, in conjunction with the success of a major Iraqi Congress in Vienna presently planned, will in the belief of the ICFI deliver the necessary institutional tools for the undermining of the system of fear imposed by dictatorship in Baghdad.

The way forward was outlined clearly in the conclusion of the statement: "Against the background of elections in liberated Iraq, the historic Iraq delegation and the Iraqi Congress will constitute landmarks for free elections and the protection of human rights in the country as a whole. The ICFI will help ensure the success of all three initiatives."[11]

Thus, the ICFI worked first to support the Kurdish elections in Northern Iraq. Many patrons were Kurds, including Jalal Talibani and the senior aides to Mas'ud Barzani, and the very step of conducting elections was a delicate one because of its consequences for the Arab opposition, which once more feared Kurdish separatist schemes. At the same time, the challenge to hold elections in the Iraqi safe haven was formidable, and it strengthened the ICFI's resolve to show the world how eager for democracy Iraqis were.

The largest "international" delegation of observers was sent by the ICFI, comprising seven members. The assistant of Richard Murphy, the influential former United States Assistant Secretary of State for the Middle East and himself an ICFI founding patron, also went to Kurdistan and helped on the American end to allay the pressure brought to bear by an administration that was also worried by the separatist bent on which the Kurdish elections could turn. Most remarkably, the ICFI delegation included the only Arab Iraqis who came to support the elections,[12] thus creating a vital bridge (however tenuous) between Arabs and Kurds on this delicate occasion.

---

[11] ICFI, "Statement of 22 April 1992," *Newsletter* 2, May 1992, 10.

[12] With the exception of Hani al-Fukaiki, who is not a patron of the ICFI. The other Arab Iraqis were Ahmed Chalabi, Saheb al-Hakim, and Ghanem Jawad.

The elections were remarkably successful.[13] Beyond the democratic message they conveyed, however, lay the more important tactical goal of oppositional unity. How would the elected leaders who emerged from the popular vote develop their contacts with the rest of the opposition? On the answer to this question depended the future of Iraq. In view of the dependence of the northern safe haven on Turkey and the mistrust of Turks towards the elections, the future of the zone was also dependent on the Turks being assured that the Kurds were not going it alone.

The enthusiasm and pleasure of the reception of the few Iraqi Arabs who came to support the elections undoubtedly offered some hope of future cooperation. At the same time, Kurdish nationalism was extremely vocal. If separatism was in the cards, nothing could stand in its way.

Too much confusion surrounded and continues to surround this issue. The collapse of the Soviet Union and of Yugoslavia offered an example of the exercise of self-determination in areas where it was out of the question a few years ago. At the same time, the experience of Yugoslavia, of Nagorno-Karabakh, of South Ossetia has proved extremely costly in terms of human lives, and has opened a Pandora's box of instability, which the countries neighboring Iraq and the Bush administration were determined to avoid.

In this maelstrom, the work of international committees does not weigh much, but in the view of the ICFI only the creation of a "democratic, nonsectarian form of government, preserving the unity of the country in its present frontiers but allowing full self-expression and effective representation to the different national identities that coexist within those frontiers," would prevent a descent into chaos. This was a vast program, considering the uncertainties. Much as elections in Kurdistan were important to show to the rest of Iraqis and to the world how feasible a decent electoral consultation could be, they needed to be, like safe havens, a temporary first step. This is why the joint Iraqi delegation and

---

[13] See Michael Meadowcroft and Martin Lunn, from the Electoral Reform Society, "Kurdistan: Monitoring Report," London, June 1992; International Human Rights Law Group, "Ballots without Borders," Washington, D.C., July 1992.

the Vienna conference were essential to a development towards further coordination and unity of oppositional Iraqis. The two other steps called for by the ICFI in April 1992 (a joint Iraqi delegation to visit Washington, an Iraqi oppositional congress planned in Vienna) had to be quickly completed.

The question was: Which had to come first, the Iraqi delegation or the Vienna Congress? The idea of the delegation had emerged on the occasion of a visit to the West by Mas'ud Barzani in February 1992. While in Ankara, he was appraised of a cable signed by the United States Secretary of State, in which it was pointed out that a delegation comprising Jalal Talibani and Sunni and Shi'i Iraqis would receive better attention in Washington than a solo visit of the Kurdish Democratic party leader. At the same time, the ICFI saw the possible visit to Washington as an occasion to propel a more "united" program of the opposition. At several meetings in London with Mas'ud Barzani, the proposed visit and the nature of the delegation were discussed by Barzani and the coordinators of the ICFI—Edward Mortimer, Ahmad Chalabi, and myself. The idea of a "historic Iraq delegation," that is, a delegation including two Arab Sunnis, two Arab Shi'is, and the two Kurdish leaders then took a more distinctive form, but it had to wait until the summer to materialize.

Meanwhile, many ICFI patrons were working on the success of the Vienna meeting. Pivotal to the Vienna meeting and to the ICFI was Ahmad Chalabi. His remarkable organizational talents, as well as an acute sense of historical opportunities, made such a difficult event possible. Much could be written about Vienna. But here was the best that could be achieved, considering the relentless opposition of the Arab and Iranian governments bordering Iraq, which are terrorized at the thought of a democratic Iraq emerging from the ruins of the Ba'th, and the haughty cynicism of the United States administration.

A delegation from Vienna visited Washington in July 1992, and the six-person "historic Iraq delegation" met with the Secretary of State. The three goals of the ICFI had been fulfilled, and four patrons of the ICFI were part of the team that met James Baker (Salah Shaykhli, Jalal Talibani, Laith Kubba, and Muhammad Bahr al-'Ulum). At the time of writing, much remains to be done, but the next discussions were clearly delineated as well by the

ICFI, in a short study circulated in advance of the meeting. The most significant passages are reproduced here:

The range of possible discussions with the Iraqi National Congress' [delegates to Washington] is wide, and must be based on clear parameters: first, no non-Iraqi blood should be spilled to liberate Iraq for Iraqis; two, mere well-wishing would be a disaster for an opposition that had to battle countless obscurantist Middle Eastern regimes in order to establish an independent and democratic agenda; three, the basis of the discussions must be the end of repression *now and after Saddam.*

Practical measures in support of the Iraqi peoples have already found their way to Security Council resolutions 706 and 712, which tie the proceeds of oil sale to effective international monitoring of the buying and distribution of medication and foodstuff to the peoples of Iraq, and to Resolution 688, which "insists that Iraq allow immediate access by the international humanitarian organization to all those in need of assistance in all parts of Iraq." These resolutions must be given teeth: as suggested by President Bush, there is no reason why their non-application by the regime should not see them implemented under Chapter 7 of the United Nations Charter.

An indictment of Saddam Hussein and his cronies is needed. The list of violations of international law is long. It runs the gamut from the time-honoured ugly device of naked aggression against a small neighbour, to "new" crimes against the environment. Revelations resulting from the liberation of Iraqi Kurdistan appear to make a clear case of ethnic genocide, especially in the Anfal operation of 1987–88. It is important that an indictment process gets under way. The concern for its difficult implementation should not stifle the efforts to give a legal formulation [to the international community's response to the unpunished crimes of Saddam Hussein]. As for the completion of the trial, it will depend, as for any vulgar criminal, on justice laying its hand on him. But the indictment process can be started immediately.

An exercise in delegitimization of the regime must develop in parallel to an increased recognition of Iraqis who are not associated with the regime. This can be achieved by a freezing of Iraqi ambassadors and representatives in a unanimous United Nations move. This is particularly important in the case of Barzan al-Takriti, the notorious half brother of Saddam, who is still Iraq's internationally accredited representative on the United Nations commission for human rights in Geneva. Such sanctions would clearly penalize the rulers of Iraq, as opposed to Iraqi citizens.

Meanwhile, the opposition cannot function without funding. Determined financial and military support to the democratically elected institutions of Iraqi Kurdistan and to the joint action of Arabs and Kurds within the wide-based INC [the Vienna Iraqi National Congress] in Kurdish Iraq is crucial for the effective undoing of the regime. Funding can either be offered directly through a specially established United Nations fund, or through the unfreezing of some of the Iraqi assets held abroad since August 1990. The legal consequences of this move may be complex, but claims of aggrieved governments and individuals can be accommodated in part on a realistic time-scale that will be a function of the rolling back and eventual replacement of the regime.

The opposition will be effective only if it has a firm foot in Iraq, which is now possible thanks to Operation Provide Comfort in Iraqi Kurdistan. This will require a lifeline, which Turkey gracefully provides but which must be reaffirmed. As for the plan to liberate Baghdad, this is of course not a subject for *public* discussions between the Iraqi National Congress representatives and the West. Some parameters can however be established. The most important is the necessity to operate the change with a minimum possible bloodletting. This means many efforts invested in devastated Iraqi soldiers, simultaneously on various fronts, to rally to the side of the Opposition. This is what effectively happened in Iraqi Kurdistan beneath the 36th parallel last October, when the large city of Suleymaniyya fell without a battle.

An immediate positive result of the meeting between the United States administration and the Iraqi opposition can take the form of Washington and its allies prohibiting Saddam Hussein from using Iraqi airspace for military purposes, and from continuing massive repression in the North and in the Southern marshes with sophisticated artillery and armor.

At the time of writing, the delegation had just met the United States Secretary of State and the head of the National Security Council. This visit is a fitting moment to end this chapter.

PART 4

The Shadow of Law

Public Confessions in
the Islamic Republic of Iran

ERVAND ABRAHAMIAN

The confession of the accused is a medieval principle of jurisprudence.
NIKOLAI BUKHARIN, at the Moscow Trials of 1938

My story will demonstrate to you how the slightest deflection from the line of the Party must inevitably end in counterrevolutionary banditry. The necessary result of our oppositional struggle was that we were pushed further and further into the morass. I will describe my fall, that it may be a warning to those who in this decisive hour still waver, and have hidden doubts.... Covered with shame, trampled in the dust, about to die, I will describe to you the sad progress of a traitor, that it may serve as a lesson and terrifying example to the millions of our country.
PRISONER RUBASHOV, in A. Koestler's *Darkness at Noon*

To be killed was what you expected. But before death there was the routine of confession that had to be gone through: the grovelling on the floor and screaming for mercy, the crack of broken bones, the smashed teeth, and bloody clots of hair.
GEORGE ORWELL, *Nineteen Eighty-Four*

Confessions as Theater

PUBLIC recantations in the form of open letters, press interviews, mea culpa memoirs, or, most common of all, pretrial confessions, became a staple of political life in Iran during the 1980s. A long array of political figures—monarchists, liberals, leftists, secular nationalists, and even former Khomeinists—were paraded before the mass media to repent their political sins, to thank the authorities for exposing them, to beseech others not to succumb to the same temptations, and to plead for appropriately dire punishments. Their confessions resemble those exacted by the Medieval Inquisition, by seventeenth-century European monarchs,

191

and, of course, by Stalinist prosecutors at the Moscow, Slansky, and other East European show trials.[1]

The aim of this chapter is to examine the confessions produced in Iran. I will argue that their chief function was to assert the power of the clerical state, underline the legitimacy of the ruling 'ulama and their ideology, and reaffirm the truth as seen by Imam Khomeini. The confessions, presented as entirely voluntary, were designed to give an aura of legitimacy to the new revolutionary institutions and to help transform clerical power into clerical authority. To that end, the confessions laced religious themes with a populist rhetoric, depicting the Islamic Republic as the fortress of the downtrodden masses in a hostile sea of ever-conspiring, antirevolutionary foreign enemies.

Besides providing positive publicity to the regime, the confessions were designed as negative propaganda against the opposition. They tried to demonstrate the opposition's political weaknesses, social isolation, foreign links, and even moral depravity— especially its "treacherous," "subversive," and "counterrevolutionary" activities. At times the target was a specific politician or organization. At other times it was a broad ideological movement or a social stratum—particularly the intelligentsia. Occasionally the target was dissenters within the clerical establishment.

In short, the recantations were part of an ongoing theater staged by the clerical authorities to display their own omnipotence and their opponents' impotence. The authorities entered the stage to underline the power of the clerical state. The victims were brought in to submit to that authority, and to participate in their own

---

[1] For confessions in medieval Europe, see E. Peters, *Torture* (New York, Blackwell, 1985). For early modern Europe, see P. Spierenburg, *The Spectacle of Suffering* (New York, Cambridge University Press, 1984); J. Sharpe, " 'Last Dying Speeches': Religion, Ideology and Public Executions in Seventeenth-Century England," *Past and Present* 107 (May 1985) 142–67; L. Smith, "English Treason Trials and Confessions in the Sixteenth Century," *Journal of Historical Ideas* 15 (1954) 471–98. For the Stalinist show trials, see A. Vaksberg, *Stalin's Prosecutor: The Life of Andre Vyshinsky* (New York, Grove Weidenfeld, 1990); G. Hodos, *Stalinist Purges in Eastern Europe, 1948–1954* (New York, Praeger, 1987); J. Kaplan, *Report on the Murder of the General Secretary* (London, Tauris, 1991); T. Judt, "Justice as Theatre," *Times Literary Supplement*, 18 January 1991.

political, ideological, and sometimes physical destruction. Some were executed, some imprisoned, and some given amnesties. But almost all the prominent recanters had their confessions aired extensively by the mass media—more so than in any other regime.

A number of factors explain why the Islamic Republic has outdone preceding regimes in this form of public theater. First, the age of television has provided the regime with a much larger audience. Stalin, by contrast, had to rely on the printed word and, at most, the radio. The Iranian regime relies not only on newspapers, pamphlets, and radio, but also on television in millions of homes.

Second, the video cassette has allowed the regime to control fully both the timing and the exact content of the show. Stalin, having invited foreign observers into the Moscow Trials, could not fully determine what was reported. The Iranian regime, however, has been able to decide exactly what is aired and when. Ayatollah Khomeini himself previewed some videos to determine what should be edited out.[2] Third, in a society that attaches importance to personal honor, shame, and martyrdom, these public recantations can utterly devastate the victim's reputation (*aberu*)—they are tantamount to political suicide. Finally, the Iranian public, including much of the educated public, was—until the late 1980s—surprisingly innocent about the means used to obtain such recantations. Unlike its Western counterpart, it had not yet been exposed to such potent works as Arthur Koestler's *Darkness at Noon*, George Orwell's *Nineteen Eighty-Four*, Berthold Brecht's *Life of Galileo*, and Victor Serge's *L'affaire Toulaev*.[3] In fact, the

---

[2] Intelligence Minister, "Announcing the Arrest of Sayyid Mehdi Hashemi ... ," *Kayhan-e Hava'i*, 24 December 1986.

[3] At the Moscow Trials, a surprising number of Western observers were fooled into accepting the public recantations at face value. Why else, argued the American ambassador, would prominent Bolsheviks, many of whom had endured years in prison, get up freely to confess unless they were guilty? But by the Slansky Trials of the early 1950s, few Western observers were taken in, having been exposed to the works of Koestler, Orwell, and Brecht. Victor Serge was not a household name in Europe, but his works were extremely influential on Orwell and Koestler. A leading Comintern organizer, Serge was imprisoned by Stalin from 1933 to 1936 and would have met the same fate as his Bolshevik colleagues if it had not been for the last-minute intervention of former literary friends in Paris. Orwell, who helped publish his works, was

means used by the Islamic Republic have been strikingly similar to those of Stalin and the Medieval Inquisition.

Preparations

The Islamic Republic often imprisoned its opponents with one major aim in mind—to obtain a public recantation. The usual procedure was for the prison wardens to place new arrivals into solitary cells, to provide them with pen and paper, and to demand a full confession about themselves and their colleagues, including their political beliefs. If the demand was not met, the wardens proceeded to exert various forms of physical and psychological pressures. The physical ones included beatings, whippings, cigarette burnings, electrical shocks, crushing of fingers, incarceration in small cubicles, sleep deprivation, and prolonged blindfolding sometimes lasting months. Psychological pressures involved extensive solitary confinement, mock executions, viewing of real executions, participation in the removal of bodies from mass executions, claims of betrayal by colleagues, as well as detention of and threats against family members. In return for full cooperation, jail wardens held out the possibility of leniency, even of amnesty and future exoneration.[4]

---

deeply influenced by his revelations about Soviet prisons, especially by his essays (collected in *From Lenin to Stalin* [1937]). For Brecht and the Moscow Trials, see I. Deutscher, *The Prophet Outcast* (New York, Vintage Books, 1963) 370.

[4] For prison conditions see Amnesty International, *Human Rights Violations in Iran* (London, Amnesty, 1982); idem, *Evidence of Torture in Iran* (New York, Amnesty, 1984); idem, *Iran: Violations of Human Rights, 1987–1990* (New York, Amnesty 1990); idem, *Iran* (London, Amnesty, 1987); Human Rights Watch, *World Report: 1990* (New York, Human Rights Watch, 1991); United Nations Economic and Social Council, *Situation of Human Rights in the Islamic Republic of Iran* (New York, United Nations, February 1990); idem, *Situation of Human Rights in the Islamic Republic of Iran* (New York, United Nations, February 1990); idem, *Situation of Human Rights in the Islamic Republic of Iran* (New York, United Nations, November 1990). For reliable Iranian sources see: Anonymous, *Evin's Gate* (unpublished manuscript written in 1986 by a former prisoner who was released after signing an affidavit that she was mentally unstable); Anonymous, *Bazandeh* (The loser) (Umea, Sweden 1984); Anonymous, *Az Arman-e keh Mejushad* (From the desire that burns) (Umea, Sweden 1984).

The prisoners faced a deadly dilemma. To avoid torture, they could make the required confession. But a confession—even to the vague charge of "ideological deviation"—could very well seal their fate. The regime considered verbal and public confession to be adequate proof of guilt. And it judged ideological deviation to be tantamount to "sowing corruption on earth"—a capital offense according to its interpretation of the Shari'a. Besides, a public confession inevitably resulted in complete "loss of face"—in short, in political suicide.

The regime's attitude towards confessions, especially coerced ones, was problematic. On one hand, Islamic law had a long tradition of frowning upon forced recantations. Had not the Prophet himself been outraged when the pagans of Mecca tortured his companion Bilal into renouncing Allah? According to the early Muslims, Bilal would have accepted anything as the true God, even a beetle, to stop the unbearable torment.[5] Had not the Prophet declared, "God shall torture on the Day of Judgement those who inflict torture on people in life"?[6] Had not the early Caliphs ruled out the use of forced confessions on the grounds that force, starvation, and fear could lead the innocent to incriminate themselves?[7] The constitution of the Islamic Republic itself explicitly prohibited not only "physical torture," but also the presentation in court of evidence obtained "through the use of force."[8] What is more, the Shari'a had placed strict rules on the types of evidence acceptable in religious courts—especially for capital offenses.[9] More than one witness was required. The evidence had to be presented

---

[5] The story of Bilal's forced recantation is recounted by M. Rodinson, *Mohammed* (London, Allen, 1971) 100–11.

[6] M. Bassiouni, ed., *The Islamic Criminal Justice System* (New York, Oceana Publications, 1982) 70.

[7] Ibid., 72.

[8] "The Complete Text of the Iranian Constitution," *Iran Times*, 30 November 1979.

[9] For rules of evidence in Shari'a courts, see J. Schacht, *An Introduction to Islamic Law* (Oxford, Clarendon Press, 1964) 177, 197; N. Coulson, *History of Islamic Law* (Edinburgh, Edinburgh University, 1964) 124–27; and O. Abd-el-Malek al-Saleh, "The Right of the Individual to Personal Security in Islam," in *The Islamic Criminal Justice System*, ed. M. Bassiouni (New York, Oceana Publications, 1982) 55–90.

orally. Circumstantial evidence was inadequate. The defendants had to be given the opportunity to withdraw any pretrial confessions they had made. And witnesses were required to possess the "highest moral and ethical qualities"—something presumably self-confessed "traitors," "terrorists," and "sowers of corruption" could not possess.

On the other hand, judicial precedent throughout the Middle East had been less meticulous. State courts had accepted circumstantial evidence, testimony from dubious sources, and self-incriminating testimonials. Islamic rulers, including Shi'a ones, had at times retorted to inquisitions known as *mihnas*.[10] The Shari'a itself left gaping loopholes. It encouraged *tawba* (repentance). It permitted clerical judges to inflict corporal punishments—especially floggings. It also permitted judges to mete out *ta'zir* (discriminatory punishments) both as "chastisement" and as "deterrence" for sundry types of activities that could feasibly "threaten Islam."[11] In the words of a contemporary jurist, qualified judges have the right to inflict "discriminatory punishments" on those who endanger the public interest or the social order of Islam.[12]

The Islamic Republic followed more lax precedents and interpretations. It functioned on the premise that the accused were guilty, and, therefore, the judicial authorities had the responsibility to expose their guilt. It viewed confession (*e'teraf*) as an acceptable sign of repentance (*tawba*). It defined physical punishment, especially floggings, not as torture but as lawful *ta'zir*. One leading judge argued that clerical magistrates could inflict floggings so long as they set guidelines on the amount of force to be used.[13] What is more, the Islamic Republic felt that these forms of friendly persuasion were legitimate when used to "reintegrate" deviants

[10] For an example of such inquisitions, see I. Lapidus, "The Separation of State and Religion in the Development of Early Islamic History," *International Journal of Middle East History* 6 (1975) 363–85.

[11] Schacht, *An Introduction to Islamic Law*, 207.

[12] M. Salama, "General Principles of Evidence in Islamic Jurisprudence," in *The Islamic Criminal Justice System*, 109–23.

[13] Mohammad Yazdi writing in *Ressalat* (11 August 1986) and quoted in *Iran Liberation*, 27 August 1986.

back into society. Assadollah Ladjevardi, the hanging judge at the notorious Evin Prison, told foreign visitors that the revolutionary regime had converted jails into rehabilitation centers where inmates could see their errors, make appropriate confessions, study Islam, and do penance before being reintegrated into society. He even went as far as to boast that the Islamic Republic was the first state in the world to "transform prisons into universities."[14] Little did he realize that Vyshinsky, Stalin's chief prosecutor, had on the eve of the Moscow Trials published with much fanfare a book entitled *From Prisons to Educational Institutions.*

No doubt, some in Iran, like Brecht's Galileo, recanted at the mere sight of the torture instruments. But others endured torture until they died—each political group has a long list of martyrs killed under torture. Still others were secretly executed once it became clear they would not take on the roles cast for them. In some cases the wardens told relatives that they had been executed because prison had failed to bring about their full repentance and rehabilitation.[15] But many—according to Ladjevardi, 95 percent of the prisoners—agreed to make videotaped confessions.[16] The tapes actually aired on television tended to be those of prominent prisoners. Only such stars could give the show an air of grand theater.

Once the victim agreed to recant, the investigators drafted a sketchy outline with an introduction and conclusion, but left the main text to the individual. This produced an aura of authenticity; the speakers could address their audience with their own particular imagery, vocabulary, and rationale. The introduction included salutations to Khomeini, invariably hailing him as *Rahbar-e Mostazafin* (Leader of the Oppressed), *Rahbar-e Kabir-e Inqelab-e Islami* (Great Leader of the Islamic Revolution), and *Bonyadgozar-e Jomhuri-ye Islami* (Founder of the Islamic Republic). It also contained a biographical sketch, stressing the author's importance within their organization. The conclusion

[14] "Prison Repentancies: Real or Phoney?" Reprinted from the *Manchester Guardian* in *Iran Times*, 30 December 1983.
[15] Amnesty International, *Iran: Violations of Human Rights, 1987–1990*, 14, 16.
[16] *Iran Times*, 11 February 1982.

apologized to the Imam, the *mostazafin* (oppressed), and the "martyr-producing people of Iran." It also insisted that the recantation was completely voluntary and done entirely to educate fellow citizens about the pitfalls of straying from the *Khatt-e Imam* (Imam's Line).[17]

A rare insider's glimpse of the whole investigatory process can be found in the memoirs of Hojjat al-Islam Rayshahri, the Minister of Intelligence from 1985 to 1987.[18] Although the relevant passages are intentionally abstruse—obviously to avoid the subject of torture—the reader can easily read between the lines. He writes that the hardest case he had to crack was that of Sayyid Mehdi Hashemi, the protégé of Ayatollah Montazeri, who at that time was Khomeini's designated successor. Rayshahri adds that the ordinary interrogators were afraid to do their job properly since the criminal had friends in high places. "The month-long investigation," he declared, "had come to a dead end." All they had obtained was a taped interview into which this "wise guy" had cleverly planted his "deviant" views.

Rayshahri claims he obtained a more complete confession—including that of murder, kidnapping, betraying Islam, and plotting against the Islamic Republic—after this brief verbal exchange:

> I said, "Are you not afraid of God?"
> He said, "Yes."
> I said, "God knows the type of person you are and what you have done. You yourself know. Why don't you tell us everything?"
> He said, "I already have."
> I said, "Have you told us everything?"
> He said, "No."
> I said, "All right, tell us everything."
> He said, "Fine. I will tell everything."

---

[17] The term *khatt-e* (line) has a Stalinist genealogy. Religious militants had borrowed it in the 1970s from the Confederation of Iranian Students. The confederation had taken it in the 1960s from the Chinese Cultural Revolution. Mao, of course, had borrowed it from Stalin's Russia. The Party Line had become the Imam's Line.

[18] M. Rayshahri, *Khaterat-e siyasi* (Political memoires) (Tehran, Motala'at Foundation, 1990) 43–95.

The text, however, can also provide a more believable story. Before beginning his own investigation, Rayshahri consulted the Imam and the Koran. The former told him to treat the prisoner as he would any ordinary citizen or grocer. The Koran, presumably opened at random, inspired him to use the utmost vigilance to achieve his purpose. Had not God said that He would forgive the sins of those who bought victory to His cause (29.7; 48.1–2)? These could be interpreted to mean that the Almighty's end justifies the means.[19]

After interviewing Hashemi, Rayshahri instructed his "brother investigators" to question him thoroughly. Meanwhile, the authorities obtained confessions from forty of his associates, including his brother, Montazeri's brother-in-law. Cornered, Hashemi agreed to appear before the cameras confessing to a long list of crimes. For some reason, this was not deemed fully satisfactory, so the judge responsible for the case prescribed eighty lashes. This completed the job. In this second tape, he ended the confession with tears in his eyes seeking forgiveness from the Imam. When Khomeini saw the final tape, he said, "Don't be fooled. He lies. His gestures [of repentance] are false." Brought before a special clerical court, Hashemi was found guilty of "sowing corruption on earth" and was promptly hanged. In announcing the trial, Rayshahri declared that the confession was yet another proof of the Imam's great foresight, for years earlier he had warned others that Hashemi harbored "deviant thoughts" (*fekraha-ye enheraf*).[20] The regime added that Hashemi had made a true confession since he had been eager to meet God fully cleansed of all his sins.[21] The Spanish Inquisition could not have staged a better spectacle.

---

[19] Chapter 29, verse 7 declares: "And (as for) those who believe and do good, We will most certainly do away with their evil deeds and We will most certainly reward them the best of what they did." Chapter 48, verses 1–2 state: "Surely We have given to you a clear victory. That Allah may forgive your community their past faults and those to follow and complete His favor to you and keep you on a right path." See *The Holy Qur'an* (Elmhurst, Tarikhe Tarsile Qur'an, 1982).

[20] Intelligence Minister, "Announcing the Arrest of Mehdi Hashemi ... ," *Kayhan-e Hava'i*, 24 December 1987.

[21] Anonymous, *Ranjnameh-e Hazrat Hojjat al-Islam va al-Muslamin Aga-ye Hajj Sayyid Ahmad Khomeini beh Hazrat Ayatallah Montazeri* (The pained

Precedents

Public confessions were not entirely unprecedented in Iran. The Pahlavi regime had discovered their usefulness in the early 1970s—at a time when it became more aware of the importance of winning over "hearts and minds." But, on the whole, these early recantations had been short, infrequent, restricted to the Left, and, preceding the video age, somewhat risky. In one famous and embarrassing case, Khosrow Golsorkhi, an intellectual accused of plotting to kidnap the royal family, tricked the secret police into giving him a live television appearance. But instead of the expected confession, he denounced the government and forthrightly expounded his Marxist beliefs. His courage and the subsequent execution brought him widespread admiration—even from those who did not share his political sentiments. So much so that for the next few years, the censors did not allow poets to compose odes to *gols* (flowers) on the suspicion the word would be an allusion to Golsorkhi.

Between 1970 and 1977, eight former leaders of the left-wing Confederation of Iranian Students gave three separate "press conferences" in which they "shared" with their listeners how their views had changed once they had returned home after years of study abroad.[22] They said that the country had been abysmally backward when they had first departed for Europe. But, on their return, they had been surprised to discover that the Shah's White Revolution had thoroughly transformed society. It had, they waxed eloquent, implemented land reform, eliminated feudal overlords, built roads, bridges, and dams, set up medical clinics and rural cooperatives, electrified the countryside, launched a literacy campaign, industrialized the economy, nationalized the oil industry, and made Iran truly independent of all foreign powers.

letters of His Excellency Hojjat al-Islam and al-Muslim Mr. Hajj Sayyid Ahmad Khomeini to His Excellency Ayatollah Montazeri) (n.p., n.d) 52.
[22] "Interview with Five Former Members of the Revolutionary Organization of the Tudeh Party," *Ettela'at*, 11 August 1970; "Message from a Confederation Leader to its Members," *Kayhan-e Hava'i*, 30 December 1972; Anonymous, *Mosahebeh* (Press conference) (n.p. n.d.); Anonymous, *Matne-e Mosahebeh-e Bahram Malayi Daryani* (The text of Bahram Malayi Daryani's press conference) (n.p, n.d).

In short, the White Revolution was accomplishing everything they had strived for—"social, economic, and political justice."

They advised students abroad not to be misled by subversive groups, like the Tudeh and the National Front, that kept their members ignorant, retained an outdated image of Iran, and denied the accomplishments of the White Revolution. Some accused the opposition leaders of being "bureaucratic," "self-seeking," "opportunistic," and "servants of foreign powers." One claimed that the National Front in America was heavily infiltrated with FBI and CIA agents. Why else, he asked rhetorically, would the Americans permit the confederation to demonstrate against the Shah? They concluded the interviews by confessing that they had returned to Iran with the intention of overthrowing the regime—even launching a guerrilla war—but now that they had seen reality with their own eyes, they wanted to partake in the Great Shah's and People's White Revolution. One stressed that he retained the same *dīn* (faith) he had always lived with—the faith of serving the masses. Another argued that as an intellectual he had been "divorced" from reality, but now he wanted to study the masses and learn how to become a full member of the community. "Iran," he declared, "was neither China nor Cuba, for it had its own particular customs, traditions, religion, history, and popular culture."

"Interviews" with two prominent literary figures, Reza Barahani and Ghulam-Hosayn Sa'edi, caused somewhat more stir. Barahani, in a televised interview, enumerated the failings of Marxism, criticized those who mimicked the West, denounced all forms of terrorism, and stressed that Marxism and Islam were incompatible—this was directed at the Mojahedin guerrillas who combined religious fervor with a radical analysis of society and history.[23] After this performance, Barahani traveled to North America, where his speaking engagements were constantly disrupted by students who accused him of "collaborating with the regime." Sa'edi, in what was billed as a newspaper "chitchat," criticized Marxists in exile for "exploiting" his works, serving as

---

[23] J. Lordman, "The Iranian Solzhenitzyn" (unpublished paper on Reza Barahani).

"tools of foreign powers," completely misunderstanding the country's religious culture, and refusing to recognize the Shah's historic accomplishments.[24] He conceded that his works were negative and obsessed with social problems, but argued that they had all been written before the recent White Revolution. He ended the interview by promising to make his future works more positive and respectful of the achievements of the White Revolution, especially the "nationalization of the forests."[25] Friends believe that this whole experience drove Sa'edi into alcoholism and eventually into an early grave.

These interviews and press conferences left much unsaid—particularly that the recanters had spent the previous months in prison; that some of their relatives had also been incarcerated; that they had been tortured—even shot in the head with blanks; that they had been promised a royal amnesty; and that the final statements were the result of a prolonged bargaining process, albeit an uneven one, between the torturers eager to extract as full a submission as possible and the tortured anxious to salvage as much of their personal honor and political integrity as possible.

Most opposition groups failed to recognize the potential dangers of such recantations. Some ignored them completely. Others denounced the victims for "selling out" to the regime. Not a single opposition newspaper discussed how these public confessions had been obtained. Even the victims, once freed, shied away from linking their release to their recantations. To have done so would have been seen as admitting moral and physical weakness. Meanwhile, Khomeini's disciples in Najaf were struck by the ability of the Iraqi Ba'thists to extract "outrageous" television confessions from leading opposition figures—even from the "relatives of the

----

[24] "Chitchat with Dr. Ghulam-Reza Sa'edi," *Kayhan*, 19 June 1975.

[25] The regime also arrested Ali Shariati, the famous radical religious intellectual, and tried to get him to make a similar television appearance. But failing to do so, it released him and published in *Kayhan* an article he had written years earlier denouncing Marxism from a Muslim standpoint. The regime created the impression that Shariati had been released in exchange for writing these denunciations. To save his reputation, Shariati spent weeks visiting his acquaintances and explaining that this article had been published without his permission.

highest-ranking Shi'a ulama."[26] No one, however, discussed the legality or illegality of such public confessions in Islam.

The Mojahedin

The Islamic Republic began to televise confessions in a concerted fashion after June 1981, when the religious but anticlerical Mojahedin tried to overthrow Khomeini. The regime used the abortive uprising as an opportunity to crack down not only on the Mojahedin, but also on much of the secular Left. The first to appear before the cameras were members of the Mojahedin and smaller Marxist groups, including many that had opposed the attempted uprising. The cast was drastically expanded in 1983 when the Tudeh (Communist party) started to criticize the government for continuing the war into Iraqi territory. Moreover, throughout the decade the Islamic Republic periodically extracted public confessions from its former supporters who, for one reason or another, had fallen by the wayside. This revolution, like many others, devoured its own children.

With the Mojahedin confessions, the Islamic Republic had to rely mainly on a minor cast of characters, since most of the top leaders had either been killed in shoot-outs or else managed to escape into exile. For example, in the midst of the 1981 crackdown, Mrs. Rajavi—the elderly apolitical mother of the organization's leader—told reporters that she wished her son would return from exile and fall at the Imam's feet to seek his forgiveness.[27] All parents, she added, must cooperate with the authorities to prevent their sons and daughters from being led astray by "foreign plotters."

The Mojahedin who appeared before the cameras tended to repeat the government's main accusations against themselves— that they were "terrorists" who assassinated innocent citizens; "fifth columnists" (sotun-e panjom) working for the foreign enemy, particularly Iraq and the United States; ideological "eclectics" (elteqati) who contaminated Islam with alien ideas, especially

[26] H. Ruhani, Nahzat-e Imam Khomeini (Imam Khomeini's movement), vol. 2 (Tehran, Imam's Way Press, 1984) 415–16.
[27] "Interview with the Mother of Masoud Rajavi," Ettela'at, 26 November 1981.

Marxism; and, most serious of all, "hypocrites" (*monafeqin*) who used religion to cover their true intentions. In fact, in 1987 the regime eased the prison overcrowding problem by executing inmates who persisted in using the term Mojahedin instead of monafeqin—it is reported that this purge eliminated over three hundred prisoners.

The Mojahedin opened their confessions with the conventional "In the Name of God the Merciful, the Compassionate" rather than their organization's "In the Name of God, In the Name of the Heroic People of Iran."[28] They saluted the "martyrs of the Islamic Revolution" as well as Imam Khomeini, "the leader of the Islamic Revolution in Iran." They continued with an autobiographical sketch, and a list of their personal crimes—arson, arms storage, muggings, bombings, and assassinations. They went on to accuse their leaders of sacrificing innocent lives, collaborating with "liberals" (*libralha*) such as Bani-Sadr and Bazargan, and serving the interests of America, France, Iraq, and the Soviet Union. Some accused Rajavi of creating an "American Islam." Others claimed that their former colleagues came mostly from privileged homes and did not perform the obligatory Muslim rituals—such as fasting during Ramadan. They invariably ended by calling on their former colleagues to repent and turn themselves in. They also thanked the revolutionary guards for their "brotherly" conduct and for teaching them about true Islam. One doomed Mojahed wrote in his final testament that responsibility for his death lay on America and its "despicable stooge" Rajavi.[29] Those who went overboard in their recantations do not appear in the Mojahedin book of dead heroes entitled *The Eternal Martyrs of Freedom*.[30]

---

[28] For a long series of Mojahedin confessions, see *Ettela'at*, September 1981–November 1981. See also *Kayhan-e Hava'i*, 18–25 June 1986, 5–19 October 1987, 4 June 1987, 28 September–12 October 1988, and 23 October 1991.
[29] "The Final Testament of Ahmad Janefshan-Vazifeh," *Ettela'at*, 29 September 1981.
[30] Mojahedin Organization, *Shaheda-ye javedan-e azadi, parchmdaran-e inqelab-e novin-e khalq-e qahraman-e Iran: Asme-e va moshkhasat-e bakhsh-e (12,028) az shaheda-ye inqelab-e novin-e Iran* (The eternal martyrs of freedom, the flagbearers of the new revolution of the heroic people of Iran: A partial list of 12,028 martyrs of the new Iranian revolution), Special Issue of *Mojahed*, 261 (6 September 1985) 1–182.

In 1983 Evin Prison convened some thirty former Mojahedin for a series of "roundtable discussions" (*mizgard*), which were televised, printed in the daily press, and quickly reprinted in a five-volume book entitled *Karnemeh-e siyah* (Black report card).[31] The avowed purpose was to answer some 450 questions submitted by the public. The group included one minor and eight women—including Rajavi's youngest sister. The program host was the organization's former link between the central committee and Khurasan province—obviously he was the highest-ranking Mojahed the regime could produce. Gathered in the prison's assembly room, now called a "religious lecture hall," the participants sat behind two tables—one for the men, the other for the women. A large crowd of inmates sat on the floor in front of them, chanting at the appropriate times. The recanters looked healthy, but repentant, sincere, and thoughtful. Hovering over them were a thirty-foot mural of Khomeini, photographs of clerics assassinated by the Mojahedin, and a large Koranic inscription pronouncing the monafeqin to be more dangerous than infidels.

Since these recanters were mostly rank-and-file members, their confessions focused on terrorism, not on ideology. They claimed that in the 1981 uprising their organization had shot innocent bystanders, bombed ambulances, and placed children, especially young girls, at the forefront of violent demonstrations. Some confessed to participating in horrendous crimes—bombing city buses, shooting into Friday prayer meetings, burning down stores merely for displaying the Imam's picture, stealing medical supplies needed badly at the Iraqi war front, assassinating bearded citizens who looked like true believers, machine-gunning anti-Mojahedin demonstrators, and kidnapping, torturing, and killing the families, even the children, of revolutionary guards.

One member of the trade union section argued that the Mojahedin had been an organization of *rawshanfekran* (intellectuals), not of *mostazafin* (masses) and *zahmatkeshan* (toilers). He also argued that the trade union branches had had no more than a

---

[31] Justice Ministry, *Karnameh-e Siyah* (Tehran, Justice Ministry Press, 1983). These "roundtable discussions" were originally published in *Ettela'at*, 31 August–4 September 1983. They were also reprinted in *Kayhan-e Hava'i*, 7 September–7 December 1983.

handful of factory workers, and that ordinary wage earners rejected rabble-rousing demands because they were willing to make economic sacrifices for the Islamic Revolution. The same recanter argued that the Mojahedin had carried out a number of damaging strikes by working through Marxists and well-off factory managers. Another thanked the revolutionary guards for having saved him from a lynch mob. The program host insisted that all his guests were there not because of pressure or fear of execution, but because they wanted to sever their links with the monafeqin and make amends to the Islamic Republic. "The monafeqin," he concluded, "are against Islam and against the people."

The regime produced its first, and so far sole, high-ranking Mojahed in 1989—after the Mojahedin had made an unsuccessful military incursion into western Iran from their base in Iraq. The captured leader was Sa'ed Shahsavandi, the director of the organization's radio station. A veteran of the movement, he had been sentenced to life imprisonment in 1974, and had run for a majles seat in the 1980 parliamentary elections. The Mojahedin tried to contain the damage of his capture by insisting that he was a mere rank-and-file member.

Shahsavandi expounded on the Mojahedin's "hypocritical nature" in a series of open letters, television interviews, and lectures given at the Industrial University in Tehran.[32] He declared that from the very beginning there had been major discrepancies between what the organization espoused and what it actually did and believed in. He claimed that his former colleagues had paid lip service to Islam, but had been more interested in Lenin, Che Guevara, Ho Chi Minh, and Mao Tse-Tung. They had talked about "true Islam," but in actual fact showed absolutely no interest in what thousands of religious scholars had written over the centuries. They had disliked the title Imam Khomeini, but nevertheless had used it to keep pace with the public. They had initially paid allegiance to the Islamic Republic, but in the

---

[32] "Television Interview with Sa'ed Shahsavandi," *Kayhan-e Hava'i*, 1 February–18 April 1989; "Sa'ed Shahsavandi's Lecture at the Industrial University," *Kayhan-e Hava'i*, 17 May 1989; "Shahsavandi's Letter to 'Le Monde,'" *Kayhan-e Hava'i*, 22 February 1989; "Shahsavandi's Open Letter to Rajavi," *Kayhan-e Hava'i*, 29 August 1990.

meantime had made military preparations to overthrow it. They waved the Iranian flag, but quietly consorted with King Hussein, American senators, and the CIA. They talked much about the virtues of democracy, but functioned as the paid agents of the Iraqi fascists and the "thief of Baghdad."

Shahsavandi also claimed that the Mojahedin no longer existed within Iran, that many of the casualties in the ill-fated attack had been untrained youngsters rushed into battle from Paris, London, and New York, and that the exiled organization was riddled with factionalism, disillusionment, suicides, and desertions. He made no attempt to explain why, in light of these problems, the regime could not produce a single voluntary recantation from a prominent defector.

Former Regime Members

Over the years there have been a number of astounding confessions from figures previously prominent within the Islamic Republic. For example, in 1983 Taher Ahmadzadeh, a well-known prisoner under the Shah and the governor of Khurasan immediately after the revolution, made an hour-long recantation from Evin Prison. The speech, which was televised, sought forgiveness for helping imperialism, betraying Islam and Iran, and allying himself with the Mojahedin in an opportunistic gamble to gain power for himself.[33] He concluded with a salutation to "our dear Imam and other leaders who struggle to liberate the world mostazafin."

His friend Abdulkarim Lahiji, then a human rights lawyer in Paris, wrote that only undescribable forms of torture could have produced this outlandish statement, since Ahmadzadeh had been considered for ten years "the symbol of resistance within the shah's prisons."[34] Comparing the speech to the Moscow show trials, Lahiji argued that the regime was threatening to execute children in order to extract public recantations from their parents. This was one of the very few articles to appear in Persian discussing the whole issue of public confessions.

---

[33] "The Text of Taher Ahmazadeh's Confession," *Kayhan-e Hava'i*, 14 December 1983.

[34] K. Lahiji, "Public Confessions," *Iranshahr*, 9 September 1983.

A similar confession was made in 1990 by Farhad Behbehani, a member of Bazargan's Liberation Movement. He admitted on television that a recently formed human rights group had been in touch with a certain Iranian woman in America, who, in turn, had been in touch with the Persian-language section of Voice of America.[35] "This," he added, "is proof enough that we are linked to the West." He described his colleagues as secular "liberals" eager to sabotage the Islamic Revolution, as scions of the "privileged class" with no understanding of the mostazafin, as enemies of the new order using the cover of human rights to rally royalists and other counterrevolutionaries, and as *rawshanfekran-e gharbzadeh* (intellectuals contaminated with the Western plague) who took their political cues from Washington. "We are," he concluded, "a fifth column within Iran." Following this television show, the judge, who presided over a closed court, congratulated the authorities for having obtained this "successful confession." He sentenced eight members of the group to prison terms varying from six months to three years. Behbehani himself was released.[36]

The most astounding of this type of confession, however, came from Sadeq Qotbzadeh and Mehdi Hashemi. Qotbzadeh had been Khomeini's main English-language spokesman in Paris. After the revolutions, he headed the National Radio and Television Network and for a brief period served as foreign minister. Hashemi, Rayshahri's chief protagonist, was a well-known figure in Montazeri's entourage. In fact, in 1976 he had been sentenced to death for masterminding the assassination of a conservative cleric who had publicly insulted Montazeri and made fun of the new notion that Shi'ism was a religion of popular revolution.

Qotbzadeh, in his pretrial television interview, confessed that he had plotted with disgruntled army officers to overthrow the regime and blow up Khomeini.[37] He also implicated Grand Ayatollah Shariatmadari, one of the most senior clerics in Qom and the chief

---

[35] "The Confession of Farhad Behbehani Concerning the Links with America of the So-Called Society of Freedom," *Kayhan-e Hava'i*, 15 August 1990.

[36] Middle East Watch, Press Release on Iran, 3 September 1991.

[37] "The Text of Sadeq Qotbzadeh's Shocking Confession," *Ettela'at*, 20 April 1982.

hope of the liberal opposition. Shariatmadari was probably the main target of the whole show. The chief prosecutor provided the press with a an elaborate chart linking Qotbzadeh to the CIA via a little-known socialist society in exile and to an Argentina-born businessman in Paris.[38]

At the "open trial" in a special military court, Qotbzadeh modified his previous confession. He insisted that his friends had intended to change the government, not overthrow the regime, and to apprehend the Imam, not kill him.[39] His main codefendant, Shariatmadari's son-in-law, confessed to having links with the Saudis and passing on funds to the plotters. Another defendant claimed to have collected money for the coup from unnamed capitalists in West Germany.[40] The judge, in his summing up, declared that the accused deserved no pity since they had plotted against the revolution, against humanity, and against Islam. Qotbzadeh's supporters claim that he was executed after refusing Khomeini's offer of clemency if he groveled publicly for forgiveness.[41]

Meanwhile, Shariatmadari made his own television appearance—probably as a deal to save his son-in-law. The regime billed this as an *e'teraf* (confession). On prime time, Shariatmadari apologized to God for not informing the authorities about the plot as soon as he had heard about it. He explained he had not taken the "childish harebrained" scheme seriously. Besides, he added, he presumed the authorities knew all about it.[42] He promised never again to make such a horrendous mistake. He also beseeched "Grand Ayatollah Imam Khomeini" to intercede to halt the media campaign against him. Shariatmadari's son, living in Europe, declared the so-called confession to be absolutely meaningless on the grounds that the Shari'a regarded coerced confessions as null and void.[43] Liberal clerics would have agreed with him. But *Ettela'at*, the main daily, asked rhetorically

---

[38] Chief Prosecutor, "The Plotters Exposed," *Ettela'at*, 20 April 1982.

[39] *Ettela'at*, 23 August 1982.

[40] "Trial of Qotbzadeh and his Four Co-Defendants," *Ettela'at*, 28 August 1982.

[41] C. Jerome, *The Man in the Mirror* (Toronto, Unwin Hyman, 1987) 289.

[42] "Shariatmadari's Confession," *Ettela'at*, 3 May 1982.

[43] *Iranshahr*, 5 May 1982.

"what better proof of a plot than confessions from the mouths
of the plotters themselves?"[44]   Hojjat al-Islam Rafsanjani, at
that time the imam jom'eh (Friday prayer leader) of Tehran, declared that anyone who had "confessed" to being privy to such a
heinous plot had no right to remain a *maraj'-e taqlid* (high-ranking
cleric).[45]

To further undermine Shariatmadari, the regime released a
photo of him in the presence of the Shah—the photo had been
taken in 1946. It gathered crowds outside his home shouting
"Death to Shariatmadari—the Traitor and American Hireling." It
insinuated that revolutionary guards had found in his house roy-
alist speeches, love songs, and pornographic pictures. It claimed
secret documents proved that he had collaborated with the American embassy as well as with SAVAK, that palace influence had
elevated him to the rank of Grand Ayatollah, and that he had
tried to derail the Islamic Revolution by talking about the need
to return to the 1906 constitution.

Meanwhile, a group of local imam jom'ehs issued a broadsheet
against Shariatmadari. It began with a quote from the Prophet
denouncing "corrupt clerics to be the worst of all people," and
argued that Shariatmadari fitted this bill on account of his subversive activities—opposing the principles of the *velayat-e faqih*
(jurist's trusteeship), sowing dissension in the seminaries, and encouraging the liberals against the Islamic Republic.[46] What is
more, clerics at the apex of the regime declared that "Mr. Shariatmadari" had ceased to be a *maraj'-e taqlid*, and, therefore, could
no longer collect religious dues and hold the title of ayatollah.[47] In
effect, they defrocked him—an act extremely rare in Shi'i history.
Shariatmadari then became a nonperson, confined to his home
until his death in 1986. The chief prosecutor even claimed that
Shariatmadari had never been an ayatollah.[48]

Mehdi Hashemi's pretrial confession was intended mainly for
fellow junior clerics—especially those with radical leanings. Using

[44] "Why Shariatmadari Fell?" editorial, *Ettela'at*, 4 May 1982.
[45] *Ettela'at*, 21 April 1982.
[46] *Ettela'at*, 4 May 1982.
[47] Society of Militant Clerics, "Announcement," *Ettela'at*, 30 April 1982.
[48] *Ettela'at*, 26 April 1982.

many Arabic and Koranic phrases, Hashemi held himself up as a pitiful example and "manifest proof" of what happens to those who stray from true Islam.[49] He began by greeting His Excellency Imam Khomeini, the "Representative to the Great Messiah." He went on to stress that he had requested this television interview on his own initiative so as to "educate" the public about the mortal pitfalls awaiting those who deviate from the Imam's line. He then listed his own sins: carrying the "disease of eclecticism" (*bimari-y elteqati*) even in the 1960s when he had been a seminary student; indulging in "extremism" (*efrati*) and "mindless activism" (*'amalzadegi*); assassinating in 1976 a fellow cleric; making a deal with SAVAK to have his death sentence commuted; creating dissension among the revolutionary guards and murdering innocent citizens from 1979 to 1985; inducing youth into thuggery and instigating trouble within the seminaries; storing arms and heroin; and, politically most serious of all, using Montazeri's office to slander the ministers, undermine the government, and create a subversive faction within the Islamic Republic.

Hashemi ended by stressing that small mistakes had led to ideological deviations, and these, in turn, had led to treason against the community, the Imam, and the Islamic Republic, as well as the greatest crime of all—apostasy against Islam. In tears, he beseeched God and the Imam to forgive him so that he could make amends and devote the rest of his humble life to serving the state, the revolution, and Islam.

The confession carefully avoided the real issues that prompted his arrest. No mention was made of Hashemi's objections to the United States arms deal, his leaking of the information about the deal to the foreign press, and the demonstrations he had organized against the visit to Tehran of President Reagan's emissaries. No mention was made of the events surrounding the recent "murders"; they had occurred when Hashemi's supporters had tried to distribute land among peasants outside Isfahan. No mention was made of Montazeri's protests against the mass executions of political prisoners. Of course, the regime gave no explanation why it had taken so long to punish Hashemi for the murder committed

---

[49] "The Complete Text of Sayyid Mehdi Hashemi's Confession," *Kayhan-e Hava'i*, 17 December 1987.

ten years earlier. This was a particularly glaring omission in light of the fact that the government claimed that from 1976 to 1979 other prisoners had shunned the Hashemi associates because they had collaborated with SAVAK, paid homage to the Shah, and even praised the so-called White Revolution.[50]

The Hashemi confession precipitated—as it was probably intended to—Montazeri's fall. When Montazeri complained that Hashemi's arrest insulted his "honor" (aberu), the regime retorted that the suspect should be treated like any other citizen, since Islam believed in equality.[51] When he vouched for Hashemi's religiosity, arguing that he had known him since childhood, the regime cited the confession admitting that he had been influenced by the devil.[52] When Montazeri offered his resignation as designated successor, describing how he had initially declined the office because the burden of leadership was too heavy for him, Khomeini replied curtly that the two had always agreed on this. "It was the Assembly of Experts," Khomeini now revealed, "that had insisted on appointing you the designated successor."[53] Montazeri promptly became a nonperson. He was confined to a seminary in Qom, and his pictures and books disappeared from public view.

Marxists

Of all the recantations, the Islamic Republic has given by far the most prominence to those of Marxists—an indication that the regime has considered Marxism to be its main ideological rival. The recanters came from diverse organizations—the pro-Soviet Tudeh, the pro-Chinese Toilers party, the diehard Maoist Paykar, the pro-Albanian Tofan, the Castroist Fedayin, both majority and minority factions, as well as smaller groups such as the Workers Road, the Communist party, and the Union of Militant Communists.

One of the first such recantations came from Hosayn Ruhani, a figure well known among dissidents since the 1960s. A member

[50] Hojjat al-Islam Ansari, "The Cause and Roots of Ayatollah Montazeri's Resignation," Kayhan-e Hava'i, 26 April 1989.
[51] Rayshahri, Political Memoirs, 81–82.
[52] Anonymous, Ranjnameh-e Hazrat Hojjat al-Islam, 21–31.
[53] Rayshahri, Political Memoirs, 269.

of the Mojahedin since the mid-1960s, he headed its ideological section in the late 1960s, and negotiated with Khomeini on its behalf in the early 1970s. Converting to Marxism in the mid-1970s, he had led the Mojahedin's Marxist offshoot, which, after the revolution, adopted the name Sazeman-e Paykar dar Rah-e Azadi-ye Tabaqeh-ye Kargar (Combat organization on the road to the emancipation of the working class)—better known as Paykar. Ruhani had also coauthored a highly controversial manifesto that argued that dialectical materialism was on all counts far more revolutionary than Islam.[54] What is more, immediately after the revolution he had given a series of press interviews in which he detailed his earlier negotiations with Khomeini. In them he depicted Khomeini as an "obscurantist" more interested in protecting his fellow "reactionary mullahs" than in overthrowing the Pahlavi regime.[55] This was the first direct attack on Khomeini in the post-1979 Iranian press.

Ruhani gave his first recantation in May 1983—almost three months after his arrest. It became the prototype of those presented by the Left. It glossed over religion, never mentioning the concept of *velayat-e faqih* (jurist's trusteeship), and instead stressed populist reasons for supporting the Islamic Republic. It cited no concrete "crimes," but general ideological deviations against the regime. It made no pretense of conversion to Islam. Instead it depicted Islam as an "authentic ideology," and Marxism as an "alien" import with no indigenous mass roots.

In his television appearance, Ruhani stressed that his sole purpose in speaking was to educate the public—especially his former colleagues in the communist movement.[56] He accused the latter of factional infighting, personal bickering, grossly miscalculating the revolutionary potential of Islam, and, most serious of all, blatantly insulting the republic as a "reactionary anti-people's regime." "Now I understand," he declared, "this is truly a people's

---

[54] Mojahedin Organization, *Bayanieh-e e'lam mavaze'-e ideolozhik-e sazeman-e Mojahedin-e Khalq-e Iran* (Manifesto explaining the ideological position of the People's Mojahedin Organization of Iran) (Mojahedin Press, 1975).

[55] "Interviews of Comrades Hosayn Ruhani and Torab Haqshenas," *Paykar*, 1 September–23 November 1980.

[56] "Hosayn Ruhani's Revealing Interview," *Ettela'at*, 9 May 1982.

anti-imperialist regime." He also claimed that in his early interviews with the Imam he had tried to deceive him by hiding his "eclecticism" and Marxism. He denounced the Tudeh as "revisionists" and "social imperialists," and the National Front as "liberals" dependent on the West. He ended by asking for an audience with the Imam and thanking his wardens for teaching him the truth about the Islamic Republic. He argued that in the underground his mind had been bound by his organization's dogmatism, but in prison it had been free suddenly to explore new horizons. In short, incarceration was liberation—a slogan worthy of Orwell's Big Brother.

Ruhani expanded on these themes a few months later in what was billed as a "roundtable discussion" for former "mini-group" supporters.[57] Ruhani stated that Paykar, unlike the Mojahedin, had not called for an armed uprising, but nevertheless had disseminated insidious propaganda, smearing the Islamic Republic as a "reactionary petty bourgeois state." We were so divorced from reality, he argued, that we refused to recognize February 1979 as a historic revolution, insisting that it was no more than a political squabble between the petty and the comprador bourgeoisie. He declared that in prison he had realized that the Imam, representing Islam, had freed the masses from the clutches of imperialism. He traced his organization's gross errors to two fundamental sources: the intelligentsia's social isolation and *zehnegiri* (subjectiveness), and Marxism's "deviant" (*enheraf*) ideology—he did not explain what it was a deviation from. He concluded by stating that he hoped his "brother" guards would arrange more such roundtable discussions so that he could further elaborate on these themes. Ruhani made no more public appearances, and it was rumored that he had helped interrogate the next batch of prisoners, the Tudeh—before being quietly executed.[58]

Between May and December 1983, twenty-one Tudeh leaders appeared on television to make their recantations—most of

[57] "Roundtable Discussion with Twenty-nine Leaders of the Mini-Groups," *Ettela'at*, 19 October–18 November 1982. The twenty-nine included members of Paykar, Fedayan, the National Front, and Bani-Sadr's Presidential Office.
[58] *Bazandeh* (The loser) (supra n. 4), 54–55.

them in yet another "roundtable discussion."[59] Their statements had two consistent themes: allegiance to the Imam and the Islamic Republic, and self-denunciations for having "betrayed" Iran during the last forty years. The media—with much fanfare and editorializing—declared that these "traitors" had confessed to advocating an alien ideology, admiring an alien society, obtaining their inspiration from alien books, receiving funds from an alien source, carrying out instructions for an alien state, spying for an alien intelligence service, and conspiring with an alien superpower to overthrow the Islamic Republic. In fact, the statements tended to be long on generalities, short on specifics, and were more like ideological recantations than actual confessions. Of course, none were permitted to mention what had triggered their arrest—their party's criticism of the decision to continue the war into Iraq.

Hojjat al-Islam Hojjati-Kermani, one of Khomeini's disciples, promptly congratulated the Imam and the Muslim community for their glorious ideological victory (*fateh-e ideolozgik*) over Marxism. He argued that such confessions from self-admitted "spies" and "traitors" proved to all the vast "superiority of religion over the so-called scientific philosophy."[60] Meanwhile, the chief prosecutor announced that these confessions proved that the Tudeh leaders had betrayed not only Iran but also the Soviet Union.[61] He urged other party members to turn themselves in without delay, arguing that the Shari'a dealt less harshly with those who recanted before combat. This, he argued, is a combat situation, since the Tudeh was preparing to overthrow the Islamic Republic. His logic would have been more acceptable to Stalin's chief prosecutor than to most Shari'a-trained jurists.

Of the twenty-one Tudeh recantations, by far the longest came from three elderly leaders in their late sixties and early seventies:

---

[59] "The Text of the Confessions of Eighteen Tudeh Leaders," *Ettela'at*, 4–10 October 1983. Reprinted in pamphlet form by the Center of Islamic Culture in Europe as *Jam'ehbani-yi chehel-u-du sal-e 'amalkar-e Hezb-e Tudeh* (Forty-two years of Tudeh party activities) (Rome, Center of Islamic Culture, 1984) 1–64.

[60] M. Hojjati-Kermani, "Congratulations to the Imam and the Muslim Community for Its Ideological Victory," *Ettela'at*, 15 May–6 June 1983.

[61] "Interview with the Chief Prosecutor," *Ettela'at*, 31 May 1983.

Nuraldin Kianuri, the organization's first secretary and a member of the central committee since 1948; Ehsan Tabari, a well-known essayist and the party's chief theoretician since the 1940s; and Mahmud Behazin, a prominent writer, translator, and the head of a writer's association.

Kianuri described—in three separate television appearances in 1983—his party's major acts of "treachery."[62] These included the support given in 1945-46 to the Qavam government, to the Soviet oil demands, and to the Azerbaijan rebellion; the support not given from 1951 to 1953 to Ayatollah Kashani and Mossadeq; the secret sympathy felt towards the White Revolution; the temptation in 1978-79 to prefer the 1906 constitution to the Islamic Revolution; the failure to believe genuinely in the slogan "Neither East nor West"; the creation of secret cells within the military; the eventual goal of someday overthrowing the Islamic Republic; and the heavy dependence on the Soviets—receiving funds from them and giving them information about the country's politics and armed forces. "The root cause of our mistakes," he argued, "was our lack of knowledge of Iran. This led us into dependence on a foreign power. This, in turn, led us into deceit, espionage, and treason." He insisted that his statements were entirely voluntary, that his "eyes had been opened in prison," and that he was grateful for the recent opportunity in jail to study the history of his party's treachery.

Seven years later, Kianuri informed a United Nations commission on human rights visiting his prison cell that he had been tortured into making these false confessions, especially those pertaining to spying and plotting to overthrow the regime.[63] As proof of torture, he showed his crushed fingers and partly paralyzed hands. The commission also found that his wife, Maryam Firuz, was so badly damaged as a result of her 1983 interrogations

---

[62] "Leaders of the Treacherous Tudeh Party Confess to Spying for the Soviets and Betraying the Country," *Ettela'at*, 1 May 1983; "Kianuri Reveals Half a Century of Treachery Committed by the Soviets, Marxists, and the Tudeh," *Ettela'at*, 28 August 1983; "The Text of the Confessions of Eighteen Tudeh Leaders," *Ettela'at*, 4-10 October 1983.

[63] United Nations Economic and Social Council, *Situation of Human Rights in the Islamic Republic of Iran* (February 1990) 32.

sessions that she still could not sit on a chair or hear from one ear.[64]

Tabari read his confession, explaining that he had to work from a written text because he was "recovering from a recent stroke."[65] In this statement, Tabari dismissed his whole life as "spurious" on the grounds that all his publications had been influenced not only by a foreign ideology, namely Marxism, but also by such nonbelieving Iranians as the iconoclastic historian Ahmad Kasravi. He now rejected his previous works because in prison—according to the authorities he had been in jail for only nine days—he had the opportunity to debate with sincere Muslims, especially the wardens, and to study the great Muslim thinkers, especially Farabi, Ibn Sina, Tusi, and, most important of all, Ayatollah Mottaheri—Khomeini's disciple who had been assassinated in 1979. He now understood that Marxism was not "scientific," that Leninism was Machiavellianism, and that internationalism was a cover for subversion and espionage.

Tabari spent the next six years—until his death in a prison hospital—elaborating on the same arguments, and, for the first time, mentioning spiritual themes. In his *Zed Khatereh* (Antimemoirs), published in 1985, he began with "In the Name of God the Merciful, the Compassionate," and retraced not only his own life but also the history of the socialist movement in Iran.[66] He criticized the movement for being isolated from the masses, betraying the country in crucial crises, catering to the whims of the intelligentsia, misunderstanding society, favoring secularism over religion, and, most serious of all, trying to undermine the spiritual authority of Islam. What is more, in a series of articles on the Marxist philosophy, he argued that dialectical materialism had been roundly debunked by Ayatollah Mottaheri, Mullah Sadr, Einstein, the "big bang theory," and an "eminent American

---

[64] United Nations Economic and Social Council, *Situation of Human Rights in the Islamic Republic of Iran* (October 1990) 53.

[65] "The Text of Ehsan Tabari's Confession," *Ettela'at*, 7–9 May 1983.

[66] E. Tabari, "Anti-Memoirs," *Ettela'at*, 7 February–5 March 1985. This was later reprinted in book form under the title of *Kez Raheh: Khaterati az Tarikh-e Hezb-e Tudeh* (The crooked road: Memoirs from the history of the Tudeh party).

scientist" who had proved that God directs living organisms.[67] It
is said that in prison he genuinely found God. It is possible—after
all, Winston Smith in *Nineteen Eighty-Four* learned to love Big
Brother. In his obituary, *Kayhan-e Hava'i* eulogized him as "one
of the world's greatest Marxist theoreticians."[68]

Behazin—whom the media described as another leading party
"theoretician"—proclaimed the final end of the Iranian Left.[69] It
had ended, he argued, both because of the strengths of Islam
and because of the inherent weaknesses of Marxism. He described
the former as the clergy's deep "one thousand year" roots among
the masses, and the success of the Imam's revolutionary Islam in
leading "the way for the liberation of the oppressed people." The
latter he traced to its alien ideology, which had led the whole of
the Left, not just the Tudeh, to become dependent on the Eastern
Bloc. This, he claimed, had created seventy years of "betrayal,"
in which the socialists had consistently failed to safeguard the
nation—from the Constitutional Revolution, through the Jangali
Rebellion and the rise of Reza Shah, to the Mossadeq era and
now the Islamic Republic. Behazin held himself responsible for
participating in a party that a foreign power manipulated from
"behind the scenes" (*poshteh-e pardeh*) and persistently used as its
"servant" (*nokar*) and "spy" (*jasouz*). Our history, he concluded,
is a history of "plots" (*tuteah*) and "treason" (*khianat*).

The other twenty-one gave shorter statements. Muhammad
Amoui, a veteran member, who had spent quarter of a century in
the Shah's prisons, declared that, on one hand, he was shocked by
his colleague's revelations and, on the other, was deeply impressed
by the "sincerity, honesty, genuineness, devotion, and kindness of
his young prison wardens and interrogators."[70] He added that he
now realized that the party's main aim was to lead astray the

---

[67] E. Tabari, "Marxism Recognized and Considered," *Kayhan-e Hava'i*, 27
September 1989–1 August 1990. See also E. Tabari, "Historical Materialism,"
Kayhan International, 21 October 1984–17 February 1985.

[68] "Ehsan Tabari Died," *Kayhan-e Hava'i*, 10 May 1989.

[69] "The Leaders of the Treacherous Tudeh Party Confess to Spying for the
Soviets and Betraying the Country," *Ettela'at*, 1 May 1983.

[70] "Text of the Confession of Eighteen Tudeh Leaders," *Ettela'at*, 4–10 October 1983.

youth of Iran. Ghulam-Hosayn Qaempanha, a seventy-year-old ex-officer, admitted that during his twenty-five years of exile he had come in "contact" with the KGB.[71]

Mehdi Kayhan, the head of the party's labor organizations, reminisced that as head of the clandestine Tudeh radio station he had broadcast programs favorable to the Shah, especially in the 1960s, when the Soviets had begun to build a steel mill in Iran.[72] Reza Shaltuki, another veteran member who had spent twenty-five years in prison, criticized the Tudeh for having supported the Soviet oil demands in 1946 and for failing to act against the CIA coup in 1953.[73] He also mentioned that Marxism had little relevance to contemporary Iran. Hosayn Jowdat, a seventy-five-year old physics professor, who had spent twenty-four years in exile and had retired from the central committee in 1982 because of ill health, confined his "confession" mostly to sketching his own political career since 1942.[74] Finally, Manoucher Behzadi, the editor of the party's main newspaper, declared that the Tudeh had organized workers, peasants, and students with "the aim of weakening the Islamic Republic, and, thereby, preparing the ground for its eventual overthrow."[75] He concluded his statement with this paragraph:

> It is obvious that the crimes the party and we committed are extremely grave. The courts must judge us, but I hope the heroic and revolutionary people of Iran, as well as the Great Leader of the Revolution and Founder of the Islamic Republic, will forgive us with their Islamic affection and compassion. The right to forgive resides with the Imam, and I hope he will forgive me so I can make amends. My message to the people of Iran, especially to Tudeh supporters, is this: Experience has shown that the only way the people of Iran can be saved is through the Islamic Revolution with its slogan "Neither East nor West" and through the Islamic Republic guided by Imam Khomeini, the Great Leader of the

[71] Ibid.
[72] Ibid.
[73] Ibid.
[74] Ibid.
[75] "Tudeh Leader Confesses that the Aim was the Overthrow of the Islamic Republic,' Ettela'at, 4 September 1984.

Revolution and Founder of the Islamic Republic. No other way
exists. I hope others will learn from me that the only correct road
is to defend the Islamic Revolution and the Islamic Republic.

These recantations laid the stage for a series of trials of Tudeh
members within the armed forces. Totaling 101, the accused included the former commander of the fleet and three colonels.
Rayshahri, presiding over the military court, declared this to be
one of the largest espionage trials in world history, and, in the same
breath, assured the public that the Tudeh, despite all their efforts,
had recruited a mere two hundred from all the armed forces.[76]
Those in the dock were accused of "sowing corruption on earth"
by gathering arms, spying on behalf of the Soviet Union, violating
the Imam's ban against party activities within the armed forces,
and organizing secret cells with the eventual aim of overthrowing
the Islamic Republic.

The main pieces of evidence presented were a radio, an ordinary camera, and, of course, "confessions" from some of the accused. It is not clear exactly what these confessions were. The
press reported only summaries of the trials, with many pictures
of repentant-looking defendants, but only cursory sketches of the
"confessions." To confuse matters, in the course of the proceedings
Rayshahri constantly referred to pretrial "confessions"—but some
of the defendants seemed to reject the content of those statements.
The most many of them admitted to in court was that they had
held secret meetings, gathered some two hundred guns, and sent
political and military reports, including assessments of the war
front, to Kianuri. As one of the accused stressed, their reports
on the war front would have been completely out of date within
forty-eight hours.[77]

Nevertheless, Rayshahri sentenced ten to death, six to life imprisonment, five to twenty years, fifteen to ten years, and the
others to lesser terms varying from five years to one year. Many
of those receiving long sentences were later executed without

[76] "Details of the First Session of the Trial of the Secret Organization of the
Tudeh Party," Ettela'at, 7 December 1984.
[77] For a summary of all the trials, see Ettela'at, 7 December 1983–17 January
1984.

explanation. Rayshahri announced that many were given light sentences because they had convinced the court that they were "genuinely repentant."[78] In a press conference held to announce the executions, a French journalist asked Rayshahri if the court had seen any other evidence beside that described in the newspapers.[79] Rayshahri replied that, in addition to the "electronic equipment" and the confessions, there were some secret documents that could not be discussed publicly. At the end of the press conference, the correspondent of *Tehran Times* asked how the court went about "evaluating these genuine confessions." Rayshahri replied,

> The answer is clear. I have elsewhere discussed how one can evaluate confessions and repentances from individuals who for years had fixed ideas and acted upon them.... One should keep in mind that never before in world history have we seen what we have seen here—the guilty coming to court, completely voluntarily accusing themselves of the highest crimes, and even acting as their own prosecutors. It is especially difficult for materialists (*madifekr*) to be able to reflect and analyze. But if you think a little, the answer becomes clear. When human beings, who have committed mistakes and moral crimes, are apprehended and confronted by upright and honest authorities then the veil of obstinacy falls off. They quickly see the enormity of their crimes. As Kianuri himself stated "We were blind." Once confronted with "why have I committed these crimes? why have I betrayed my nation?" then they want to make their confessions and even lighten their guilt. One of the revolution's great assets is that it can force criminals to face their own nature and remove the veils of deception from their eyes. In other words, my answer to your question involves psychology.

Gletkin, the main interrogator in *Darkness at Noon*, also considered himself to be a psychologist.

Epilogue

These public confessions reached a flood in the mid-1980s, but gradually diminished in the late 1980s, dwindling to a mere trickle by the early 1990s. A number of factors account for this decline. First, the Islamic Republic, once it was fully institutionalized, felt

---

[78] *Iran Times*, 27 January 1984.
[79] "Court Verdicts," *Ettela'at*, 22 February 1984.

less need to attain and retain the public's "hearts and minds." Power now came from state institutions rather than from grass-roots organizations and street demonstrations. The government could punish dissidents quietly, dispensing with public displays and ideological lessons. Second, the execution of those who had given public confessions diminished the incentive for others to give similar recantations. For example, of the twenty-one Tudeh leaders who recanted in 1983, as many as thirteen were later killed in prison—some under torture, others by execution.[80] The choice ceased to be one of recanting to save one's life. Instead, it became one of heroic martyrdom or dying after negating one's whole life commitment. Third, some of the main arguments cited by the re-canters for supporting the Islamic Republic sounded hollow by the end of the decade. In the early 1980s, the theme that the regime was the vanguard of a "people's anti-imperialist revolution" carried far. But by the late 1980s, after the embarrassing revelations of Irangate, the October Surprise, and the Israeli arms deals, not to mention the regime's dismal social record, these themes sounded like hot air—except perhaps to diehard believers. The more conservative the regime became the less it could resort to these populist arguments.

Fourth, the overuse of public confessions reduced the theater into soap opera—if not for the victims, at least for the bored viewers. By the early 1990s, the public had been barraged by an endless cast of characters with similar scripts, similar salutations, similar arguments, similar forlorn expressions, and similar sins, crimes, and misdemeanors. Confessions that earlier had sounded astounding now appeared to be worn-out clichés.

Finally, the ever-widening net of victims gradually produced empathy among the opposition and thereby among the general public. For example, when the Mojahedin were first carted before the cameras, the Tudeh, as well as many other groups, accepted the confessions at face value and even applauded the authorities for their vigilance. When the Tudeh leaders first made their recantations, their old-time enemies, especially Bazargan's Liberation Movement, gloated and reminded the public that for decades they

[80] For the names of 163 Tudeh members killed in prison between 1983 and 1988, see "List of Martyrs," *Mardom*, 11 March 1988.

had warned that these Marxists were a "fifth column." But by the time Bazargan's own supporters confessed to "spying for United States imperialism," most opposition groups, including the Tudeh and the Mojahedin, were willing to denounce the statements as false, coerced, and therefore meaningless. To paraphrase Brecht, few worried when the regime went after the religious Left. More worried when it went after the Left in general. Yet more worried when it went after the liberals and the center. And yet even more worried when it came after anyone suspected of subversion. It is no accident that it was in these later years the intelligentsia discovered the importance of Koestler's *Darkness at Noon*—a work that in the past they had tended to dismiss as a worthless piece of Cold-War propaganda. Harsh experience had raised both social awareness and political consciousness. In the 1980s, public confessions helped legitimize and strengthen the Islamic Republic. By the 1990s, the same confessions and the means to obtain them threatened to delegitimize and weaken the Islamic Republic.

Obstacles to Democratization in Iraq

A Reading of Postrevolutionary Iraqi History through the Gulf War

CHIBLI MALLAT

THE great enemy of the peoples of Iraq has been the law. It was primarily international law that forced, in the decade-long tragedy of republican Iraq, the mute observation by foreign actors of a government's systematic repression of its own people. The principle of this law is known as "non-intervention in the domestic affairs of a sovereign country," and is enshrined in Article 2.7 of the United Nations Charter. More relentlessly, the playing out of the domestic shadow of the rule of law imposed a straitjacket on progress to a more open society. The interplay of domestic and international legal constraints led Iraqi rulers at least twice into major foreign adventures. In the first Gulf War, begun on 22 September 1980 against Iran, and in the second Gulf War, initiated on 2 August 1990, they chose to invade neighboring countries as an escape from the pressing shadow of the rule of law. International law dovetailed with the refusal of the Iraqi government to answer to domestic pressures for democracy.

This essay argues the centrality of law to the State of Iraq's descent into domestic and regional violence since 1958. Two propositions derive from this argument: (1) The (negative) impact of the noninterference principle in unchecked governmental repression; and (2) the transformation of a quest for legitimacy into foreign adventures.

To root these propositions in Iraqi history, two major scholarly contributions on twentieth-century Iraq will offer the counterpoint to my propositions: Hanna Batatu's *Old Social Classes* and Samir al-Khalil's *Republic of Fear*.[1]

The Domestic Shadow of the Rule of Law

In assessing Batatu's masterpiece two decades after its publication, the Palestinian scholar's work appears unbalanced. There is no doubt that the old classes lost political power brutally in the summer of 1958. The successive revolutionary councils and governments had effectively obliterated the guardians of the *ancien régime*. Such disappearance, however, *must* have been largely on the surface. The liberal currents were there, and remained politically subdued but active in various ways, including, I would like to suggest, in some of their religious-sectarian dimensions. The long muted struggle between the southern Iraqi town of Najaf, with its strong Shi'i influence, and Baghdad—a struggle largely ignored by Batatu—reflects a fundamental conflict in Iraq between mass

---

[1] H. Batatu, *The Old Social Classes and the Revolutionary Movements of Iraq: a Study of Iraq's Landed and Commercial Classes and of its Communists, Ba'thists, and Free Officers* (Princeton 1978) [hereafter *OSC*]; Samir al-Khalil, *The Republic of Fear* (London 1989) (hereafter *RF*). The two books have been widely reviewed. A conference on Batatu's work organized by the University of Texas resulted in Robert Fernea and William Roger Louis eds., *The Iraqi Revolution of 1958: The Old Social Classes Revisited* (London 1991). The most remarkable review of the *RF* is by Edward Mortimer, "The Thief of Baghdad," *The New York Review of Books*, 27 September 1990, 7–15. Although scholarship on Iraq has remained limited in the West, partly because of the constraints on research in Baghdad, there was a significant and generally remarkable pool of studies even before the invasion of Kuwait. Most noteworthy are books by Peter Sluglett and Marion Farouk-Sluglett, Phebe Marr, Charles Tripp and Shahram Chubin, and Majid Khadduri. Since the second Gulf War, a number of works have appeared, some of which were written by journalists and policymakers, but their concern and shorter historical focus are addressed to a different audience. They include works by John Bulloch and Harvey Morris; Judith Miller and Laurie Mylroie; Pierre Salinger and Eric Laurent. These works appeared after the invasion of Kuwait and before the ground war started in February. Later, other shorter works, mainly articles, were published taking into account the Iraqi revolt of March 1991 (the Iraqi *intifada*) and its aftermath, as well as the conducting of military operations. Most remarkable are Bob Woodward's *The Commanders* (New York, Simon and Schuster, 1991), and Laurie Mylroie's *The Future of Iraq*, Policy Paper 24 (Washington, D.C., The Washington Institute for Near East Policy, 1991).

protest against dictatorship and brutal repression. By 1981, even Batatu had to acknowledge that there were more causes of unrest in the Shi'i-populated Iraqi South than he had in 1978, when he pointed to a drought resulting from "the decrease in the level of the Euphrates river" and "alleged curbs on Shi'i study circles and religious processions."[2] For any observer of the Iraqi scene, full-fledged confrontation between Najaf and Baghdad culminated in the arrest of Muhammad Baqer al-Sadr, the most politically active, and most intellectually creative Shi'i (and arguably Islamic) scholar of the century, and his sister Bint al-Huda, and their execution in April 1980.[3]

Sadr was a politically involved, innovative thinker who set out to offer a detailed theory of "the Islamic way." He wrote profusely, and contributed scholarly analyses in philosophy, logic, and especially economics and constitutional law, for which he became widely known in the Arab and Muslim world and achieved prominence on the Iraqi Islamic scene. Since the 1960s and after the death of his mentor Muhsin al-Hakim in 1970, he increasingly became the point of reference of political Islam in Iraq. His opposition to Saddam Hussein, for which he was arrested and imprisoned several times, took a dramatic turn after the success of his colleague in Najaf, Ruhollah al-Khomeini, in taking over the Iranian state. As for Iraq, the focus on Sadr is important throughout the postrevolutionary period for three reasons.

---

[2] Cf. *OSC*, 1093, and H. Batatu, "Iraq's Underground Shi'a Movements: Characteristics, Causes and Prospects," *Middle East Journal* 35 (Spring 1981) 577–94; published also with slight alterations as "Shi'i Organizations in Iraq: al-da'wah al-islamiyya and al-mujahidin," in *Shi'ism and Social Protest*, ed. J. Cole and N. Keddie (New Haven 1986) 179–200.

[3] I have completed a book on Sadr's legal contributions: *The Renewal of Islamic Law: Muhamad Baqer al-Sadr, Najaf, and the Shi'i International* (Cambridge University Press, 1993). On Sadr and the circles around him, see also my "Religious Militancy in Contemporary Iraq: Muhammad Baqer al-Sadr and the Sunni-Shi'a Paradigm," *Third World Quarterly* (Spring 1988) 699–729; "Iraq," in *The Politics of Islamic Revivalism: Diversity and Unity*, ed. Shireen Hunter (Center for Strategic and International Studies and Indiana University Press, 1988) 71–87; "Le féminisme islamique de Bint al-Houdâ," *Maghreb-Machrek* (June 1987) 45–58.

The first is one of style: Sadr represents the opposite of Saddam Hussein in his openminded discussion of topics, which is the hallmark of disputation in Shi'i law, both in theory and practice. This is not to say that Sadr was a liberal in the Western sense, but his style is distinctively persuasive and in law stands in its traditional approach in clear opposition to the revolutionary law heralded by Saddam Hussein. The second contrast is regional, in that Sadr is the symbol of the Shi'i, deprived, peripheral South (symbolized by Najaf) against Sunni, affluent, central Baghdad. The third contrast is organizational. Saddam's rule can be described as a ring of concentric circles—immediate family, then Takritis (that is, people who, like Saddam Hussein, hail from Takrit, a small Sunni city north of Baghdad), then Ba'thists, then Sunnis, then Arab Iraqis. These circles intersect with other concentric circles of raw power—bodyguards, security apparatuses, Presidential and Republican guards, and the army. Sadr did not operate through a normal political party, and certainly not through the so-called Da'wa party (*hizb al-da'wa*), even though some have ascribed the birth of the Da'wa directly to him.

This is why Batatu's appraisal in 1981 remained off the mark; his insistence on a secondary, shadowy movement called al-Da'wa shows how the Islamic phenomenon in Iraq was still being read incorrectly as an essentially extremist, underground, and narrow expression of discontent. The search for a classical political party carrying the torch of the Islamic Shi'i rebellion in Iraq made the investigation mistake the forest for the trees. The Da'wa was never the significant organization that it was later depicted to be. In fact, it was a bizarre and probably unwitting creation of the Iraqi Ba'th's Revolutionary Command Council (RCC).

This is how the Da'wa's exaggerated importance happened. The word Da'wa appeared in the West, and started enjoying credibility when it was first mentioned in Western media, as well as being a clear concern of intelligence services, after 9 April 1980. On that day, the highest collective authority in Iraq, the RCC, issued a decree that reads as a retroactive and automatic condemnation to death of all members of the Da'wa party.[4] The date is important.

---

[4] See the Arabic text of the decree in the appendix to *Dima' al-'ulama fi tariq al-jihad* (The blood of the 'ulama on the way of struggle) (Tehran 1984). In

On Saturday April 5, Muhammad Baqer al-Sadr and Bint al-Huda
were arrested and transferred from Najaf to Baghdad. There is little doubt that in accordance with the sinister practice of the Ba'th
the usual torture operations on the siblings will have been carried
out, but the only established fact in the momentous executions
is the identification of the body of Muhammad Baqer al-Sadr, at
dawn on April 9, by relatives who were summoned to the grave-
yard for the purpose.[5] Sadr must have been killed between the
fifth and the eighth, and it is generally acknowledged that the
death of the two siblings took place on the eighth of April. This is
confirmed by the infamous anti-Da'wa decree, which in effect legitimized from the point of view of the Iraqi Ba'th the suppression
of the Najaf *'alim.*

That the death sentence was carried out retrospectively did not
matter, so long as revolutionary law Iraqi-style was meted out. In
line with the habit of the RCC, this was another instance of a
forced consensus to a "legal" decision that clearly came from the
top leadership. Saddam Hussein was repeating a practice that had
succeeded a few months earlier, when his party was decimated in
a notorious "Night of the Long Knives," recorded on a video that
circulated in Arab circles after the event and was broadcast on
Western television programs in variously edited versions. It shows,
in a Macbeth-type atmosphere, a large meeting of leading Ba'th
personalities, in which people are called up from the audience and
charged with treason. Heavily sweating, in total silence, each one
confesses, stays mute, or cries, before being whisked off to (presumably) his death, and another victim stands up. The presence of
silent fellow Ba'thists secured "the collectiveness" of the decision.

Even more significantly, in April 1980, exactly as in July 1979,
Hussein and his cronies collectively endorsed the killing of the
most famous Najaf scholar (thus for Saddam Hussein sealing
survival through common responsibility), and shrouded it with

---

English, see translation and reports in Foreign Broadcast Information Service,
Daily Report: Middle East and Africa (Washington, D.C.) 10 April 1980;
Summary of World Broadcasts, pt. 4 (London) 11 April 1980.

[5] Kazem al-Ha'eri, "Tarjamat hayat al-sayyid al-shahid," (Biography of the
martyred sayyid) in Muhammad Baqer al-Sadr, *Mabaheth al-usul* (Studies in
usul) (Tehran 1988) 139.

the universality of Ba'thi law. It was by law that his assassination was retroactively legitimized. The fact that it was dressed up by alleging his leadership of the Da'wa (said to have carried out the bombings at the Baghdad universities of Waziriyya and Nasiriyya on April 1 and 5 that were the trigger for Sadr's arrest) fooled only those who were not in the know—the Iraqis at large, the West, and possibly even the RCC colleagues who signed the April 9 decree.[6] The security apparatus knew better. In fact, Sadr had long disassociated himself from any movement called Da'wa. As early as 1974, he had issued a *fatwa* (religious decree) prohibiting his students of Najaf from adhering to the Da'wa.[7]

Whatever the cloak-and-dagger dimension of this episode, the veil will never be totally removed from the fateful days of April 1980, which were indicative of the atmosphere in Iraq of the late 1970s. This atmosphere cannot be adequately described, as in Batatu's successive analyses, as the result of violent operations by a small underground movement called the Da'wa. Nor did the phenomenon—active and important resistance to the Ba'th— actually start in the 1970s. The first sparks of the confrontation between the Saddam-Bakr tandem and the Najaf leaders went back to the early days of the Ba'th's second access to power on 17 July 1968.

An initial major spark resulted from the confrontation that took place over an educational project: the university of Kufa. The master architect of the Kufa project was Muhammad Makkiyye, who, at the request of a large Shi'i constituency including the tur- baned leaders of Najaf and Karbala', embarked in the mid-1960s on the construction of a regional university, which would offer obvious advantages to the backward South. The Kufa project was brutally interrupted as soon as the Ba'th came to power,

---

[6] The names of the RCC are not always known. The RCC itself became eventually meaningless, as the key to the security of the system is the existence in parallel of a number of intelligence services that check and counterbalance each another, the ultimate arbiter and manipulator being Hussein himself.

[7] I have never seen the text of the *fatwa*, but it is referred to in several Islamic publications: e.g., Ghaleb Hasan Abu 'Ammar, *Al-shahid al-Sadr, ra'id al-thawra al-islamiyya fil-Iraq* (Martyr al-Sadr, pioneer of the Islamic Revolution in Iraq) (Tehran 1981) 58.

despite the availability of large funds and international talent. The university at Kufa had involved a cross-section of the population that was distinctly Shi'i, but that included religious and nonreligious figures. Further, although it was a secular university, it had the blessing of the leading *marja'* at the time, Ayatollah Muhsin al-Hakim, who clearly saw the benefit of such a venture, even if it meant a strong competition with the theological colleges of Najaf. The aborting of the Kufa university plan signaled the first move of the Ba'th to stifle development in the South. It was also an early example of the stifling of pluralism, regional and political, by Baghdad.[8]

Kufa was the tip of an iceberg of hatred and mistrust between Baghdad and Najaf that built itself up very rapidly. In the recurring showdowns, Najaf consistently lost. After the failure of the Kufa project, another defeat showed in the impotence of the Najaf network before a widespread policy of expulsions of "Iranian" Shi'is by the Ba'th. The basis for these expulsions was the Iraqi Nationality Law, which gives stringent criteria for Iraqi citizenship, excluding in the process a large number of settled Iraqis of Shi'i persuasion.

A similar process was afoot in the North, but it was more distinctly political than in the Kufa episode and more brutal in that it targeted a large ethnic community: the Kurds. While the confrontation between Baghdad and Kurdish Iraq abated with the agreement on Kurdish autonomy of March 1970, a number of features, which would last to the present, can be identified in the text itself. The first element, which is clear in the 1970 text, is the concern for legalism. The agreement is a long document, with treaty features and a language that, along with the revolutionary and messianic message to the Arab nation by the glorious Ba'th,

---

[8] I have had the pleasure of meeting many of the protagonists directly and indirectly linked to that project. The land was earmarked, and the considerable sum at the time of 4,530,000 dinars was also mentioned, which was confiscated by the government. See al-Khatib ibn al-Najaf, *Tarikh al-haraka al-islamiyya fi'l-Iraq* (History of the Islamic movement in Iraq) (Damascus? 1981) 72. In English, the episode is counted in a remarkable article on the Makkiyye family. Lawrence Wechsler, "Profiles: Architects amid the Ruins," *The New Yorker*, 6 January 1992, 46, 48. I am grateful to Bob Annibale for this reference.

shows a distinct legal bent. Concern for legalism is most patent in the minute institutional arrangements. The rule of law constitutes the main guiding point for the agreement, and this would eventually carry through in the discussions between the Kurds and the rest of the opposition after all ties with Baghdad were severed by the gassing at Halabcha. All the parties have been holding on to the Holy Grail of a poorly thought-out but apparently middle-of-the-road text. But there was law in it, and this seemed enough to warrant it being taken seriously, well after the lure of revolutionary Pan-Arab phraseology had lost its initial impetus.[9]

Politically, two features appear prominently in the context surrounding the signing of the 1970 pact. First, a simultaneous look at events in the North and in the South shows the easy dividing by the Baghdad government of regionally based oppositional forces. Time and again, Baghdad would either set Kurds against Kurds or, through well-timed truces and other sweeteners, Kurdish Iraqis against Arab Iraqis.

The second political lesson, which would endure from the early days of the Ba'th regime, relates to the uses and misuses of political and religious sectarianism. It is not that Sunnis did not suffer from repression. But rulers from Saddam's circle, although they may be described on the whole as straight espousers of a godless and/or religiously eclectic and opportunist doctrine, had Sunni origins over at least one decade of the Bakr-Hussein regime.[10]

---

[9] Until the Vienna meeting of the Iraqi opposition in June 1992, one could still find a systematic reference to the agreement in oppositional programs. See my *Iraqi Opposition: a Dossier* (London, SOAS, 15 February 1991) for a brief analysis and critique of the text. In Vienna (see above, pages 184–87) the loose "self-government" (*hukm dhati*) was finally replaced by the concept of Kurdish "right to self-determination, excluding secession, within one Iraqi nation" (*haqq taqrir al-masir li-kurdistan al-'Iraq min dun al-infisal, dimn al-watan al-'Iraqi al-wahid*). I attended in Vienna some of the heated discussions that led to this compromise. The reader can find a remarkable account of the discussions by the rapporteur of the constitutional commission, Professor Hasan Chalabi, "*Al-mu'tamar al-watani al-'Iraqi: al-injazat al-siyasiyya wa'l-dusturiyya*," *Al-Hayat* (London) 7 July 1992, 13.

[10] *OSC*, 1077–79, summarizing various tables. One can find a continuation of these tables in the appendix of the *RF*. The relatively meaningless dimension of these statistics since 1979 must be noted in the case of Iraq, for the

The modus operandi of the Ba'th in power rests on three pillars: legal obsession, divide and rule, and sectarianism.[11] The very blueprint that appeared in the period from 1968 to 1970 has haunted, with intensities varying according to political expedient, the rule of Iraq in the past quarter of a century. How the model differs from Batatu's works and from al-Khalil's thesis is the subject of the rest of this section.

The absence of Najaf from Batatu's post-1958 history has been noted. The consequence of this absence on the appreciation of modern Iraqi history must now be developed. For it is not just that Najaf does not exist in the *Old Social Classes*, save for passing mention of the Euphrates water level and the anti-Communist *fatwa*s of the early 1960s. In the span of twentieth-century Iraq covered by the book, Najaf is relegated to appendices and constantly appraised against the rise of Iraqi Communism.[12] This disinterest fails to take account of the wider angle of what the small Southern city stood for: opposition to Baghdad. For Najaf was (and remains) much more than its underground movements and more than its 'ulama and colleges, in the way Baghdad is, in my analysis, much less than its variegated people. Here, only the metaphors of Najaf and Baghdad count: Najaf, especially in republican Iraq, stands for mass protest against dictatorial practice. It is also the voice of the Shi'is as underdogs,[13] a stance that

---

Iraqi government had become highly aware of the narrow sectarian basis that Batatu established beyond appeal. The way Saddam Hussein proceeded was through the appointment of Shi'is to apparently prestigious posts, such as prime minister (Sa'dun Hammadi was the first such appointee in the wake of the second Gulf War) and speaker of the National Assembly, and by avoiding the naming of participants to the RCC meeting, while the RCC remained constitutionally and effectively the center of power in Iraq. Though muted by the Iraqi regime, Batatu-type statistics have found their way to the analysis of regimes in the Gulf that are less sophisticated in repression, but equally narrowly based. A remarkable analysis of the sectarian and tribal affiliation of the various Gulf countries' councils of ministers can be found in Bahgat Korany's recent chapter on the region in R. Mantran, et al., ed., *Les régimes politiques des pays arabes* (Paris 1991) 451–538.

[11] Cf. the new book by Amatzia Baram, *Culture, History, and Ideology in the Formation of Ba'thist Iraq, 1968–89* (London 1991).

[12] See *OSC*, 752–54, 1137–48.

[13] *OSC*, 45.

became more intense as Saddam relied more on sectarianism.[14] Shi'ism became an expression of dissent in Iraq as a whole. This includes Najaf's defence of prisoners of conscience and liberal figures excluded by Pan-Arab ideologies, the protection of private property against the excesses of land reform and nationalization for the benefit of ruling Ba'thists, or, even earlier, its stand against forced molding of family laws into a single code.[15]

The Baghdad metaphor must also be appraised more closely. Baghdad is not here Sunni Iraq, insofar as the rulers did not hesitate to exclude the best Sunni talents from all sectors. But Baghdad may also be Sunni, especially in times of acute crisis. Nor is that avoidable in the contemporary Middle East, when weak and poorly representative governments systematically play the sectarian card to increase their hold on power.

Nor is sectarianism, as state policy, ever absolute. The writings of Saddam Hussein the socialist in the 1970s were those of a leader whose Arab ambitions had no patience for religion. These theoretical expatiations reeked of clear atheism, and so they were perceived by similarly inclined leftist intellectuals collected in Beirut at the time. The beginning of the first Gulf War changed the picture overnight. It was not possible to counter the Khomeini message with socialist-atheist talk for two essential reasons: there was dire need for Saudi and Kuwaiti support, and religion was an unnecessary bone of contention. More importantly,

---

[14] Sami Zubaida has summarized this policy, which he calls communalism: "The Baath regime rules in a situation in which the power of the traditional elites ... [has] been eliminated or firmly subordinated to the state.... At the same time, state patronage proceeds on particularistic bases of kinship, religious and regional networks. This, together with constant feelings of threat and insecurity, encourages the formation and maintenance of particularistic solidarities on the bases of kinship and religion, with leaders and patrons negotiating privileges with government departments and personnel. That is to say, communalism is reconstructed, not necessarily in terms of historical continuities with traditional formations, but on bases favored by the current situation." Zubaida, "Communities, Class and Minorities in Iraqi Politics," in *The Iraqi Revolution of 1958* (supra n. 1) 209.

[15] Mallat, "Introduction," in *Islamic Family Law*, ed. C. Mallat and J. Connors (London, Graham & Trotman, 1990) 1–8, and "Sunnism and Shi'ism in Iraq: Revisiting the Codes," in ibid., 71–91.

a religious redirecting of Saddam Hussein's discourse became increasingly vital to avoid hurting the sensitivities of the mainly Shi'i rank and file who were sent to their deaths on the eastern front.

Divide and rule, with or without its sectarian garb, must remain. In the case of the Kurds of Iraq, the story is well known. But it was not restricted to creating factionalism among the Kurds; it was also true of fighting within the Ba'th. Samir al-Khalil has drawn a telling chronological list of coups and purges.[16] The remarkable feature of the consolidation of Saddam Hussein's rule is the timing of the purges, which has allowed him to avoid confronting a large chunk of resistance at once.

The most controversial pillar in my depiction of Iraqi post-1958 history is the rule of law and the strength of the shadow it casts on domestic and regional policies. Yet this element emerges from the surprising care given in Ba'thi Iraq to the production of laws by the state. As in the case of the March 11 agreement, which was noted earlier, there has been a serious investment of the state in legal phraseology. I am talking here about legalism, not legality. Legalism is a special effort exerted by the government to apply a legalistic language and legally based arguments to a clear policy of repression. In contrast to other dictatorships, which care little for the way a message is conveyed, the envelope of the message is important and takes therefore the shape of law. But the intention and spirit of the law are insignificant, as is the separation between the power that dictates the law and the power that implements it. There is no concept of separation of powers in Ba'thist Iraq, yet there is great concern for legalism.[17]

One is surprised at the legislative production of Ba'thi Iraq, which is centered on *Al-waqa'i' al-'iraqiyya* (the official journal of Iraq), published both in Arabic and in English. Occasionally, the state sponsors legal encyclopedias, such as the reproduction of Ba'thi laws and statutes (already published in the *Al-waqa'i' al-'iraqiyya*) in twenty volumes with full indexing, covering the

---

[16] *RF*, xxii–xxiv, 292–96.

[17] I am grateful to Ellis Goldberg for clarifying the concepts used in this section.

period from 1968 to 1981.[18] Similarly, officials are very precise and technical in the formulation of legal drafts, even if everyone knows, including the two parties involved, that the legal paper signed will be ignored before the ink is dry. The concern for legalism and legal forms suffuses the whole bureaucracy of Iraq, from visas to presidential decrees. It is a phenomenon that requires further study, and probably involves a psychological dimension to which social sciences have not been attentive in the Middle East.[19]

This is perhaps where my reading of contemporary Iraqi history differs essentially from al-Khalil's in the *Republic of Fear*. In my thesis, it is concern for legalism and the shadow cast by the demands of the rule of law that offer the key to the structure and philosophy of the system and explain the aggressive foreign policy of the rulers of Iraq. Three examples drawn from observing Ba'thism in action in Iraq will illustrate this theme: the constitutional framework of the system, the United Nations discussion over the ceasefire resolution with Iran, and the legal deadlocks of 1979 and, more significant, of 1989.

The departing point is the interim constitution of 1970 and the constellations of legal texts around it, including the March 1970 agreement with the Kurds and such texts as the 1971–1973 National Action Charter. It is sufficient to read the 1970 constitution, which vests power primarily (almost exclusively) with the Revolutionary Command Council. The constitution was careful to obliterate any scheme of separation of powers. Legislative and executive powers were merged, and the authority exercising both was vested in the RCC. To the extent that other authorities mentioned—on the side of the Ba'th, the Regional Command, and on the side of classical constitutionalism, the President of the Republic, the Council of Ministers, and in 1979 the newly established National Assembly—exist, they do not wield any power, even on paper. The National Assembly, for instance, is not entrusted with

---

[18] *Al-mawsu'a al-qanuniyya al-iraqiyya* (The Iraq legal encyclopedia) (Baghdad 1981).

[19] A remarkable analysis, which contrasts the profiles of Saddam Hussein and Hafez al-Asad, was recently published in the French journal *Esprit*. See "Le battant et le joueur: Saddam Hussein et Hafez El Assad—Entretien avec Percy Kemp," June 1991, 249–54.

any power to enact legislation. The meager powers that other figures once had were concentrated, on the legal level, in the hands
of Saddam Hussein. Since 1979, he has become the head of the
RCC, head of the Ba'th Regional Command, president, head of
the Council of Ministers, and commander in chief of the army.
Each step was taken according to the devolution of powers set out
in the 1970 interim constitution, which entrusts the RCC to carry
out such concentration.

Legalism is also the hallmark of international argumentation.
Discussions on the implementation of the ceasefire resolution of
July 1987 show the legal tenacity of Iraqi negotiators. Faced with
the clause assigning responsibility to the party that started the
war, the Iraqi party advocated a "successive implementation" of
the resolution. Clause 6 on responsibility was to be addressed
only after the other clauses were carried out and it was, of course,
for Iraq to decide whether all prisoners of war were effectively
surrendered and the delimitation of boundaries was finalized, in
agreement with the earlier clauses.[20] The same legalistic attitude
became all too familiar in Saddam Hussein's efforts to link the
United Nations Security Council resolutions 660 (condemning the
occupation of Kuwait on 2 August 1990) and 242 (The United Security Resolution of 22 November 1967, which "rejects the acquisition of territory by [Israeli] force"). Saddam would have remained
in Kuwait until he had determined that Israel had adequately
performed its obligations under Resolution 242.

It is argued in the *Republic of Fear*, with great talent, that
Ba'thism produced war as a "logic of madness" rooted in the
established psychology of intimidation and fear. "Madness in this
strictly political sense is expressed in the act of subordinating
each particular incident, every development on the battlefield,

---

[20] It was for the UN Secretary General to decide, as his last important
verdict before the end of his mandate, that Iraq was responsible for the
war. But that was well after the second Gulf War had transformed Saddam
Hussein into an international pariah. See Perez de Cuellar's statement on the
implementation of Security Council Resolution 598, 9 December 1991, and the
reaction in Baghdad: e.g., *Al-thawra*, 18 December 1991, accusing Perez de
Cuellar of not reflecting the legal requirements for consultation, and attacking
his "irresponsible, unfair practices and positions."

each human life regardless of status, wealth or rank, and of course the sum of all lives to ... indefinite, distant and fictional goals."[21]

The argument is powerful, especially given the author's style and scholarship, which is steeped in Hannah Arendt's works on totalitarianism. Even more powerfully, the arguments for the first Gulf War can be borrowed, word by word, to explain the second Gulf War, when absurdity, brutality, and madness had been augmented with time and the consolidation of personal power in Baghdad.

Enticing as the madness argument may be, my reading of the wars of Saddam Hussein does not correspond to the mass psychology depicted in the *Republic of Fear*. It is much more prosaic, and can be summarized as the shadow of the rule of law, hovering over Iraq.

In the case of the first Gulf War, Khalil's undermining of arguments other than "madness" is correct, except for an important detail. There is little doubt that sovereignty disputes, rife and numerous as they are in the Middle East, cannot be a significant explanation of the invasion of Iran. Nor is the alleged historical enmity between Arabs and Persians of significance in the first Gulf war, as the ideological battlefield was more seriously conducted over the truer Islam than over Arabism. Argument about Iranian instigation of the Shi'i community, however, is more difficult to write off. As presented by Khalil, it goes:

> Once Iraq was put on the defensive, it became common to allege that Shi'i unrest inside Iraq, fomented by Iran, compelled the Ba'th to take defensive action to forestall the export of the Iranian revolution.

Khalil's response is that,

> notwithstanding Ba'thi paranoia, the view is untenable for various reasons. First, by the late 1970s the Ba'thi state was wealthier and stronger than any state has ever been in the modern history of Iraq, and it had crushed all organized opposition. Second, growing Shi'i sectarianism inside Iraq was not principally a product of the 1979 revolution, even if this helped to foster it; sectarianism in the social

[21] *RF*, 286.

and personal domain was produced by Ba'thism. Third, unlike
Iran, this sectarianism was not overtly, or in the first place, political
but reflected growing social and cultural antipathy between Sunnis
and Shi'is. Fourth, the relatively new Shi'i political organizations
(like al-Da'wa), which probably received Iranian backing, were
small and largely crushed *before* the outbreak of war.[22]

I do not think that what Najaf stands for can be dismissed so
easily, and the general ignoring of it in *The Republic of Fear* carries
through from Batatu's opus. The rebellion was crushed before the
war, in the person of Muhammad Baqer al-Sadr, but the mood
conveyed by two decades of resistance is a different matter, and it
was fueled by a conjunction of pressures from other Iraqi sectors.
Rather than being a product of Ba'thist "madness," the attack
against Iran must be seen in terms of the domestic shadow of
the rule of law.[23] Saddam's first adventure was not a response to
Iran's fomenting unrest in the Iraqi south; it was a *fuite en avant*
from powerful questions of legitimacy inside the Ba'th and in Iraq
at large.

The fateful years of 1979 and 1980 saw general disapproval
of Hussein inside and outside the Ba'th. The National front of
progressive parties was a hollow skeleton, the highly emotional
union with Ba'thi Syria floundered (another mini-foreign adventure), Muhammad Baqer al-Sadr and his sister were killed in cold
blood, and, probably most importantly, unease reverberated at
the highest echelons of the party, with the dramatic purges of the
summer of 1979 and the seizure by Hussein of all power, against
even old cronies like Ahmad Hasan al-Bakr. Unrest was there for
all to see inside and outside the Ba'th. The coffers of the state
might have been full, but the political possibilities had shrunk
beyond imagination: that is, beyond domestic imagination. The
only way to distract unrest was to go outside—to the weakest link
in the region, Khomeini's Iran.

The second Gulf War is a similar case. But here, again, it is
the political situation that must be assessed against the peculiar

---

[22] *RF*, 265.

[23] This point was argued earlier, in more details, in my "A l'origine de la
Guerre Iran-Irak: l'axe Najaf-Téhéran," *Les Cahiers de l'Orient* (Paris, Fall
1986) 119–36.

circumstances resulting from the "victory" over Iran—and now the coffers of the state were empty. Again, fear was what confronted Saddam, besieged with demands for liberalizing measures from the top of the state to its bottom.

Here the rule of law must be presented literally, in a succinct formula to be tested against history: the collapse of the search by Saddam Hussein for a constitution for Iraq. For this was the main political activity in Baghdad between the 1988 ceasefire with Iran and August 1990. A text indeed emerged, but its main feature was the consecration of Saddam Hussein's power.[24] That the constitution was never passed is testimony to the forms of resistance that have occurred in Baghdad, even inside the Ba'th, which tried to use the constitution to voice a desire for some relaxation. From a legal point of view, the only, and then much noted, opening up was to allow bereaved Iraqis to travel abroad.

Given the economic crisis, it was necessary to find a foreign weak link: that was the little kingdom of Kuwait. Then, international law failed the people of Iraq and came to the succor of dictatorship. This issue is examined next.

The Failures of International Law

On the scale of human tragedies, one may wonder which was worse: the Gulf War itself or the ceasefire.[25] If the Gulf War was epitomized by a brief and brutal military confrontation, the

---

[24] See the study of 'Abd al-Husayn Sha'ban, "Min asl 179 madda, hunak 69 tatahaddath 'an salahiyyat ra'is al-jumhuriyya" (Of 179 articles, 69 define the power of the president), Al-hayat, 18 June 1992.

[25] This section is part of a work in progress on the inadequacy of international law and diplomacy in light of the Gulf War. The arguments were put publicly for the first time in "Harb al-khalij min khilal al-manzur al-duwali wa darurat tajdidihi" (The Gulf War from the point of view of international law and the necessity of renewal), Al-hayat, London, 30 June 1991 (in Arabic), from a lecture at the Kufa Gallery in London on June 12. For a critical perspective from an international relations point of view, see "Towards New Orders in the Middle East: The Role of US Policy," a report of a workshop held under the auspices of the Center of International Studies, Princeton University, 18–19 May 1991. I am grateful for the text to the rapporteur at the meeting, Professor John Waterbury.

ceasefire (in which fire was ceased only by one side, while the other continued firing at another kind of enemy) has now been followed by so many misfortunes that victory or defeat in the Gulf War have become meaningless concepts. It is appropriate to ask which of the two tragedies was harsher.

In war and in peace the same unavoidable truth was revealed: international law failed to prevent the violent confrontation and failed to control its aftermath. The bloody confrontation and the ensuing peace will remain in this waning century the epitome of absolute diplomatic and political impotence. For people whose professional life is dedicated to the law the failure is far greater. They can see international law at a total loss before events on the move.

The question is whether, independently of the mercurial game of nations, it is possible for renewal to take place on the level of international law, when the law's limits have been made clear in the ugly and bloody results so far achieved. For a realistic answer to the question, it is necessary to address the ways of international law as the principles developed during the Gulf crisis.

First, there was a failure in preventing war. Would it have been possible for international law to offer the tools that could have avoided the war launched by the Allies on January 17? The answer is difficult. For if international law provided the framework that was necessary for the use of force through "all necessary means needed for the application of Resolution 660," as stated in Resolution 678 of 29 November 1990, the proposition of international sanctions as a valid and effective alternative to outright hostilities remains in question because of the difficulty of assessing the practical incidence of sanctions and their effectiveness.

Independently of the political value of sanctions, international law did allow the choice, from within a number of tools included in Articles 660 and following, of some military and nonmilitary sanctions. Both came under its competence. From a strict legal viewpoint, it is therefore possible to provide an answer to the question whether the law dictates a particular course for the avoidance of war. The answer is no. What international law offered was a choice and not a resolution, and the decision rested with the influential parties in the United Nations who consecrated the option of open war and deepened the impotence of international law, as it now stands, to avert it.

The most crying contradictions took place after the war. At a time when the Allies occupied most of Iraq's desert South, a major popular revolt shook the country for four weeks. Silence suddenly descended upon America and its allies, with the excuse, based on international law, of nonintervention in a sovereign country's domestic matters.

The suppression of the revolt in the South and in the North, with the world's governments in silent witness, came at a time of insistence on the application of Resolution 687, which has remained the main criterion for the Allies' handling of Iraq, despite what the resolution entails in terms of intervention in the domestic economic and security structure of the country. International handling of Iraq is at the heart of the matter. In the fifteen resolutions that separate the second of August from the ceasefire, the observer does not see a single trace of the Iraqis as people. Dealing with Iraq as an equation that comprised people and government has meant that people were ignored.

This is the essential legal failure: international law did not distinguish—not for a moment between August 1990 and March 1991—between the two elements of state and society, and this failure played itself out on three levels, which correspond to the three phases of the conflict. In the first phase, international law was incapable of preventing the war because it is not equipped with the preventive tools that such an operation would need.[26] Because of the doctrine of noninterference in domestic affairs, international law was unable to recognize a popular element that could counterbalance the rigidity of the leadership. During the war, in the second phase, international law proved incapable of separating civil society and military apparatus, and within the

---

[26] The argument of supporting the Iraqi opposition against Saddam Hussein rather than launch a classical war, has to my knowledge been voiced only by Professor Bernard Lewis, in articles published in the *Wall Street Journal* on the eve of the hostilities. I have more modestly (and unsuccessfully) tried to put it in action in private conversations with President Carter (November 1991) and the British FCO, and developed it in a lecture at the University of London Student Union on 15 January 1991.

military apparatus, between commanders and helpless rank and file. In the third phase, the country was split asunder by the revolt of the ruled in the immediate aftermath of the hostilities, after the rulers had been defeated militarily. International law was incapable of resolving the problem because it had still to uphold the principle of nonintervention in a sovereign country's internal affairs. Yet the rulers of Iraq had violated, from the standpoint of international law, all imaginable principles by brutal invasion, sequestration of innocent civilians and diplomats, and new crimes best illustrated by the wanton destruction of the environment.

The call of the United States president "for the people of Iraq, or the military, to set aside the dictator, Saddam Hussein" remains in everybody's ears. But this was a political ploy: should one remain with international law in its pristine principles, there is little doubt that the panoply of measures under which some indictment could have taken place was sacrificed at the altar of the principle of nonintervention in domestic affairs.

Perhaps the most significant legal landmark in the Gulf crisis is the ceasefire resolution, Resolution 687. In the longest Security Council resolution ever, in page after page of humiliation for the state and the people of a country for the present and the future, the drawing of boundaries with Kuwait was determined, the destruction of Iraq's military machine was established, a costly mechanism of supervision was forced on the technical reconstruction, and war compensation was imposed on generations of Iraqis to come.

Curiously enough, only the Iraqi government, in all these long and harsh pages, was effectively protected. And, as in the case of the first Gulf War, the second Gulf War has proved its point: a breathing space for dictatorship, which has so far bought another few years of survival. As for drawing borders, war compensation, or even the destruction of the military machine that was its pride, these are of concern to the Iraqi rulers only to the extent that they may threaten or constrain their hold on power. This is why there was such a universal sense of frustration, which included the Western leaders themselves. For when President Bush and Prime Minister Major declared that Iraq would remain a pariah nation until the demise of the present government, they were in effect expressing politically what remained blunted by international law. The problem was in the shortcomings of the law, which worked at destroying Iraq as a state and as a people, while the rulers who were responsible for the tragedy remain at the helm, still prowling and boasting of their superior might. The need is clear: international law must be renewed on bases that will allow its glacial progress to reach the essential needs of a world community craving a new order.

How is that to be achieved? It is difficult today, and probably unwise, to reject established international rules altogether. Nor is it conceivable for the principle of nonintervention of one country in the internal affairs of another to disappear overnight. Here, for us to keep our feet on the ground, it is worth examining, within the manifestations of the Gulf War itself, some of the ideas that suggest that a discussion over substance has started, even though it will remain undecisive until dictatorship is brought to an end in Baghdad.

A first significant occasion was missed with the abandonment of the call to establish the present Iraqi regime's responsibility. This principle had found its way into the draft of the ceasefire resolution, as the United States lawyers of the State Department had included in it a clause giving the Iraqi president responsibility for the disasters in the Gulf. As to why this clause did not find its way to the final text, it seems that European circles in the Security Council had shown unease toward a clause that appeared difficult to apply without arresting the leader in person.

Whether in the framework of an international tribunal or by a similar mechanism, the principle of responsibility constitutes the beginning of separation between people and government, and between a state, which will endure, and a government, which by nature is limited in time. The international community should have endeavored to put on trial the persons who are responsible for the war, in a challenge best expressed by the Egyptian Nobel Prize winner Nagib Mahfuz: "In truth, if the tyrant and his aides are not presented before an international tribunal, then there is no meaning to values in this life."

As for the difficulties in implementing such a responsibility clause, which calls for producing the criminal, they are real, but the choice between the humiliation of country and people and the establishment of a principle of responsibility for rulers who have taken country and people to the brink should have been clear in international law. The route taken by Resolution 687 in dropping the responsibility clause is but another throwing away of a chance that could have been a key to some renewal in the diplomatic and legal field.

The features of the second opportunity appear in Resolution 688, which urges the government to stop its aggression against its people. In the second paragraph of the resolution, the Security Council demands that Iraq, as a contribution to removing the threat to international peace and security, stop its repression. And in the third paragraph, the Security Council demands that the Iraqi government allow relief operations of humanitarian organizations to be carried out unimpeded in the areas of Iraq where repression continues.[27] It is clear in this text that the principles of nonintervention in the internal affairs of a country, and the restriction of international recognition to a government as the sole legitimate interlocutor in a given country, have lost their usual sway.

Mention of Iraqi civilians and Iraqi repression is new in international law, even though the framers of the resolution tried to pursue a conciliation between the traditional legal view and the requirements triggered by widescale repression. For those who have followed the discussions that resulted in Resolution 688, especially the position of the British government over the necessity to establish "safe havens" and the demand by French Minister of Humanitarian Affairs Kouchner to reconsider the principles of international relations, and the resistance of the United States, Soviet, and Chinese governments to these positions, it is clear how the text ended up as an uneasy equation between the old and the new. The obsession with the absolute legitimacy of the government remains patent in the talk of Iraq in the two clauses mentioned.

The concept of safe havens was established in parallel to Resolution 688, and has, from a practical point of view, yielded a

[27] S/RES/688 (5 April 1991).

remarkably efficient result. But safe havens were not established by any form of concerted agreement in a Security Council resolution that would be blessed by international law. Safe havens resulted from a combination of *realpolitik* pressures exerted by the Turkish government, which was worried about the destabilizing effect of Kurdish Iraqis fleeing *en masse* to its southeastern areas,[28] and the genuine concern, particularly in ruling circles in Britain and France, for the fate of thousands of people. The safe haven concept was eventually adopted by the United States, in the form of the "Poised Hammer–Provide Comfort" operation, which is run under the label of some of the multinational forces involved in the war against Iraq. It still lacks the imprimatur of the United Nations and the effective seal of comprehensive legitimacy under international law.

Still, the inching away in Resolution 688 from a recognized international principle such as intervention in the domestic affairs of a country, and the resolution's separation of people and government, do constitute significant precedents that might introduce tension into international relations. Foreign intervention supporting a nongovernmental faction against a legitimate government is a worrying novelty for many a country in the world, as it opens doors that may be difficult to close.

The answer to the worry may be twofold. It might be possible to give this change an exceptional dimension related to the special case of Iraq. There, the internal collapse and the emergence of a wide popular revolt have come in the wake of an international military operation. To distinguish between the military operation and the revolt is difficult, as the revolt is but the continuation of opposition to the rulers on an internal level, after the international community opposed these rulers militarily and imposed military sanctions on them. The Iraqi case may be considered specifically, in contrast with other domestic troubles in the world, since the Iraqi internal unrest took place in the context of the international crisis resulting from the invasion of Kuwait. In this narrow view of the precedent introduced by Resolution 688, the repression of unrest in a given country will remain an internal affair so long

---

[28] See William Hale, "Turkey, the Middle East and the Gulf Crisis," *International Affairs*, December 1992.

as the government of that country does not operate beyond its boundaries.

The second possibility is to look at Resolution 688 as a first phase in a historic course that sees the renewal of international law in a significant manner. The new principle entails furthering the idea that the absolute sovereignty of a state must be overridden by human rights issues, and adopts the point of view defended in this essay that the foreign adventures of the rulers of Iraq cannot be separated from domestic constraints. The principle of absolute representation vested in a government, the refusal to take into account civil society, the principle of the illegality of intervention in internal affairs—all these established pillars of the international system must lose their absoluteness in issues of human rights, not only as a matter of morality, but out of calculated reasoning of the inside effect on the outside. This is what Resolution 688 starts timidly to acknowledge, if it is to be taken seriously and not as an embarrassed reaction of Western governments to the flight of civilian Kurds.

As for Iraq in particular, the investigation of the separation between the present government and civil society on the basis of a significant renewal of international law brings up a question that is no less important than the effect of its impact on international relations. The question is one of the persistence of acceptance of foreign intervention for the sake of human rights. Those who would benefit from the intervention of the international community in the domestic affairs of Iraq must be ready to accept it as a principle in the future. In other words, those new "subjects of international law" who benefit from foreign intervention—Iraqi civil society and those who represent it among the opposition—need, in order to strengthen the resolve and legitimacy of this intervention, to show their readiness to accept a similar intervention in the future, should their behavior once in power be similarly repressive. The principle of humanitarian intervention cannot be an exception tailored for the Iraqi Ba'th. This principle must attach to the present as well as to future governments if indeed it is intended to take root. It is only in this way that Iraq may escape from the present shadow of the rule of law and turn the legalism of repression into a legality marked by institutional checks within government and an autonomous civil society. Iraq needs a strategy that refuses to distinguish between domestic law and international law, and that looks for the protection of the rule of law at the time of Saddam Hussein *and beyond*.

Private Goods, Public Wrongs, and Civil Society in Some Medieval Arab Theory and Practice

In a nation of subjects or of citizens civil society refers to all institutions in which individuals can pursue common interests without detailed direction or interference from the government.

REINHARD BENDIX, *Kings or People*

CONTEMPORARY Middle Eastern political practice and theory cannot trace an institutional heritage of parliamentary (or any other) democracy back to the high Middle Ages. For much of this century, however, there have been Muslim thinkers who claim that Islam is deeply imbued with a concept of freedom that would underpin any viable democratic government. Some of this is undoubtedly mere rhetorical posture, but as even so trenchant a critic of Islamic fundamentalism and its apologists as Martin Kramer has suggested that "the reinterpretation of Islamic sources, done with enough imagination, could conceivably produce an opposing argument for Islamic democracy."[1] Thus it seems possible that political theorists and actors could trace a conceptual heritage of liberty. Muslim actors and thinkers are indeed

Research for this article was supported by National Science Foundation grant SES 90010816.

[1] Martin Kramer, "Islam vs. Democracy," *Commentary* (January 1993) 35–42. For a trenchant statement that this has not yet happened from someone who is attempting it, see Muhammad Arkoun, "Al-haraka al-islamiyya (qira'a awwaliyya)," *Al-Wahda* (September 1992) 10. For a remarkable essay on a variety of aspects of this problem, see Franz Rosenthal, *The Muslim Concept of Freedom* (Leiden, E. J. Brill, 1960. Rosenthal's concluding words (p. 122) strike me as the place where further work ought to begin: "Freedom, as an ideal, was not unknown. As a political force it lacked the support which only a central position within the political organism and system of thought could give it."

likely to look to the primary sources of Islam, but a purely genetic approach is likely to hide as much as it reveals.[2] if Islamic
law (Shariʻa) were an eternal and constant truth and were fully
present in the original sources, its virtue would remain normative
rather than explanatory for the simple reason that human history
varies and a constant can never explain variation.[3] To evaluate
claims (from whatever source) about a relationship between Islam and democracy (or any institution in society) we will still
require some positive theory that allows us to focus on historical
development. What I want to suggest is that we begin with an
appreciation for the development of medieval Muslim civil society, although no one called it that and although there often seems
doubt that it existed.[4] In making this argument, I hope to expose the historical importance of law as a political instrument
in the hands of private actors to shield themselves and others
from the demands of an absolutist monarchy.[5] The shadow of

[2] For an impressive analysis of how a contemporary legal system develops
adaptively and in unforeseen ways, see Aharon Layish, "Saudi Arabian Legal
Reform as a Mechanism to Moderate Wahhabi Doctrine," *Journal of the
American Oriental Society* 107 (1987) 279–92.

[3] Tariq al-Bishri made a similar point in a slightly different way in a brief
essay aimed at convincing Islamic researchers to accept the distinction between
commitment and detachment: "Shaykh Hassan al-Banna speaks of the reason
for the decline of [Muslim] society and refers it to abandoning [the Koranic
injunction of] 'commanding the good and proscribing the evil,' but this causal
chain [tasbib] cannot be correct from a scientific viewpoint because it does
not explain why people leave off commanding the good...." Tariq al-Bishri,
introduction to Ibrahim al-Bayoumi Ghanim, *Al-fikr al-siyasi li'l-imam Hasan
al-Banna* (Cairo, Islamic Publishing and Distribution House, 1992) 22.

[4] Although the popularity of the concept of civil society is somewhat recent,
this is a very widespread claim. Even Elia Zureik, who argues that we should
not "assume a distinct watershed between precapitalist/capitalist or precolo-
nial/colonial societies," nevertheless tells us, "the absence of civil society (i.e.,
autonomous corporate institutions that operate with minimal state control) is
an equally visible feature of Arab society." See "Theoretical Considerations for
a Sociological Study of the Arab State" *Arab Studies Quarterly* 3 (1981), 256.
As will become apparent, I believe Zureik goes wrong by including "corporate"
as a necessary adjective for institutions to exist as a form of civil society.

[5] Patricia Crone and Martin Hinds have remarked more strongly than anyone
else on the constitutional role of law in the medieval Islamic setting, although
they concentrate (as do all other authors) too heavily on electoral mechanisms

law, to borrow the felicitous phrase of Chibli Mallat, provided some respite for society from the sometimes necessary but often destructive intervention of arbitrary Sun Kings.[6] Thinking about law in this way, and especially in terms of shielding individuals from the exactions of the state, may still be of utility in the creation of liberal (and possibly democratic) regimes. However, I am also going to argue that the institutional context within which this approach to thinking about law grew was markedly different from that in medieval Europe or in the contemporary world. Analytically, there are two ways a subject can affect his relation to the state: speaking up (voice) or moving out (exit). My argument is that the relatively great mobility of merchants within the Islamic Mediterranean area conditioned a way of thinking about the state and society in which direct bargaining with the king was at best of secondary importance. States developed in a world in which leaving a political community (exit) was as easy as and possibly more effective than bargaining within it (voice).[7] Thus we can imagine elements of contact between this classical tradition of thought and our own as well as profound differences.

I want first of all to dispose of the idea that we have a single and agreed-upon picture of the medieval Arab world, both empirically and in terms of the presumed political theory of its inhabitants. I shall then present elements of what is taken to be a dominant view and then a brief opposing view, largely derived from the work of the late Marshall Hodgson. I want then to look briefly at some of the classical literature in Arabic on politics, as well as some of the

---

as the only way to limit royal prerogative. See *God's Caliph* (Cambridge University Press, 1986) 108–9. For a review of the pertinent sources on the completeness of this prerogative unlimited by voice, see Malcolm Kerr, *Islamic Reform* (Berkeley and Los Angeles, University of California Press, 1966) 33–41.

[6] For a fuller account of the metaphors of sun and shade in Islamic writing, see Bernard Lewis, *The Political Language of Islam* (University of Chicago Press, 1988) 21–22. See also the Koran, *Surat al-furqan*, *ayas* 45 and 47 on shade and night.

[7] For an account of the development of voting institutions as mechanisms by which rulers bind themselves (for their own reasons) not to confiscate the wealth of subjects, see Yoram Barzel and Edgar Kiser, "The Development and Decline of Medieval Voting Institutions" (unpublished paper).

medieval chronicle literature. I shall conclude by arguing that we can assert that there was civil society in a world in which men (and for the most part we will be talking about men) managed to assert claims to and defend their property from kings on a systematic basis.

My most important claim is that there was a civil society in the medieval Arab world. In making this claim I stand in opposition to much of the recent research and writing on the medieval world.[8] As one reviews the existing literature on the medieval state and society, it is striking how contradictory are the pictures that arise and how poorly formed the arguments can be. In describing political developments in an era between about 750 and 1525 C.E., P. J. Vatikiotis tells us of a dramatic separation of an increasingly centralized state from society:

> The state, in effect, ceased to lay claim to religious authority that ended in the exclusive hands of the *ulema*. State power however was often shared by local satraps, notables, dynasties and others. The rest of the burgeoning urban society, concerned with commercial and other wealth became non-political.... [M]ore and more groups in society, if not society in its entirety, avoided the state, so that a disjunction occurred between the exponents of state authority and those of religion.[9]

The picture presented here we can find elsewhere. Daniel Pipes tells us "Muslim subjects in normal times concentrated on personal matters. They were principally interested in leading the good life and much less in who administered it. Intense family, communal, and religious involvements ... took the place of power politics and warfare."[10] Pipes makes medieval Muslims sound rather like

---

[8] Besides the work of Marshall Hodgson, of which more below, see also the work of Patricia Springborg for an attempt to take a very different look at the record and to cast the argument in a much longer time span. See her *Western Republicanism and the Oriental Prince* (London, Polity Press, 1992), and the comment "the state in the East, which includes Greece, was essentially pluralistic, aggregating the institutions of civil society in a classically Hegelian manner" (p. 4).

[9] P. J. Vatikiotis, *Islam and the State* (London, Croom Helm, 1987) 26.

[10] Daniel Pipes, *Slave Soldiers in Islam* (New Haven, Yale University Press, 1982) 73.

contemporary American non-voters, and the reasoning that would lead them to avoid politics could then be found in any elementary textbook account of the voting paradox. For Pipes, however, lack of political involvement on the part of Muslims arises because of profound psychological conflicts experienced by Muslims as they confront a state that does not live up to the ideals of the Shari'a.[11]

To me, the implications of Vatikiotis's statement are unmistakable and I think remarkably insightful: in medieval Muslim society there were significant and significantly successful attempts by the wealthy and the educated to construct patterns of social relationships that existed apart from and probably in opposition to the coercive rule of the state.

Vatikiotis does not dwell on the implications of his argument; he also goes on to make a different and (to my mind) contradictory argument: "Islam is a political religion: it presumes political duties for the believers."[12] Thus "the political obligation of obedience [to any secular ruler] remained a religious duty, [and] the legitimacy of the ruler could be rationalized or justified as necessary for the existence and perpetuation of the *umma* (Sura 22.22), who protects and enforces the sacred law, in order to lead Muslims to prosperity in this world and salvation in the next."[13]

The problem here is that either individuals in society managed themselves into prosperity in this world (in which case they had a civil society) without reference to the state or they required

---

[11] Pipes, *Slave Soldiers*, 62–65. There are many problems with Pipes's use of evidence and his poorly specified analytic framework. A significant portion of his confusion, however, might have been resolved if he had read more deeply with the Chicago economists than with the Chicago sociologists. His work would have been better had he understood the nature of the agent-principal relationship as it has been developed in contemporary micro-economic and political-science literature.

[12] Pipes, *Slave Soldiers*, 30.

[13] Pipes, *Slave Soldiers*, 34. See also E. I. J. Rosenthal, *Political Thought in Medieval Islam* (Cambridge University Press, 1962) 8–9: "Politics [in Islam] is part of religion, so to speak; in other words, *siyasa*, or *siyasat al-dunya*, is the scene of religion as life on this earth as long as the law of the state is the *Shari'a*." The reference to verse 22 of *surat al-hajj* is, unfortunately, not explained. The tortures to which it refers (boiling water, iron rods, intense heat, and constant motion) appear in context to be punishments in the next world rather than prescriptions for this one.

the state to do it for them and lacked a civil society. There is no straightforward manner in which both of these accounts about medieval history can be correct. It is possible, of course, that an unresolved tension existed in Islamic political thought about the relation between civil society and the state. Classical Islamic political theory had at least two strands, which Bernard Lewis characterizes as authoritarian (or quietist) and radical (and activist) in regard to the obedience those in society owe their rulers.[14]

Any holder of effective power must be obeyed for normative and instrumental reasons. As Lewis tells us, "the same point is made in such oft-repeated dicta as that 'tyranny is better than anarchy' or 'sixty years of tyranny are better than an hour of civil strife.'"[15] This latter aphorism is so widely found both in the writings of Muslim thinkers and in contemporary writings about them that it probably deserves its own treatment. E. I. J. Rosenthal alludes to its importance in an argument about Islamic political thought preferring any authority to anarchy in *Political Thought in Medieval Islam*.[16]

Even authors highly critical of Rosenthal dwell on this Hadith-aphorism. Charles Butterworth disapproves of what he calls Rosenthal's anti-Muslim attitude, but raises this citation in "State and Authority in Arabic Political Thought."[17] In placing classical Arabic political thought in relation to Hobbes, Butterworth suggests an alternative reading not only of Ibn Taymiyya but of much of the classical literature. "Because of their pessimistic view of what humans might do if left to their own devices," Butterworth says, "the jurists and theologians are little concerned with safeguarding human freedom." Thus, better sixty years with a bad ruler than a single night with anarchy. Butterworth's quite

---

[14] Lewis, *Political Language*, 91–94.

[15] Bernard Lewis, "Islam and Development: The Revaluation of Values," in *Islam and History* (New York, The Library Press, 1973) 296.

[16] E. I. J. Rosenthal, *Political Thought*, 44, 55, and associated footnotes 58 and 99.

[17] Charles Butterworth, "State and Authority in Arabic Political Thought," in *The Foundations of the Arab State*, ed. Ghassan Salamé (London, Croom Helm, 1987). Aziz al-Azmeh, in *Arabic Thought and Islamic Societies* (London, Croom Helm, 1986) 258–59, also brings this up.

sympathetic account, however, lays bare a critical point: such an attitude makes sense only if one is attempting to construct a political theory out of the assumption that human beings are selfish egoists. Remarkably, Butterworth contrasts this political theory of Ibn Taymiyya's with that developed slightly later in Europe. I say remarkably, because Butterworth's own description of Thomas Hobbes's work makes the parallelism of the assumptions in Ibn Taymiyya apparent. Hobbes, Butterworth tells us, "deems human beings to be so concupiscent that they will seize the goods and threaten the well-being of others unless restrained by force," thereby creating a situation in which "the alternative to political order—namely a state [of nature] that must result in continuous war of all against all, one in which as Hobbes puts it, life is 'solitary, poor, nasty, brutish, and short'—is so frightening that he considers any regime preferable to anarchy."[18]

What I want to propose is that we take at face value the similarity that Butterworth suggests: that at least some Islamic political theory is better understood by recognizing it as political theorizing based on the assumption that human beings are rational egoists and that they must (and in fact do) cooperate.[19] I am not claiming that Islamic political philosophy is the source of Hobbes, nor am I claiming that the Muslim philosophers were the first theoreticians of what is now called rational or social choice theory. What I do claim amounts to a significant revision of our picture of them and suggests that we should take their work at least as seriously as we take the work of Machiavelli or Hobbes or Aquinas or Augustine, if not more so. They recognized that it was awfully difficult to explain how it was that men cooperated if they were egoistical individuals.[20] They recognized, as any serious thinker

[18] Butterworth, "State and Authority," 107.

[19] Note that for Ibn Taymiyya, for example, those in charge of public funds (*wulat al-amwal*) must be unlike private owners of property. The former must not divide their property on the basis of their own desires, while the very hallmark of private ownership is that one can do so. See *Al-siyasa al-shar'iyya fi islah al-ra'i wa al-ra'iyya* (Beirut, Dar al-kutub al-'arabiyya, 1966) 28.

[20] If one believes that human beings are not egoistic maximizers, then of course there is no "problem of cooperation." People cooperate because they are cooperative just as, to paraphrase Molière, sleeping pills work because they are soporific.

using an analytic system based on formal deductive reasoning must, that one had to come up with some explanation since people did indeed manage to cooperate.[21] They also realized what I believe most Western thinkers tended to miss until recently: that not only were social actors egoists but so too were kings; that is, they recognized the universality of the assumption they made. It is beyond the scope of this paper to suggest how such thinkers might have solved such an intellectual problem, but it may not be going too far to suggest that for them, as often for us, human cooperation clearly had its miraculous component.

Recognizing that similar tensions might pervade both Islamic and European philosophies has an honorable pedigree, for Shaykh 'Ali 'Abd al-Razak, in his famous argument that there is no uniquely Islamic form of government, suggested that the tension between Locke and Hobbes on the source of governmental legitimacy parallels one in Islamic thought.[22] A sharper sense of Jewish and Islamic thinking about the necessity for absolute obedience to rulers whose authority partakes of divine authority coupled with a profound distrust of and discomfiture with those who actually hold positions of royal authority was provided by the late S. D. Goitein.[23]

To the degree that any particular Islamic thinker generalized the problem of selfishness, he was caught in a very difficult problem for which we ourselves have discovered no particularly brilliant solution. Society might do better with a bad ruler than with no ruler at all, but what could protect society from the exactions—both in terms of money and service—of such rulers?

Perhaps the conundrum of selfish rulers and selfish society would not have been so acute for medieval Muslim thinkers if

---

[21] For an interesting (but regrettably too brief) argument about similarities in formal reasoning between Ibn Taymiyya and J. S. Mill, John Locke, and David Hume see Nicholas Heer's "Ibn Taymiyyah's Empiricism," in *A Way Prepared*, ed. Farhad Kazemi, et al. (New York University Press, 1988).

[22] See 'Ali 'Abd al-Razak, *Al-islam wa usul al-hukm* (with a critical commentary by Mamduh Haqqi) (Beirut, Dar maktabat al-hayah, 1966) 23–24.

[23] "Attitudes toward Government in Judaism and Islam," in *Studies on Islamic History and Institutions* (Leiden, E. J. Brill, 1966) 203, 205. Goitein's argument about the prophetic role superseding any political role is worth considering in its own right, and also appears to follow the same line as 'Abd al-Razak, *Usul*, 141.

they had not placed so much of their hope precisely on freely given human cooperation as the best form of social order. The symbol and instrument of cooperation between rational egoists was, of course, the contract, and I find myself largely convinced by Marshall Hodgson, that we can make the most sense out of social relations in the post-'Abbasi and pre-Ottoman period as well as of state-society relations if we look at them as expressing an essentially contractarian view of life: "The Muslim principle, in contrast, denied any special status to public acts at all, stressing egalitarian and moralistic considerations to the point where it ruled out all corporate status and reduced all acts to the acts of personally responsible individuals."[24]

Here, after what may seem like a very long prologue, we come to the heart of the question: property and property rights (as opposed to political rights). It seems clear that the classical Islamic thinkers believed (as suggested in the citation to Ibn Taymiyya in note 19) in relatively unrestricted rights to property in the goods, including land, found in urban locations.[25] David Santillana, for example, tells us that the "concept of private property is exceptionally clear in the minds of the Muslim legal thinkers."[26] He tells us,

[24] Marshall Hodgson, *The Venture of Islam*, vol. 2 (Chicago, University of Chicago Press, 1974) 347. Hodgson's work is a remarkable piece of explanation in the human sciences, as well as a vision of what the medieval Islamic world was all about.

[25] See Maxime Rodinson, *Islam and Capitalism* (New York, Pantheon Press, 1973) 172–175. I draw this from an unpublished paper that Farhat Ziadeh has been kind enough to share with me. Majid Khadduri takes a somewhat contrary view, and argues that private interests must be subordinated to public ones, but in fact the limitations on private disposal of property are so minimal that his argument seems hard to sustain on its face. See his "Legal Justice," in *The Islamic Conception of Justice* (Baltimore, The Johns Hopkins University Press, 1984) 138–39, where the restrictions on private ownership amount to the right of the state to tax, certain rights of co-owners, and certain basic definitions of legal capacity.

[26] David Santillana, *Istituzioni di diritto musulmana malichita (con riguardo anche al sistema sciafiita)*, vol. 1 (Rome, Istituto per l'Oriente, n.d.) 355. Santillana's word is "limpidissimo."

Property ("milk, mulk") is generally defined as "the right to enjoy and dispose completely of any thing to the exclusion of any other person" (*kamal at-tassaruf al-mutlaq*), which corresponds exactly to the Roman concept of ownership, *plena in re potestas*.[27]

Santillana's research led him to conclude that the inviolability of property was "an absolute rule" between private parties as well as between private parties and the state in all the schools of Islamic law.[28] He only lists three possible derogations of private property's inviolability: for the payment of debts by an insolvent creditor when ordered by a court, for pressing public interests, for the prevention of intergenerational transfers of wealth illegally gained by state officials.[29]

What kinds of goods were available to become private property? Relying again on Santillana, it is apparent that the range of what were considered as private goods was extremely broad: any utility not consumed as a very fact of its existence.[30] It appears to have been easier to identify what were not private goods than what were. Dead animals, clots of blood, grubs, piles of dust were not private goods because they had no usefulness. The perfume of a rose and the heat of a burning piece of wood also were not private goods because their existence was brief and they only existed in being consumed, as opposed, of course, to the garden in which the rose was found or the fireplace in which the wood was burned. The only other substances not considered private goods were those held to be illegitimate, such as stupefying drink, musical instruments, or books on magic.

There is one other category of private goods in medieval Muslim thought to which, as far as I am concerned, we pay far too little attention: debt and instruments of debt. Law protected not only the 'ayn (property) but the *dayn* (debt). Islam, to paraphrase the common aphorism, is not only concerned with *din* and *dawla* but with *dayn* and *dawla*—not only with religion and the state, but debt and the state. Obligations themselves were private property

[27] Ibid., 355–56.
[28] Ibid.
[29] Ibid., 357–58.
[30] Ibid., 307–310.

in the medieval Islamic world, and the creditor had an absolute right to recover his property, whether originally the loan of a numeraire or other fungible good or a particular thing.[31]

It is incontestable that medieval Muslim thinkers and medieval Muslim society recognized an extensive category of private goods that private individuals had full rights to control. There is even good reason to believe that within the urban setting, at least, the assumption was that collective or public space ought to be cut to an absolute minimum and that the urban environment was in essence an agglomeration of private spaces.[32] Janet Abu-Lughod has suggested that we should see in the "privatization of public space," which appears clearly in Jacques Sauvaget's diagrams of the marketplace of Aleppo, a commonplace phenomenon (which is especially unexceptional in that other society that assumes itself to be made up of freely contracting rational egoists, the United States).[33]

Muslim cities were urban markets not merely in the sense of the great market fairs of medieval Europe but in the sense of regular and routine multiple transactions that helped to fix prices in a public sense.[34] Individuals in them not only held their property freely, they appear to have disposed of it with great frequency through market mechanisms, and they had an extensive network

---

[31] As for ourselves, the understanding of debt as obligation had a moral as well as purely financial dimension. To be recognized as a real debt (obligation), the debtor had to recognize it as such "in his conscience" (*dayn fi al-dhimma*). On the problem of private rights and state obligations, see Sherman Jackson, "From Prophetic Actions to Constitutional Theory," *International Journal of Middle East Studies* (1993 71–90.

[32] See Hugh Kennedy, "From *Polis* to *Madina*: Urban Change in Late Antique and Early Islamic Syria," *Past and Present* 106 (1985) 3–27.

[33] Janet Abu-Lughod, "The Islamic City—Historic Myth, Islamic Essence, and Contemporary Relevance" *International Journal of Middle East Studies* 19 (1987) 155–76, n. 44. For Sauvaget, see *Alep* (Paris, Librairie Orientaliste Paul Guethner, 1941) 104. Obviously, I do not see the transformation of public or collective property into private property as necessarily as "degradation," to use Sauvaget's words, any more than I can agree with von Grunebaum's vision of Islamic urban reality as a decadent version of the Greek polis.

[34] Springborg, *Western Republicanism and the Oriental Prince*, 7, makes a similar case for a large volume of transactions creating both "more" power and "more sites" for power.

of legal institutions predicated upon, as well as symbolized by, contracts to protect their properties and their markets, which had important ramifications for the city structure itself. Thus it appears that in the built environment the greater role accorded private property in Islamic law than in Roman law was significant: "a man could extend his house into the street or build an overhanging balcony without needing to seek permission from anyone."[35] In Italian city-states, the right of the state to intervene in what private individuals did with real property was greater. So, too, the subdivision of the older market-places (where this occurred) increased the number of retail locations available and thereby made urban markets more efficient, so that "urban design now responded directly to commercial pressures and no government action was taken to counter such pressures in the name of the inviolability of public lands or of æsthetic considerations."[36] Some of the institutions that protected private property arose from the state, and others apparently from outside the state, within society itself. Medieval Muslim society was not distinct from medieval European society in this regard, for there, too, multiple institutions existed by means of which urban dwellers protected their property. It would be a mistake to think that such institutions must be part of the state: under certain conditions a reputational system of merchants themselves can enforce contracts over large distances in the absence of a unitary state.[37]

The state institutions—from the state court systems to the market inspectors to the police and army—were themselves primarily the result of private entrepreneurial activity of would-be kings.

[35] Hugh Kennedy, "From *Polis* to *Madina*," 21.

[36] Ibid., 25.

[37] See Paul R. Milgrom, Douglass C. North, and Barry R. Weingast, "The Role of Institutions in the Revival of Trade: The Law Merchant, Private Judges, and the Champagne Fairs," in *Economics and Politics* 2.1 (March 1990) 1–24. The core assumptions of the model (which is more of an "existence proof" than an argument with sound empirical support) is that there be a specialized actor who "serves both as a repository of information and an adjudicator of disputes" (p. 10) and that some institutions be created that "deter the Law Merchants [judges] from soliciting or accepting bribes" (p. 18). Seen from this perspective, it might be easier to understand why there was a market for biographical dictionaries of the 'ulama, i.e., the *tabaqat* genre.

Kings and their agents (*umara*) provided certain services and required payment for them. Some of these services were public goods—everyone benefited from their provision—in a rough and ready way.[38] Not everyone wanted the goods the kings provided, nor did they always want the particular mix that kings provided and for which they expected to receive regular income through the tax mechanisms. Given the Hadith *innama al-maksi fi'l-nar* (the taxman belongs in hell), it seems medieval Muslims did not relish paying taxes any more than we do. Yet if Islam was a state and a religion it seems strange that Muslims resented paying their taxes. Did they not owe obedience to the holder of authority regardless of all other considerations?[39]

Yet it goes without saying that there were public wrongs, or else there would have been no need to compare the sixty unjust years with the single anarchic night. What I wish to touch on quite briefly, however, is some sense of how (some) Muslim thinkers thought about these public wrongs. What, in short, was wrong about them and what was public? We may then move to discuss the issue of civil society, and especially the absence of corporate institutions, which seems to hang like the albatross around the neck of the Ancient Mariner.[40] The problem, of course, is, if rational egoists in a society that had a contractarian vision faced public wrongs, why did they find it so difficult to create institutions to discipline kings?[41]

One area we might wish to think about briefly is taxation, whether general taxes or specific tax-fees for services rendered. The taxes that were supposed to be levied by kings were relatively few in number and were relatively clearly enunciated. Kings

---

[38] I am not using "public goods" in a technical sense here.

[39] This is not as unfair a question as it might seem. Voluntary compliance with tax law is generally taken to be an indicator of legitimacy, and it has historically been argued that such compliance is higher in the United States than in most European democracies.

[40] See Lapidus and Stern, "The Constitution of the Islamic City," 36, Elia Zureik, and others. I except Hodgson from this list because he suggests a way out of the dilemma.

[41] This is what I take to be the genuine and important question that Lapidus and Stern ask, and it should not be allowed to die in the rush to attack "Orientalism."

tended to extend the range of properties that they felt they could tax and to increase the rates at which they taxed them. There is nothing particularly unusual about this in human history. Ibn Khaldun noted it and suggested that only at the very beginnings of dynasties were kings likely to tell subjects to expect the message "no new taxes." Not taxing per se but the indefinite extension of the taxing power to the point of economic ruin constituted the public wrong. It was wrong because it was a form of theft, and it was public because it affected not only private individuals ("soak the rich") but was deemed to have a pernicious effect on society as a whole. The rights of individuals to their goods were both the representation of and the instantiation of their autonomy, and thus of their liberty in civil society. This was deemed to be both a constitutive value of society (given by God) and of instrumental importance in the proper working of society.

Levying taxes was not all that kings did. As long as kings protected private property, after all, taxes were going to be a fact of life. Someone has to protect private property against private persons.[42] Unfortunately, kings themselves were private persons. Of the many quite nasty things that medieval Muslim kings (like European kings) did, little seems to evoke greater distaste on the part of their contemporary observers than the arbitrary taking of private property. Opening a chronicle more or less at random will produce an account of one or another act of *nahb* or the taking of property by force. Kings took things that were not theirs either directly or by forcing private individuals to pretend to enter into valid contractual agreements with them.[43]

It is this latter aspect that I wish to spend just a bit of time on, because I think it reveals something important about the critical jurisprudential vision of the state in the medieval Arab tradition. I think it is possible to sustain the position that Ibn Taymiyya's argument is actually somewhat more sophisticated than usually presented. Elites (the *umara* and 'ulama) exist to resolve problems for the mass of people who are for a variety of

[42] This is a problem that naturally arises without a noncoercive solution to the prisoner's dilemma.

[43] This is the point of Lapidus's discussion of state-society relations, after all.

reasons going about their business living in society. In the event of a social dispute, it is the business of the elite to come up with solutions that are most suitable to everyone's interest through some consultative (but not voting) mechanism.[44] What has been overlooked is that the decision rule proposed here is unanimity. The *umara* and the 'ulama are supposed to debate until they find an appropriate solution. Such a rule is especially appropriate in a voluntary community (which is what an *umma* is supposed to be, as it is based on acceptance of a religious order by noncompulsory means) in which

> each member is guaranteed his right to preserve his own interests against those of the other members.... Each individual has the right to bring issues before the [community] which will benefit him and he thinks will benefit all.... [T]he political process implicit in the unanimity rule is one of discussion, compromise and amendment continuing until a formulation of the issue is reached benefitting all.[45]

Why does unanimity break down? Because it has what we would call high transaction costs and, as Ibn Taymiyya noted, there may not be sufficient time or capable practitioners to make the unanimity process work.[46] For Ibn Taymiyya, in the absence of a unanimous agreement individuals are free to do as seems best to them from among already established outcomes.

[44] See Ibn Taymiyya, *Al-siyasa al-shar'iyya*, 135–37 for the section on *mashwara*, but especially p. 136.

[45] Although it appears to accord quite well with Ibn Taymiyya and I believe with much of the descriptive literature on *mashwara*, this is actually a rendition of the underlying assumptions and the implications of the unanimity rule for social choice proposed by Knut Wicksell and James Buchanan. See Dennis Mueller, *Social Choice* (Cambridge University Press, 1975) 212. I am not making the claim that Ibn Taymiyya was a "rational choice" theorist. I am making the claim that he was a rather perceptive theorist who believed that politics could be a cooperative business from which everyone could benefit, and that he believed human communities were voluntary associations of individuals who did tend to seek their own advantage and ought largely (but not totally) to be allowed to do so.

[46] Contemporary social choice theory tends to focus primarily on time constraints rather than the expertise of the personnel, but generally takes the same form in its derogation of unanimity. See Mueller, *Social Choice*, 213 n. 9.

What counts in the argument here is less the substance of the decision than the procedure by which it is reached. I think it is possible to agree with al-Azmeh about what is going on in *al-siyasa al-shar'iyya* without having to share his pessimistic evaluation of it. Ibn Taymiyya represents the culmination of a trend "which attempted to inject a lawful orientation (and I will not say content) to *siyasa*, politics as such, which was never part of the theoretical or semantic fields of the caliphate, but was concerned with human husbandry as it were."[47] Process can be of far greater importance than this quotation suggests. Process implies a concern with institutions to limit the power of kings who exceed their legitimate authority. Kings who exceeded their legitimate authority are fairly common in the medieval Muslim tradition, and they are often identified with Pharaoh. The famous sixty-years aphorism, after all, is actually only a preface to a discussion of how we ought to think about rulers who do commit unjust acts. Such rulers arrogate to themselves the role of gods, as did Pharaoh and his ministers Haman and Qarun, who were fairly common figures to medieval Muslim thinkers.[48]

It is helpful, however, to contextualize how to comprehend the limits of authority and the legitimation of obedience. One thinker who attacked the problem directly was Ibn al-Jawzi, who, in his *Talbis Iblis*, destroys the claims to legitimacy of kings as divine.[49] The brief following discussion will be drawn from the chapter "Talbis iblis 'ala al-wulat wa al-salatin."[50] The initial way in which Satan or Iblis deceives kings is by convincing them that God especially loves them. This deception occurs as kings come to believe that, were it not for God's love, He would not have made them his deputies. As Ibn al-Jawzi rather acidly points out, if God had really made kings his deputies He also would have made them rule in accordance with his path. In fact, of course, kings rule in a completely different way, not only using force but

---

[47] See al-Azmeh, *Arabic Thought and Islamic Societies*, 258.

[48] See Ibn Taymiyya, *Al-Siyasa al-shar'iyya*, 140. Those who desire power and money for their own sake, Ibn Taymiyya tells us, are like Pharaoh and Qarun, and we know they came to a bad end.

[49] See Ibn al-Jawzi, *Talbis Iblis* (Cairo, Government Printing Office, 1928).

[50] Ibid., 131–34.

also choosing subordinates who are inappropriate for the positions they are given.

It thus comes as no surprise that kings tend to substitute their own judgment for that of God and (at least as I understand the tenor of the argument) by utilizing more coercion than is acceptable: they maim and kill those who do not deserve to be punished. For Ibn al-Jawzi, therefore, the demand for *siyasa*, which seems to have here a meaning more nearly akin to royal prerogative, is a claim that the Shari'a is defective and is therefore essentially an apostate claim. What is most remarkable, however, is Ibn al-Jawzi's choice of an example of such an arbitrary royal judgment, for it is not what we might expect. It is told, writes Ibn al-Jawzi of 'Adud al-Dawla,

> that he fell in love with a slave girl and she preoccupied his heart. He ordered that she be drowned so that his heart not be occupied with anything other than the bidding of his king. This is absolute madness, because killing a Muslim who has committed no crime is not permitted. His ['Adud al-Dawla's] belief that it was lawful is unbelief and I believe that it was not legitimate because even if he thought it beneficial, nothing can be beneficial that transgresses the Shari'a.[51]

All Muslims—even slave girls unlucky enough to catch the eye of a royal minister—have the right to security in their persons and property. We would be wrong to misconstrue the argument into those of our own times. The slave girl was not going to be anything other than a slave girl, but even as such she had the right to the same protection as any other member of the community. In taking her life, 'Adud al-Dawla was committing a public wrong insofar as he limited the degree to which all Muslims could rely on the royal administration for justice. In reading the chapter, the outrage is palpable, and it is outrage over the action of a powerful man in regard to a weak and helpless woman. Earlier, we heard that the point of classical Islamic arguments about royal power was that one owed obedience to kings because they were the agents of God. The point here is precisely the reverse. Kings are as likely as (and perhaps more likely than) anyone else to be fooled because of the

[51] Ibid., 132–133.

position they hold. If one continues to obey, it is only because one figures that rupturing the community might still prove to create more havoc than the royal decision has already brought about.

The interesting question turns out, I think, to be not whether there was private property or whether there were public wrongs but what people in society did to preserve their property in the face of public wrongs. One conclusion might be that they suffered in silence, but there appears to be little support for this conclusion. Another might be that they developed a few paltry and ineffective ways of preserving their lives and property.

What I hope has become clear at this point is that it seems hard to believe that, given the existence of both private goods and a sense that there were public wrongs, private actors in society did not find ways to protect themselves and their property. What I want to suggest is that we must attempt to confront the question of what kinds of institutions could have been available that allowed individuals to protect themselves and inflict significant penalties on kings without necessarily using direct political or coercive mechanisms. Of course the political and demonstrative mechanisms did exist and were used.[52] Additionally, the very existence of legal institutions in private hands has recently been held to constitute such a barrier and, on this reading, Islamic law came into existence not as the basis for a royal state but to subvert it: "The scholarly conception of Prophetic sunna was thus a threat to caliphal authority from the moment of its appearance."[53]

Clearly it was not political institutions that allowed urban property owners to try to protect their rights.[54] It is, therefore,

---

[52] See, for example, Simha Sabari, *Mouvements populaires à Bagdad à l'époque 'abbaside, XIe–XIe siècles* (Paris, Librairie d'Amérique et d'Orient Adrien Maisonneuve, 1981), or Hamdan al-Kubaisi, *Aswaq Baghdad* (Baghdad, Ministry of Culture, 1979), for recent works. The seminal work remains Claude Cahen, *Mouvements populaires et autonomisme urbain dans l'Asie musulmane du moyen age* (Leiden, E. J. Brill, 1959).

[53] Crone and Hinds, *God's Caliph*, 94. For a fascinating account of the way in which Shari'a could be taken to be a pattern for royal law, and such law even projected backwards in time, see D. O. Morgan, "The Great Yasa of Chingiz Khan," *Bulletin of the School of Oriental and African Studies* 49 (1966) 175.

[54] Institutions of the kind commonly taken in Europe to institutionalize the separation of powers neither existed nor had strict semantic equivalents. See

economic institutions and markets to which I will turn. Markets, including markets for debt, did not spring into existence in the medieval Muslim world in some magical or costless way. Medieval merchants—Muslim, Jewish, and Christian alike—were only too aware that markets were difficult to maintain. It took then (as it takes now) time, energy, and a variety of resources to allow individuals to pursue their private interests through markets. Medieval merchants were not exchanging nuts and berries on the edge of the forest. Rather,

> Medieval trade, like its modern counterpart, was not simply a matter of buying and selling. The successful prosecution of commerce involved the judicious employment of a variety of transactions. People had to be hired for the care and transportation of merchandise. Circumstances often required that goods be deposited in another person's care, either to be sold or retrieved at a later date.[55]

The costs of these transactions necessary for the maintenance of markets were borne by merchants, but were not themselves directly marketed. They were borne by extensive patterns of long-term reciprocal relationships. Udovitch called them quasi-agent relationships, but they are undoubtedly better understood, as Avner Greif has attempted to do, in terms of complex patterns of agent–principal relationships.[56] Greif's work uses the Geniza archives to analyze the patterns of cooperation among Jewish merchants, but there is every reason to believe that quite similar patterns of agency underlie the arrangements among Muslims discussed by Udovitch.

Even patterns of agency creating what Greif calls coalitions, which allow members to benefit significantly in relation to nonmembers, will have disputes, run into problems requiring solutions agreeable to all members, and require the existence of some

---

Ami Ayalon, *Language and Change in the Arab Middle East* (New York, Oxford University Press, 1987) 131.

[55] Abraham L. Udovitch, "The 'Law-Merchant' of the Medieval Islamic World," in *Logic in Classical Islamic Culture*, ed. G. E. von Grunebaum (Wiesbaden, Otto Harrassowitz, 1970) 120.

[56] See Avner Greif, "Reputation and Coalitions in Medieval Trade: Maghribi Traders," *Journal of Economic History* 59 (1989) 857–82.

conventional rules to allow business to be transacted (such as rules governing what constitutes a valid sale).

In contemporary capitalist countries many of these problems are handled directly by the state, whether through legislation, provision of judiciary, government printing offices, or a state-run banking system. It is difficult to avoid drawing the conclusion that, although state officials provided some public support for merchants (*mazalim* courts, *hisba* functions, royal mint), much of the substructure of merchant market activities was supported by merchants themselves. When the 'ulama refused to take government posts but continued to work on various commercial problems under the heading of Shari'a, they were supported by social contributions. When merchants (or even kings for that matter) provided endowments to allow the 'ulama to escape government service, they were also paying the cost of providing part of the substructure of trade. The farflung credit system of the merchants, which made bills of exchange more acceptable than tax allocations, was also wholly supported by the private activities of merchants.[57]

By creating wide-ranging networks of trade in goods and debt, merchants also created a veritable free-trade regime in the southern Mediterranean and perhaps beyond. That this is so is incontestable, but what it means in terms of civil society is largely misunderstood. Because our image of civil society is primarily that of medieval corporate urban institutions, we have difficulty recognizing the existence of noncorporate institutions that allowed individuals (in Bendix's words cited at the beginning of this paper) to pursue common interests (in this case, trade) without detailed direction or interference from the government. Markets and almost the entire institutional structure that made them up were not only locations in which individuals pursued private interests in common without state direction or interference. They were also places sustained by the collective actions of such individuals apart from, occasionally in opposition to, and largely outside the institutional structure of the various states themselves.

One remarkable result of this situation is that, in Goitein's words, "during the High Middle Ages men, goods, money, and

[57] S. D. Goitein, "The Bourgeoisie in Early Islamic Times," in *Studies in Islamic History and Institutions*, 239.

books used to travel far and almost without restrictions throughout the Mediterranean area. In many respects the area resembled
a free trade community."[58] The creation of a free-trade community
largely apart from interstate negotiation is a remarkable historical achievement and can bear considerably more research.[59] Its
implications are also of some importance, for it suggests the existence of institutions that allowed merchants to move themselves,
their goods, and their capital freely across the boundaries of states
for whatever reasons that seemed good to them. One reason that
might seem good would be onerous taxation.

Here we have come, in a sense, full circle, and may be in a position to answer some questions with which we began. In medieval
Europe, when merchants did not like royal policies regarding taxation, they voiced their discontent through a variety of political
institutions. Voice is only one mechanism available to rescue society from situations in which "misbehavior feed[s] on itself and
lead[s] to general decay."[60]

One could imagine a situation in which exit rather than voice
provided the institutional mechanism to check the appetites of
rulers. Such a mechanism might have seemed fanciful even a short
while ago, but in the aftermath of the collapse of the Berlin Wall
we may be more able to understand the pressures brought on
states by the cumulative effects of the very simple decisions of individuals to move themselves or their resources across the boundaries of one state to another. The mechanism was itself the extensive network of commercial markets for goods and debt created by
medieval merchants, a network that they maintained and that allowed them scope on occasion quite literally to escape from rulers.
The medieval Muslim credit markets and goods markets required
extensive material and ideological resources for their existence over
time and space. Merchants used them not only to exchange nuts,

---

[58] S. D. Goitein, *A Mediterranean Society*, vol. 1 (Berkeley, University of
California Press, 1967) 66.
[59] See Ellis Goldberg, "Borders, Boundaries, Taxes and States in the Medieval Islamic World," paper presented to the SSRC Conference on Revenue
Production at the University of Washington, 27 April 1990.
[60] Albert Hirschman, *Exit, Voice and Loyalty: Responses to Decline in Firms,
Organizations and States* (Cambridge, Harvard University Press, 1970) 1.

berries, ambergris, or cotton, but also to ensure that efficient ways existed to transfer resources from city to city and state to state. The credit facilities of the *suftaja* and the *hawala* allowed merchants to move resources quickly over long distances without necessarily having to transfer much physical wealth, and the relatively easy entrée into Muslim communities allowed merchants to move themselves as well. The mechanism used by merchants to protect their property and to organize civil society was not so much voice (although voice mechanisms existed as well) as exit.

Hirschman's description of how an exit mechanism would work is as follows:

> Costs also remain constant, for by definition the quality decline results from a random lapse in efficiency rather than from a calculated attempt, on the part of the firm, to reduce costs by skimping on quality. Under these conditions, any exit whatever of consumers will result in revenue losses; and, of course, the more massive the exit the greater the losses following on any given quality drop. Whereas an increase in price can result in an increase in the firm's total revenue in spite of some customer exit, revenue can at best remain unchanged and will normally decline steadily as quality drops.[61]

The mechanism described here should be familiar to students of medieval Arab history and historiography, for it is identical with Ibn Khaldun's famous analysis of why taxes are few but productive at the beginnings of dynasties and manifold but unproductive at their ends.[62]

To the extent that merchants especially could leave one situation and enter another, they might be more disposed to exit rather than to use voice. Nevertheless, as Brian Barry notes in his critique of Hirschman, exit and voice are not opposite poles of a single choice but different kinds of choice mechanisms requiring

[61] Ibid., 23.

[62] See Ibn Khaldun, *The Muqaddimah*, trans. Franz Rosenthal, ed. and abr. N. J. Dawood (Princeton University Press, 1970) 230. We must assume that cheap and "kind" (to follow Rosenthal's somewhat idiosyncratic translation) early rulers are of higher quality than more demanding and personally more aggrandizing later ones.

different kinds of institutional infrastructures.[63] The institutional infrastructures necessary for the successful use of exit for the influence of state policies would be somewhat rare, although as I have argued elsewhere I believe they existed in the medieval Muslim world and I believe they are coming to exist once again in our own world.[64]

The problem I have tried to pose here was acutely suggested by Goitein in his work on the early Islamic bourgeoisie.[65] He suggested that the "ethic" of early English capitalism and the early Islamic bourgeoisie was remarkably similar: "to prove that the vigorous striving of the new Muslim trading people for a decent living ... was actually regarded as a religious duty." For Goitein, one problem was that this class "never became an organized body and, as a class, never obtained political power." Leaving aside the question of whether classes ever obtain political power, the question can still be usefully asked: "Do not such members of such classes attempt to create institutions that allow them to retain their wealth and pass it to their offspring?"[66] Wealthy people should have sought to resolve such problems, and some form of bargaining with rulers—or seeking new ones—will at least allow us to retain the tensions we observe in Islamic political thought intact, and to regard more highly the presence of liberal ideas about property and human choice in the absence of democratic institutions.[67] It must also be recalled, however, that

---

[63] Brian Barry, "Review Article: Exit, Voice and Loyalty," *British Journal of Political Science* 4 (1974) 91.

[64] See, e.g., Jeffry A. Frieden, "Inverted Interests: The Politics of National Economic Policies in a World of Global Finance," *International Organization* 45 (Fall 1991) 425–451.

[65] Goitein, "The Bourgeoisie in Early Islamic Times," 220–21.

[66] At least in this regard a still useful insight into what we might mean by class is Joseph Schumpeter, *Social Classes in an Ethnically Homogenous Environment* (New York, Signet Books, 1971) 167.

[67] Although 'Abd al-Razak's *Al-islam wa usul al-hukm* is often taken to present of unique approval of parliamentary bodies, it is worth recalling that as early as 1899 it appears that Rashid Rida was thinking seriously about the necessity for some form of representation of social interests as a way of limiting authoritarian government in the name of Islam. See *Jam'iyyat umm al-qura (aw mu'tamar al-nahda al-islamiyya)*, which claims to be the minutes of an

representative institutions do not surge up only from society but also appear to arise from the strategies of rulers. A complete answer to our question then will require ultimately a new look not only at society but at kings in the medieval Islamic world. What remains an acute problem, however, for those who wish to revive the classical Islamic canon as a way to think through problems of democracy and sovereignty in the present, is whether guarantees can be provided to those who are not members of the religious community in which rights are created and exercised. Just as the rights of noncitizens to property can be problematic in the national state, so too can the rights to property (and the ancillary political rights needed to defend them) become problematic for those who are not Muslim in a community defined as Islamic.[68]

Islamic conference held in Mecca in 1898. It was published (and most likely written by) Rashid Rida in *Al-Manar* 5, and republished in 1899 (n.d., n.p.).

[68] For a review of the pertinent academic and political literature, see Tariq al-Bishri, "Mabda' al-muwatana," in *Al-muslimun wa'l-aqbat fi itar al-jama'a al-wataniyya* (Beirut, Dar al-Wahdah, 1982) 669–91. For a critical view of this book and the presentation of the Muslim Brothers and Hasan al-Banna in it, which at least tempers al-Bishri's optimism, see the late Ahmad Sadiq Sa'd, "Harakat al-jamahir al-tilqa'iyya fi'l-manhaj li kitabat al-tarikh al-mu'asir (ma' tarkiz 'ala fikr Tariq al-Bishri)," in *Tarikh Misr bayna al-manhaj al-'ilmi wa'l-sira' al-hizbi*, ed. Ahmad 'Abd Allah (Cairo, Dar Shuhdi, 1988). Al-Bishri's rejoinder argues that Sadiq Sa'd's Marxism failed practically because it was alien to Egyptian culture—a claim of which I am dubious.

INDEX

Abd al-Razak, Shaykh Ali, 255, 255n23
Abdelkader, Djeghloul, 116
Abu-Lughod, Janet, 258
Abrahamian, Ervand, 12
Adaham, Omran, 99
Ahmadzadeh, Taher, 207
al-'Azm, Khalid, 89
al-Azmeh, Aziz, 263
Aleppo, 258. *See also* Chambers of
   Commerce (Syrian); Chambers of
   Industry (Syrian)
Alevis, 161
Algeria, 23, 25; Berberism in, 108–9;
   democratic bargain in, 74, 74n12,
   75; Egyptian model used in, 29;
   elections in, 3, 7, 26, 30, 37, 39, 117,
   150, 168, 169; nationalism in, 104–6,
   108; results of riots in, 111
Algiers, 109
Amman, 150
Amoui, Muhammad, 218
Anatolia, 46, 52n6, 56. *See also* Turkey
Ankara, 43, 57n21, 63, 185
Arab Socialist Union (ASU) (Egypt),
   26, 27
Arabs, 25, 102; and democracy, 171; in
   Iraq, 181–84, 187; in Israel, 213; and
   Kurds, 181–84, 187; and national-
   ism, 152; in Palestine, 123; relations
   with Persians, 237
Arafat, Yassir, 167
Arendt, Hannah, 237
al-Asad, Hafiz: and Arab-Israeli peace

process, 167; and the economy, 32,
   81, 93; and the Muslim Brotherhood, 84n30; and the United States,
   165; view of democracy, 99, 100
Ashkenazi, Motti, 131, 132
Associations Law (Israel), 134
Atatürk, Mustafa Kemal, 50, 52, 55,
   155–57
Azerbaijan, 216

Ba'th: in Iraq, 13, 177, 179–80, 185,
   227–39, 246; in Syria, 82, 83n26, 85,
   87, 89, 95, 100. *See also* Hussein,
   Saddam; Iraq
Baghdad, 237, 239; demand for democ-
   racy in, 176–77; and Kurds, 178–80,
   231; al-Sadr transferred to, 228; as
   symbol of repression, 225–33 *passim*;
   universities of bombed, 229
Bahrain, 33, 35
Baker, James, 185
al-Bakr, Ahmad Hasan, 238
Barahani, Reza, 201
Barry, Brian, 269
al-Bashir, Omar (general), 31
Batatu, Hanna, 225, 226, 232
Bayar, Celal, 51, 51n5, 52n6, 54, 62
Bazargan, Mehdi, 204
Behazin, Mahmud, 216, 218
Behbehani, Farhad, 207, 208
Behzadi, Manoucher, 219
Beirut, 233
Ben-Eliezer, Uri, 118, 134

Ben Ali, Zine el-Abidine, 26, 29, 30
Ben Ayed, Abdelwaheb, 110
Benjedid, Chadli, 26, 29, 30
Berberism, 108–9
Berbers, 37–38
Bianchi, Robert, 38
Bint al-Huda, 226, 226n3, 228
al-Bishri, Tariq, 249
Black Panthers (Israel), 131, 158
Blackwell, Kenneth, 146
Bolsheviks, 193n3
Bouchrara, Moncef, 109
Boumedienne, Houari, 109
Bourgeoisie: Islamic, 270; North African, 79; Ottoman, 47
Bourguiba, Habib, 22, 29, 115
Braudel, Fernand, 43
Brecht, Berthold, 193
Britain, 19, 66, 159, 245
Burgat, François, 112–13
Bush, George, and Iraq, 176, 178, 184, 186, 242
Butterworth, Charles, 253, 254

Capitalism, 76, 106, 270
Carter, Jimmy, 11, 241n26
Caucasus, 147, 162
Ceauşescu, Nicolae, 99
Central Intelligence Agency, 201, 206, 208, 219
Chalabi, Ahmad, 174, 175n1, 183n12, 185, 231n9
Chambers of Commerce (Syrian), 88–93 passim
Chambers of Industry (Syrian), 88–89, 92
Christians, 19, 266
CIA. See Central Intelligence Agency
Civil society: definitions of, 7, 118n2, 119, 120–23, 248; in Iraq, 11, 246; in Israel, 9, 118, 120, 122, 124, 129–37 passim, 136; in the Maghreb, 10, 105, 111, 116–18; in medieval Muslim society, 249, 251, 251n8, 252, 253, 260–61, 267, 269; in Turkey, 50
Cold War, 31, 165, 166, 170, 172
Communist party: Iranian, 212; Syrian, 95, 95n51. See also Tudeh
Constitution: in Algeria, 30; in Egypt, 19, 28; in Iran (Islamic Republic of),

195, 210, 216; in Iraq, 181, 235–36, 239; in Ottoman Empire, 46, 155; in Turkey, 60–61, 64–66
Constitutionalism, 35, 235
Corruption, 10; alleged in Iran, 195, 199, 220; denounced in the Maghreb, 112; in Syria, 84; in Turkey, 59

Damascus. See Chambers of Commerce (Syrian); Chambers of Industry (Syrian)
Danet, Brenda, 129
Daniel, Jean, 117
Da'wa party (Iran), 227–29, 238
al-Dawla, 'Adud, 264
Dayan, Moshe, 131
Democracy: in Algeria, 30, 109, 115–19; current trend for, 141, 144, 164, 271; definitions of, 7, 17; and economy, 70, 70n3, 70n4, 76–77, 77n15, 142; in Egypt, 20–21, 27, 38–39; in Iraq, 174–77, 176n4, 183, 224; and Islam, 147, 149, 160, 248–49; in Israel, 125; in Jordan, 33; in Kuwait, 34; in Lebanon, 24; in the Middle East, 3, 3n1, 7–14 passim, 35, 120, 145; and Mojahedin (Iran), 207; in Morocco, 33; and the Palestinians, 171, 147–48; prerequisites for, 4–5, 6, 6n5, 142–43; and President Asad, 99–100; and President Mubarak, 28; and President Saddam Hussein, 150–51; in Turkey, 9, 43–45, 54, 57, 59, 66–68, 152, 155–57, 159, 162; United States support for, 164–65, 167–68, 170–72. See also Economy; Pluralism
Democratic party (DP) (Turkey), 51–56, 59–62, 64, 66
De Nerval, Gerard, 158
Dictatorship, 142, 143; in Iraq, 13, 174, 183, 226, 239, 242, 243
Djerijian, Edward P., 167n2

Ecevit, Bülent, 11, 12
Economy: and democracy, 70, 70n3, 70n4, 76–77, 77n15, 142; Egyptian, 27, 74n12, 79n20, 94, 98; in the Gulf, 145, 166–67; in Iran, 200; market, 142–43; and pluralism, 36;

Economy (*continued*)
  reforms of in the Maghreb, 112; and
    ruling bargain, 74, 74*n*11, 75; in
    Syria, 10, 81–84, 83*n*27, 88–90, 92–
    93, 96, 98–101; in Turkey, 45, 47, 52,
    154. *See also* Democracy; Market(s);
    Oil
Egypt, 23, 144, 170; and democratic
    bargain, 74–75; and economy, 10,
    27, 74*n*12, 79*n*20, 94, 98; and Israel,
    167; elections in, 18–21, 25–26, 28–
    29, 36–39; and pluralism, 20–21, 71
Elections, 8, 17–20, 22–27, 36, 170*n*4;
    in Algeria, 3, 7, 29, 37, 117, 168; in
    Bahrain, 33; in Egypt, 18–21, 25–
    26, 28–29, 36–39; in Iran, 206; in
    Jordan, 31, 150; and Kurds, 182–
    84; in Kuwait, 33; in Sudan 31; in
    Syria, 19, 93; in Turkey, 43–46, 51,
    53, 59–61, 67. *See also* Democracy;
    Pluralism
Enault, Louis, 158
England, 19, 66, 159, 245
Erim, Nihat, 51, 51*n*5
Evren, Kenan (general), 44
Execution(s): in Iran, 194, 200, 206,
    211–22, 226, 228; of Menderes, 62,
    65; in Turkey, 43

Fahd (king of Saudi Arabia), 166
Firuz, Maryam, 216
France: and Iraq, 245; and the Magh-
    reb, 113, 117, 168
Fromm, Erich, 142
Front Islamique de Salut (FIS) (Alge-
    ria), 7, 30, 31, 37, 168
Front de Libération Nationale (FLN)
    (Algeria), 30, 31, 116
Fundamentalism, 146, 248; in Jordan,
    145, 150; and Saudi Arabia, 150;
    and Khomeini, 161

Geertz, Clifford, 111
Ghozali, Sid Ahmad, 30
Goitein, S. D., 270
Goldberg, Ellis, 11, 118
Golsorkhi, Khosrow, 200
Gramsci, Antonio, 120, 121, 124
Gulf War, first, 224, 237–38
Gulf War, second, 11, 145, 147; British

policy in, 174; and Iraq, 224, 236*n*20,
    237–39, 239*n*25, 240, 242; and Syria,
    101
Gush Emunim (Block of the Faithful),
    132

Haj Soula, 110
al-Hakim, Muhsin (Ayatollah), 226, 230
al-Hakim, Saheb, 182, 183*n*12
al-Hakim, Tawfik, 21
Halabcha, 231
Halil Pasha, Chandarli (Ottoman grand
    vizier), 153
Harbi, Mohamed, 108,
Hashemi, Mehdi, 198, 210–12, 210*n*49
Haass, Richard, 175
Hassan II (king of Morocco), 22
Hegel, George Wilhelm F., 120, 120*n*3,
    121
Hermassi, Abdelbaki, 7, 10
Heydemann, Steven, 10
Hirschman, Albert, 269
Histadrut, 127, 128, 133
Hobbes, Thomas, 253–55
Hodgson, Marshall, 250, 256, 256*n*24,
    260*n*40
Hojjati-Kermani (Hojjat al-Islam), 215
Human rights, 3, 5*n*3, 6, 7, 13–14, 143–
    46, 167, 170–72; in Iran, 207–8,
    216; in Iraq, 174, 182, 246; in the
    Maghreb, 110
Hunter, Shireen, 150
Hussein Ibn Talal (king of Jordan), 32,
    150, 167, 207
Hussein, Saddam, 176–81 *passim*, 247;
    and aggression, 32, 236, 236*n*20,
    237–39; and constitution, 239; and
    democratization, 150, 151; and
    Kurds, 178–80; opposition to, 186–
    87, 226–28, 241*n*26, 242–43; power
    of, 229*n*6, 231–34, 235*n*19, 236; and
    United States, 165, 171, 242; writ-
    ings of, 233–34. *See also* Ba'th; Iraq

Ibn al-Jawzi, 263, 264
Ibn Khaldun, 107, 261
Ibn Taymiyya, 253, 254, 254*n*19, 256,
    262, 262*n*45, 263, 263*n*48
Imadi, Muhammad, 96
Infitah, 26–28, 111

Inönü, Ismet, 65
Intelligentsia: in the Maghreb, 116; targeted in Iran, 192, 217, 223; Turkish, 54, 61
International Committee for a Free Iraq (ICFI), 175, 175n1, 176, 178–80, 182–86 *passim*
International Monetary Fund (IMF), 27, 31, 71n4, 76, 76n14, 83n27, 101, 108
Iran, 3, 12, 13, 17, 200–201, 215–16, 219; American intervention in, 165; in Baghdad-Kurdish agreement, 180, and fundamentalism, 144, 149, 162, 150; and oil, 166; war of with Iraq, 32, 206–7, 224, 235, 237–39. *See also* Islamic Republic of Iran; Gulf War; White Revolution; Tudeh
Iraq, 3, 10–13; and democracy, 174, 177–87; elections in, 18–20; and political reform, 32; and sanctions, 176; and Saudi Arabia, 151; war of with Iran, 206, 215, 224; repression in, 144, 225–32; legalism in, 233–39; and the United States, 171–72; and the West after the Gulf War, 241–47. *See also* Baghdad; Hussein, Saddam; International Committee for a Free Iraq; Gulf War
Islam: and Ba'thi Iraq, 226, 237, and democracy, 6, 141, 147, 149, 155, 160, 164n1; and freedom, 248–49; and Islamic Republic of Islam, 198, 206–7, 209, 211–14; in the Maghreb (Islamism), 111–17; and Marxism, 201, 203–4, 217–18; and nationalism, 112, 152; and the state, 11–12, 102, 257, 260, 270; in Turkey (Ottoman), 46, 154–55; in Turkey (republican), 48, 161. *See also* Muslims
Islamic Republic of Iran, 13, 192–97, 203, 206–7, 211–16, 218–20, 222, 223. *See also* Iran
Islamism. *See* Islam, in the Maghreb
Israel, 17, 27, 124–37 *passim*; and civil society, 118, 120, 136–37; and democracy, 8–9, 144; and ombudsman, 130; and Palestinians, 147–48; and peace efforts, 167–68, 236; and public sector, 125; and U.S. Middle

East policy, 164–65
Istiqlal (Nationalist party of Morocco), 22, 23

Jangali Rebellion, 218
Janissaries, 153
Jawad, Ghanem, 183n12
Jefferson, Thomas, 166
Jews, 19, 123, 147; North African (in Israel), 124, 126, 128, 131
Jordan, 3, 71; democracy in, 144–45; economy and democracy in, 74, 74n12, 76; elections in, 19, 25, 31; fundamentalism in, 150; king's role in, 23, 24, 31–33, 150; and United States, 165–66, 167–68, 170
Jowdat, Hosayn, 219
Justice party (JP) (Turkey), 64–66

Kabyle/Kabilia, 108–9, 117
Karagöz plays, 158–59
Kasaba, Reşat, 7, 8
Kashani (Ayatollah), 216
Kasravi, Ahmad, 217
Kayhan, Mehdi, 219
Kepel, Gilles, 113, 114
al-Khalil, Samir, 225, 234, 237
Khomeini, Ruhollah (Ayatollah), 226, 233; and confessions in Iran, 192–93, 197–99; and Mojahedin, 203, 204, 206–13 *passim*; and Marxists, 212–21 *passim*
Khurasan, 205, 207
Kianuri, Nuraldin, 216, 220, 221
Kimmerling, Baruch, 118, 128
Knesset, 127, 131
Koran, 66, 154, 155, 198
Kramer, Martin, 248
Kufa University, 229, 230
Kurds: Baghdad's dealings with, 179–84, 230, 231, 234, 235; ICFI and, 187; and UN Resolution 688, 246
Kuwait, 22, 151; and democracy, 33–35; Iraqi invasion of, 239, 245; national pact in, 32; subsidizes islamization, 114; in UN Resolution 660, 236; in UN Resolution 687, 242

Labor party (Israel), 128
Ladjevardi, Assadollah, 197

Lahiji, Abdulkarim, 207
Laroui, Abdallah, 102
Law, 21, 110, 120*n*3, 143, 170, 170*n*4, 226; Algerian electoral, 30; Ba'thi, 229; civil, 14; Egyptian electoral, 28; international, 11, 13, 177, 224, 239, 240, 247; in Iraq, 181, 230–31, 234–35; Islamic, 12, 257, 154, 160, 195, 227; in Israel, 134; in Syria, 95*n*51; Tunisian electoral, 29; in Turkey, 54–56, 54*n*13, 60, 62–63, 156. *See also* Shari'a
Lebanon: electoral democracy in, 19, 20, 21–22, 24, 35; and 1982 war, 128, 132, 135; pluralism in, 36; Syrian presence in, 85, 85*n*32; tragedy of, 144; and United States, 164
Legalism, 13, 230, 231, 234–36, 246
Legality, 203, 234, 246
Legislation, 267; agricultural (Syrian), 91; in Iraq, 235–36; of junta in Turkey, 61; land reform (Turkish), 55; and women, 110
Legitimacy, 4, 86, 102, 110, 115, 120, 122, 260*n*39; and Iranian state, 192; and Iraqi state, 224, 238, 244; and Islamic law; 252, 255, 263; and Israeli state, 136; and Maghreb states, 103–4, 111; and Ottoman state, 155; and Syrian regime, 82; and Turkish political system, 67
Lenin, Vladimir, 206
Leninism, 217
Leveau, Remy, 114, 115
Lewis, Bernard, 241*n*26, 253
Liberalism, 10, 27, 47, 55, 103, 104, 111
Liberalization: economic, 10, 25, 69–71, 71*n*4, 72–73, 80–82, 101, 111; and political restructuring, 69, 75–79, 79*n*20, 116; significance of addressed, 4; in Syria, 85–88, 92–99; and United States, 168, 170
Liberty, 156, 158, 248, 261
Libya, 3, 25
Liebman, Charles, 135
Likud, 128
Locke, John, 255

Maghreb, 10, 103–5, 107, 110–12, 114, 115. *See also* North Africa

Mahfuz, Nagib, 243
Major, John, 180, 242
Makkiyye, Kan'an, 182
Makkiyye, Muhammad, 229, 230*n*8
Mallat, Chibli, 11, 13, 250
Mammeri, Mouloud, 109
Market(s): and Islamic cities, 258, 259, 266, 268; and the Maghreb, 110; mentality (Turkey), 68; oil, 83; replace controlled economy, 70*n*3, 76*n*14; and Syria, 85. *See also* Economy
Marxism: and Islam (Iran), 201, 203–4, 202*n*25, 212, 213, 215, 217–19; of Sadiq Sa'd, 271*n*68; and the state, 103, 120*n*3. *See also* Islam; Khomeini, Ruhollah (Ayatollah); Tudeh
Mehmet II (Ottoman sultan), 153
Meir, Golda, 131
Menderes, Adnan, 8, 53, 55, 56, 59, 64; execution of, 61, 62–63, 63*n*25
Migdal, Joel, 9, 69
Migration, 58, 66
Modernization: and Islam, 114; in the Middle East, 144, 145, 147–49; in Turkey, 49, 68, 151–52
Mohammad V (king of Morocco), 22
Mojahedin, prosecuted in Iran, 201, 203, 204, 204*n*28, 205–7, 212, 213*n*54, 214, 223
Moore, Clement Henry, 36
Morocco: democracy and economy in, 76, 79*n*21; elections in, 20, 22–24; nationalism in, 104–6; riots in, 108; United States and, 165, 168
Mortimer, Edward, 174, 185
Mossadegh, Mohammed, 165
Mill, Stuart, 110
Montazeri, Hosain Ali (Ayatollah), 198, 212
Mottaheri, Morteza (Ayatollah), 217
Mouvement de Tendence Islamique (MTI) (Tunisia), 30
Mubarak, Husni, 27, 28, 38
Muhammad (Prophet), 65, 195, 210
Muravchik, Joshua, 143
Murphy, Richard, 183
Muslim Brotherhood, 28, 84*n*30, 31, 39, 154, 271
Muslim(s): in the Maghreb, 117;

medieval, 251, 252, 260, 264, 266;
    thinkers, 217; early, and torture,
    195; in Turkey, 54, 67. *See also* Is-
    lam

Najaf, 202, 225–30, 232
Nasser, Gamal Abdel, 20, 26, 37
National Democratic party (NDP)
    (Egypt), 27
National Islamic Front (NIF) (Sudan),
    31
Nationalism, 7, 152; and Islam, 112;
    Kurdish, 184; in the Maghreb, 104–5
Nationality Law (Iraq), 230
Nimeiri, Ga'afar, 26
North Africa, 23, 25, 79, 166, 168. *See
    also* Maghreb
North Korea, 146

Oil, 25, 74; and ICFI, 176, 186; in Iran,
    200; in Kuwait, 34; and Syrian econ-
    omy, 32, 83–84, 101; and U.S. policy,
    145, 166–66, 172; USSR demands
    from Iran, 216, 219; and world econ-
    omy, 166–67. *See also* Economy
Ollier, Edmund, 156
Organization for Economic Cooperation
    and Development (OECD), 83
Oman, 35
Orwell, George, 193, 214
Ottoman Empire, 8; nonstate arena in,
    45–48, 67, 157–61; and Middle East-
    erners, 149; multinational character
    of, 152, 153, 155
Ottoman Parliament, 46, 155–56
Owen, Roger, 7, 8

Pahlavi, Mohammed Reza (Shah of
    Iran), 165–66, 201, 207, 211, 219
Pahlavi, Reza Khan, 218
Pahlavi regime, 200, 213
Palestine, 123, 135
Palestine Liberation Organization
    (PLO), 147, 148, 167
Palestinians: and democracy, 147–48,
    171; in Israel, 3; in Jordan, 145; in
    occupied territories, 128
Paykar party (Iran), 212–14, 214n57
Pipes, Daniel, 251, 252
Pluralism: and economy, 36, 71n5; in

Eygpt, 18–21, 71; in Iraq, 230; in
    Lebanon, 36; in Middle East, 20–
    21, 78; in Morocco, 23; and the
    Palestinians, 171; as prerequisite
    for democracy, 9, 14; and President
    Asad, 100; and President Mubarak,
    38; and President Sadat, 27; in
    Syria, 99; in Turkey, 53–54, 57–59.
    See also Democracy; Economy; Elec-
    tions
Popper, Karl, 17

Qatar, 35
Qom, 208, 212
Qotbzadeh, Sadeq, 208, 209
Quandt, William B., 10–11

Rafsanjani, Hashemi (Hojjat al-Islam),
    210
Rayshahri, Mohammed (Hojjat al-Is-
    lam), 198, 199, 208, 220, 221
Reagan, Ronald, 25
Revolution: Cultural (Chinese), 198n17;
    Egyptian, 20; French, 18; Islamic,
    203, 204, 204n30, 206, 208, 210, 237;
    White (Iran), 200–202, 212, 216
Revolutionary Command Council
    (RCC) (Iraq), 227–29, 229n6,
    231n10, 235, 236
Rosenthal, E. I. J., 253
RPP (Republican People's party)
    (Turkey), 51, 51n5, 52–55, 58, 60,
    61, 65, 66
Ruhani, Hosayn, 212, 213n55, 214

al-Sabah family (Kuwait), 34
Sadat, Anwar, 26, 27, 167
al-Sadr, Muhammad Baqer, 217; and
    Da'wa, 229; execution of, 228–29,
    238; opposes Saddam Hussein, 226–
    27
Salafi reformism, 104
Santillana, David, 256, 257
Saudi Arabia, 12; and fundamentalism,
    150; resists democratization, 144–
    46, 149, 151, 152, 162; and Saddam
    Hussein, 233; subsidizes islamization,
    114; and the United States, 165–67;
    and women's freedom, 163
SAVAK, 210, 211

Shahsavandi, Sa'ed, 206, 207

Shaltuki, Reza, 219

Shari'a (Islamic law): and confessions (Iran), 195, 195n9, 196, 209, 215; interpretions of, 160, 264, 265n53; and markets, 267; in Turkey, 154, 155. See also Law

Shariatmadari, Mohammed Kazen (Ayatollah), 208, 209, 209n44, 210

Shi'i Muslims, Shi'ism: and ICFI, 182, 185; in Iran, 208, 210; in Iraq, 151, 226–27, 230, 232–33 232n10, 237–38; in Turkey, 161; use of torture by, 196. See also al-Sadr, Muhammad Baqer; Najaf

Sidqi constitution (Egypt), 19

Socialism, 30, 99, 104

Soviet Union: influence of denounced in Iran, 204, 215, 216, 219, 220; and Iraq, 244; recent changes in, 3, 8, 27, 72n7, 143, 144, 184; show trials in, 192, 193, 193n3; and Syrian economy, 82, 99, 100; and Turkey, 50; and U.S. Middle East policy, 165

Stalin, Josef, 3, 193, 193n3, 194

Sudan, 20, 25, 26, 31, 32, 79

Sufi Muslims, Turkish, 161, 162

Sunni Muslims: and ICFI, 182, 185; in Iraq, 227, 231, 238; in Turkey, 161

Syria: Asad's ruling style in, 3, 12, 32, 81, 99–100, 144; chambers of commerce and industry in, 73, 88n38, 89–94, 97n56; controlled economy in, 74n12; and economic liberalization, 10, 73, 80–83, 83n26, 94, 98; economy of, 85n31, 87, 88n38, 89, 91, 92n44, 99–101; and elections, 19; and Iraq, 238; and military spending, 86; and peace process, 167–68; and United States, 165; women in, 20

Tabari, Ehsan, 216, 217

Taher, Ahmadzadeh, 207

Taxation, 76, 80, 260, 268

Tehran, 209, 211

Tudeh (Communist party of Iran), 201, 203, 212, 214–15, 215n59, 218, 218n69, 218n70, 219, 220, 220n76, 222, 222n80, 223. See also Marxism

Tunis, 22, 110

Tunisia: economic liberalization in, 79; elections in, 25, 26, 29, 32; national pact in, 39; as national state, 104–6; Neo-Destour in, 22; and 1991 Algerian elections, 168; riots in, 108; private sector in, 109

Turkey: and democracy, 8, 9, 17, 43, 43–45, 54, 57, 59, 66–68, 141, 144, 147, 151–52, 155–57, 159, 162; as a democratic model, 11, 162; and economy, 45, 47, 52; and elections, 43–46, 51, 53, 59–61, 67; and Islam, 46, 48–49, 66, 147, 149, 155; and the Kurds, 184, 187; and secularism, 49, 147, 149, 151–52, 160–61; and United States, 164, 170; and women, 48, 59, 64, 162. See also Islam; Turkish Republic

Turkic states, 147, 162

Turkish Republic, 47–49, 53–54, 58, 154. See also Turkey

Udovitch, Abraham L., 266

Union Nationale des Forces Populaires (UNFP) (Morocco), 23

United Arab Emirates (UAE), 35

United Nations, 182, 187, 224, 236n20, 240–41

UN Security Council Resolution: no. 660, 236, 240; no. 687, 241, 242, 244; no. 688, 244–47

United States: human rights policy of, 39; and Iranian confessions, 201, 203-4, 207, 210, 211; and Iraq, 165, 171–72, 176–79, 183, 185, 242–45 passim; and Jordan, 165–66, 167–68, 170; and Lebanon, 164; and liberalization, 168, 170; Middle East policy of and democracy, 11, 145, 164–73 passim; and Morocco, 165, 168; and Saudi Arabia, 165–67; and Syria, 165; and Turkey, 51, 164, 170. See also Bush, George; Central Intelligence Agency

Vatikiotis, P. J., 19, 251, 252

Veblen, Thorstein, 107

Wafd, 19

Waterbury, John, 23, 98
Weber, Max, 107, 182
White Revolution (Iran), 200–202, 212, 216
Wolfsfeld, Gadi, 124, 125, 132
Women: in Algeria, 116–17; among Mojahedin recanters, 205; position of, 110–11, 145–46, 162; in Saudi Arabia, 3, 163; and suffrage, 20; in Turkey, 48, 59, 64, 162

Yemen, 144, 170
Yishai, Yael, 118, 129, 133, 134

Zaganos Pasha (Ottoman grand vizier), 153
Zahlan, Rosemary, 35
Zarrouk, Makhtar, 110
Zionism, 9, 133
Zubaida, Sami, 18, 18n3, 233n14
Zu'bi, Mahmoud, 95n51, 96
Zureik, Ilia, 249n4

CONTRIBUTORS

ERVAND ABRAHAMIAN is Professor of History at Baruch College of the City University of New York. He is the author of *Iran between Two Revolutions* (1982) and *The Iranian Mojahedin* (1989).

BÜLENT ECEVİT is a former Prime Minister of Turkey, and currently the Chairman of the Democratic Left party and a member of the Turkish Parliament.

ELLIS GOLDBERG is Associate Professor of Political Science at the University of Washington. He is the author of *Tinker, Tailor, Textile Worker* (1986) and articles including "Smashing Idols and the State" in *Comparative Studies in Society and History* 33.1 (1991).

ABDELBAKI HERMASSI, formerly Professor of Sociology at the University of California at Berkeley and at the University of Tunis, is now the head of the Tunisian Delegation to UNESCO. His books include *Leadership and National Development in North Africa* (1972).

STEVEN HEYDEMANN is the staff member of the Social Science Research Council for the Joint Committee on the Near and Middle East and International Peace and Security.

REŞAT KASABA is Associate Professor of International Studies and Adjunct Professor of Sociology at the University of Washington. He is the author of *The Ottoman Empire and the World Economy: The Nineteenth Century* (1988).

CHIBLI MALLAT is Professor of Law and Politics at the School of Oriental and African Studies of the University of London, and a founding member of ICFI. He is the author of *The Renewal of Islamic Law* (1992).

JOEL MIGDAL is Professor of International Studies and Political Science at the University of Washington. His latest books are *Strong Societies, Weak States* (1989) and *Palestinians: The Making of a People* (1993).

ROGER OWEN is Professor of Middle Eastern History and Politics at St. Antony's College, Oxford. His most recent book is *State, Power, and Politics in the Making of the Modern Middle East* (1992).

WILLIAM QUANDT is Senior Fellow at the Brookings Institution, and a former member of the National Security Council, advising President Carter on the Middle East. His publications include *The Middle East: Ten Years after Camp David* (1988).